Palestinian Christians in Israel

Although Christians form a significant proportion of the Palestinian Arab minority in Israel, very little research has, until now, been undertaken to examine their complicated position within Israel. This book demonstrates the limits of analyses which characterise state–minority relations in Israel in terms of a so-called Jewish–Muslim conflict, and of studies which portray Palestinian Christians as part of a wider exclusively religious-based transnational Christian community.

This book locates its analysis of Palestinian Christians within a broader understanding of Israel as a Jewish ethnocratic state. It describes the main characteristics of the Palestinian Christian community in Israel and examines a number of problematic assumptions which have been made about them and their relationship to the state. Finally, it examines a number of intra-communal conflicts which have taken place in recent years between Christians and Muslims, and between Christians and Druze, and probes the role which the state and various state attitudes have played in influencing or determining those conflicts and, as a result, the general status of Palestinian Christians in Israel today.

Una McGahern is a visiting Research Fellow at the School of Government and International Affairs, Durham University, and part-time lecturer in Middle East Politics at the University of Newcastle, UK.

Durham Modern Middle East and Islamic World
Series editor Anoushiravan Ehteshami
University of Durham

Palestinian Christians in Israel

State attitudes towards non-Muslims in a Jewish state

Una McGahern

Routledge
Taylor & Francis Group

LONDON AND NEW YORK

First published 2011
by Routledge
2 Park Square, Milton Park, Abingdon, Oxon, OX14 4RN

Simultaneously published in the USA and Canada
by Routledge
711 Third Avenue, New York, NY 10017

Routledge is an imprint of the Taylor & Francis Group, an informa business

British Library Cataloguing in Publication Data
A catalogue record for this book is available
from the British Library

Library of Congress Cataloging-in-Publication Data
McGahern, Una.
Palestinian Christians in Israel : state attitudes towards non-Muslims in a
Jewish state / Una McGahern.
p. cm. — (Durham modern Middle East and Islamic world series ; 22)
Includes bibliographical references (p.) and index.
1. Christians—Israel. 2. Palestinian Arabs—Israel—Religion.
3. Church and state—Israel. 4. Israel—Church history. I. Title.
BR1110.M44 2011
305.6'70899274—dc22
2011004866

ISBN13: 978–0–415–60571–7 (hbk)
ISBN13: 978–0–203–80664–7 (ebk)

Typeset in Times New Roman by Swales & Willis Ltd, Exeter, Devon

MIX
Paper from
responsible sources
FSC
www.fsc.org   FSC® C004839

Printed and bound in Great Britain by the MPG Books Group

Contents

Tables

Acknowledgements

This book is based on my doctoral dissertation 'State Attitudes towards Palestinian Christians in a Jewish Ethnocracy' which was examined at Durham University's School of Government and International Affairs in January 2010. I am deeply grateful for the generous financial support of Ustinov College and the Sir Peter Ustinov Prejudice Scholarship which enabled me to carry out this research. I would also like to thank the Economic Social and Research Council 1+3 studentship scheme, as well as the Council for British Research in the Levant and the British Society for Middle Eastern Studies, for providing the financial support necessary to conduct extensive fieldwork in Israel.

Given the sensitive nature of this research, I am especially indebted to a long list of Palestinian and Jewish individuals and organisations in Israel who gave generously and unconditionally of their time to engage with this research and to answer my questions. Whilst many have preferred to remain anonymous, I am beholden to them all for their uniform graciousness, frankness and hospitality. An unequivocal debt of gratitude is in particular due to all the members of the Ashkar family of Nazareth who unreservedly opened their homes and hearts to this itinerant researcher and provided her with a much valued home away from home.

I am also grateful to Emma Murphy for her critical but always constructive feedback, and to all my colleagues and friends at Durham University, Ustinov College and further afield for their support and companionship during this whole process. And finally, for their unwavering support on every step of this journey, and for instilling in me the hope, passion, ambition and drive necessary to complete it, I owe the greatest deal of thanks, admiration and love to my parents, Harold and Margaret.

List of abbreviations

ACAP	Arab Centre for Alternative Planning
CBS	Central Bureau of Statistics
CP	Communist Party
DFPE	Democratic Front for Peace and Equality
FA	Fundamental Agreement
HRA	Arab Association for Human Rights
IDF	Israeli Defence Forces
IISS	International Institute for Strategic Studies
ILA	Israel Lands Authority
JA	Jewish Agency
JCJCR	Jerusalem Centre for Jewish-Christian Relations
JNF	Jewish National Fund
MFA	Ministry of Foreign Affairs
MK	Member of Knesset
NDA	National Democratic Assembly
NGO	Non-Governmental Organisation
NII	National Insurance Institute
NIS	New Israeli Shekel
NRP	National Religious Party
OPTs	Occupied Palestinian Territories
PA	Palestinian Authority
PINGO	Palestinian Israeli NGO
PLO	Palestine Liberation Organisation
UAL	United Arab List
UN	United Nations
WZO	World Zionist Organisation

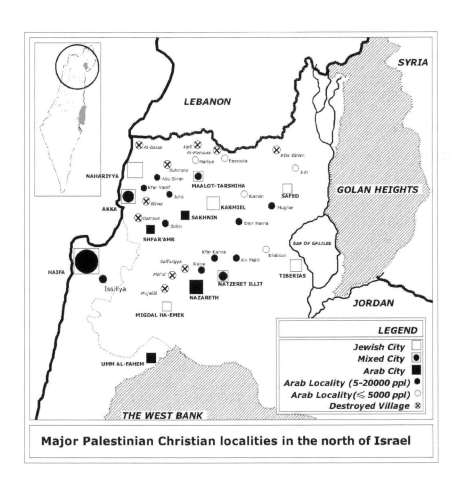

Major Palestinian Christian localities in the north of Israel

1 Introduction

> Palestinian Christians are a religious minority whose unique interests and problems have received scant attention. They are a group that has faced almost uninterrupted persecution in the years since the Oslo peace process began, suffering from the difficulties of being a religious minority living in a Palestinian Authority [PA] whose inner workings, both from a legal and societal perspective, are often governed by strict adherence to Muslim religious law. They are a group that has been abandoned by its leaders, who have chosen to curry favour with the Palestinian leadership by refusing to acknowledge the magnitude of the threat. They are a group whose persecution has gone almost entirely ignored by the international community, the relevant NGOs, and other human rights activists. Facing widespread corruption in the PA security and police forces, facing growing anarchy and lawlessness in an increasingly xenophobic and restless Muslim populace, the Palestinian Christians have been all but abandoned by the very people whose task it is to protect them.
>
> (Weiner 2005: 1)

The above excerpt is taken from the first page of a monograph entitled *Human Rights of Christians in Palestinian Society*, published by the Jerusalem Centre for Public Affairs in 2005. The report, written by Justus Reid Weiner, a scholar-in-residence at the centre, lists several problems which, he claims, face Palestinian Christian communities under PA rule today. Such problems include: increased 'Christian emigration', 'social and economic discrimination', 'boycott and extortion of Christian businesses', 'violation of [Christian] property rights', 'crimes against Christian Arab women', 'Palestinian Authority incitement against Christians', 'the failure of Palestinian security forces to protect Christians' and 'the inclusion of Sharia Law in the Palestinian Authority's draft constitution'. While these problems are understood to have been exacerbated by the ongoing Israeli-Palestinian conflict, the report finds that they are ultimately due to the growth of Islamic fundamentalist tendencies within the majority Muslim population and within the PA itself, and calls upon the US government to uphold its 1998 Freedom from Religious Persecution Act and apply economic sanctions against the PA until sufficient democratic reforms are in place to protect Christians.

Weiner's report had an immediate impact on international public opinion. Media outlets in Israel and throughout the world quickly took up the cause of

Palestinian Christians under such titles as 'The Dark Fate of Christians under Palestinian Rule', 'Christians under Cover', 'Palestinian Christians are Afraid' and 'Palestinian Christians live in Constant Fear'. While Weiner's report accurately describes the scant, superficial and rather spasmodic attention given to the study of Palestinian Christians, the particular line and focus of inquiry which it adopts, and which has since been taken up with gusto by the international press, has done little to improve the situation of Palestinian Christians or the general quality of research undertaken on this small community.

One major explanation for the poor state of research into Palestinian Christians in Israel today lies in the continued popularity of generalised studies examining Christians throughout the Middle East as a whole. The work of scholars such as Robert Betts, Kenneth Cragg, Philippe Fargues, Andrea Pacini and Anthony O'Mahony – which has been published under such titles as 'Christians in the Arab East', 'The Arab Christian: A History in the Middle East' and 'Christian Communities in the Arab Middle East' – approaches the subject of Christians in the Middle East as a single regional religious minority. In so doing, these studies have tended to centralise, or over-state, the religious component of Christian identity in their analysis of the status of various Christian communities in different Middle Eastern states. While revealing interesting points of comparison and continuity between Christian communities, the focus of these studies has often come at the direct expense of a deeper and more holistic analysis of the range of issues affecting particular Christian communities. Critically, these studies – which may be collectively dubbed as 'Holy Land' studies – have diminished the role accorded to the non-religious components of Christian identity and, by extension, the non-religious factors and processes which affect the status of Christians in society and influence inter-communal relations in the Middle East.

This is not to suggest that religion does not play an important role in the status of Christian communities throughout the Middle East and in the particular nature of Palestinian inter-group dynamics and conflicts. Indeed, the history of the Middle East is replete with instances of religiously fuelled political and territorial conflict. Religious affiliation and identity within the land commonly referred to today as 'holy' cannot be disregarded. Nonetheless, a framework of analysis which centralises the religious factor not only runs the risk of over-simplifying the complex and dynamic nature of Palestinian identity and inter-group relations but of minimising or downplaying the equally important roles played by other factors and agencies.

Connected to this problem is the rather deliberate and selective choice of case study typical of much research into Palestinian Christians today. While further research should undoubtedly be undertaken to investigate Palestinian Christians in the Occupied Palestinian Territories (OPTs) in a full and comprehensive manner – including the more unsavoury aspects of religiously fuelled violence and discrimination – the absence of a comparable level of critical inquiry into the general status of Palestinians (Muslim and Christian) living under PA rule – and Israeli occupation – not only suggests the absence of intellectual rigour but also of several politically motivated 'blind spots'.

One of the more obvious blind spots concerns the status of Palestinian Christians living inside Israel today. As three quarters of all Palestinian Christians currently resident within the combined territories of Israel-Palestine do not live under PA rule, but rather as Israeli citizens inside 'Israel proper' (the area inside the Green Line, or the pre-1967 borders of the State of Israel), it would not be unreasonable to expect that any analysis of the status of Palestinian Christians in the OPTs would be viewed relative to the status of this larger community. However, as Justus Reid Weiner's report illustrates, this has not been the case. Underlying the absence of a comparative analysis is the assumption that the problems facing Palestinian Christians in the OPTs are intrinsically connected with PA, and by extension, Muslim rule. This conclusion is, however, deeply problematic and flawed.

Weiner's statements on the 'unique' problem of Christian emigration from the OPTs have been vigorously challenged. According to Sabeel's 2006 Survey on Palestinian Christians in the West Bank in Israel, patterns of Christian emigration, whilst far more pronounced in the West Bank, also exist inside Israel. Unlike Weiner's report, the Sabeel survey indicates that the main reason underlying Christian emigration from both the OPTs and from Israel is not Muslim fundamentalism but, rather, the poor political and economic situation which Palestinians find themselves in under occupation in the West Bank or as a discriminated minority inside Israel. The 'push' factor of relative deprivation combined with the 'pull' factor of greater family connections abroad, Sabeel explains, accounts for the higher rates of Palestinian Christian emigration.

Christian emigration, however, is not the only issue of concern highlighted by Weiner's report. The report raises several questions which have, to date, not been examined with respect to the Palestinian Christian population of Israel. With regards to social and economic discrimination, for example, how have Palestinian Christians in Israel fared, not just relative to Palestinians in the OPTs, but relative to Israel's Muslim, Jewish and Druze populations? Have they been exposed to economic boycott by any segments of the Israeli population? If so, to what extent have these measures been experienced by other segments of the Israeli population (Muslim, Jewish or Druze)? As Christians, have they experienced any religiously motivated violence or violations of their property rights? In instances where discrimination, boycott or violence has taken place, who are the responsible parties (are they necessarily Muslim?), what grievances motivated them and how have the Israeli authorities and security forces responded or dealt with them?

These are just a few of the questions which can be asked in foot of Wiener's report, but which, to date, have not. The absence of critical research into the status of Palestinian Christians living in Israel is, however, symptomatic of a larger and more traditional 'blind spot' affecting critical research of Israel and its sizable Palestinian Arab national minority. The Palestinian Arab minority in Israel is faced with a unique conundrum that has often been overlooked or ignored by both international media and academic scholarship. As Israeli citizens, Palestinian Arabs have access to a wide range of democratic rights and material benefits which are otherwise unavailable to the majority of state-less Palestinians forced to eke out a deprived existence either in refugee camps throughout the region or under Israeli occupation in the Palestinian territories. As a result, many consider the status of Palestinian Arabs in Israel to be 'normal' and unproblematic. However, their Israeli citizenship does little to offset the unique dilemmas which Palestinian Arabs face in a state which was created to reflect and promote Jewish national interests and priorities over and above the interests and priorities of its large indigenous Palestinian Arab minority. Excluded and suspected, their identity and rights both as individual citizens and as a national minority have become a permanent battleground.

As a sizable non-Jewish minority, Palestinian Arabs are also deemed to constitute a 'demographic threat' to the future maintenance of the state as a Jewish state. Once viewed as a potential 'fifth column', descriptions of the minority as a veritable 'ticking time bomb' have become increasingly common following the watershed events of October 2000 in which 13 Palestinian citizens of the state were killed by Israeli police and security forces during legal demonstrations against Israeli state policy. Increasing tensions between the State of Israel and its Palestinian Arab minority and the growing number of calls from within right-wing and mainstream Jewish circles alike to make the citizenship of all Palestinian Arabs, including Palestinian Christians, in Israel conditional upon a pledge of loyalty to the state (as a Jewish state) have exacerbated the already unstable position of the Palestinian Arab minority and, by association, of Palestinian Christians inside Israel today.

This book is, therefore, motivated by the need to address the problematic status of both the Palestinian Arab minority and the equally problematic status of Palestinian Christians in Israel. Analyses of Palestinian Arabs in general, and the nature of state–minority relations in Israel in particular, have tended to overlook the diversity of Palestinian Arab society. While critical scholars such as Aziz Haidar, As'ad Ghanem, Nadim Rouhana, Amal Jamal and Ahmad Sa'di have attempted to overlook or minimise religious differences in their analyses of state–minority relations, others, such as Dov Friedlander, Ilana Kaufman, Alisa Peled and Raphael Israeli have explicitly focused their analyses upon the largest component of the Palestinian Arab minority – the Muslims. Whether motivated by particular political agendas or determined by sensitivities to alternative academic discourses, the current state of scholarship on the Palestinian Arab minority in Israel has become partially blinded to the role and significance of internal diversity within the minority and the particular experience of non-Muslim and non-Jewish groups in society.

Despite the fact that the majority of Palestinian Arabs in Israel are Muslim, almost one in five are not. Given an international discourse that is increasingly located within foreign policy concerns and which stresses the so-called 'Islamic threat' emanating from the Middle East as well as the alleged 'clash of civilisations' between Islam and the 'West', there is a marked parallel tendency to oversimplify state–minority relations in Israel along the same lines. As such, this book aims to avoid this slippage by focusing its analysis on one non-Muslim segment of the Palestinian Arab minority in Israel – the Palestinian Christians.

The choice to focus on Palestinian Christians is, therefore, influenced by two main factors. In the first instance, the neglect and marginalisation of Palestinian

Christians within the social and political sciences has served only to reify generalisations which have traditionally equated Arab ethnicity with the Muslim faith. Furthermore, the significant contribution of Christian Arabs to the development of Arab culture and the crystallisation of both Palestinian and Arab nationalist thought has often been overlooked by studies which focus on church issues or the exclusively religious aspects of Christian identity. The importance of integrating Christian political identities and orientations within any analysis of the Palestinian Arab minority is, therefore, essential to the promotion of a more nuanced understanding of Palestinian and Israeli society and politics.

This leads on to the next main factor motivating this study's particular focus, which is that Palestinian Christians represent an alternative but useful test-case for state–minority relations in Israel. An analysis of Palestinian Christians in Israel, who are a non-Muslim Arab community, can provide new insights into the nature of Israeli state attitudes and policies towards its Palestinian Arab minority as a whole. Palestinian Christians have historically played an important and high-profile role within the Palestinian Arab minority that is disproportionate to their small numbers. The contributions of such figures as Edward Said, Emil Habibi, George Habash, Emil Touma, Anton Shammas, Mahmoud Darwish and Azmi Bishara to Arabic literature, culture and poetry and, critically, to the development of Arab and Palestinian nationalism is well known. The cultural engagement and political activism of Palestinian Christians has been reflected in the system of classification used by the State of Israel to categorise the nationality of its non-Jewish population. While Christians and Muslims are both defined as 'Arab' nationals, the Druze – the only other non-Muslim Arab community in Israel – have been accorded a separate Druze nationality by the state. Similarly, both Palestinian Christians and Muslims have, on the basis of their shared Arab nationality, been exempted by the state from performing mandatory military service, while the Druze are subject, together with the majority of Jews, to compulsory service.

The decision to focus on Palestinian Christians is, therefore, a calculated one. A focus on Palestinian Christians not only liberates this study from the pitfalls associated with many contemporary investigations of Muslims in society, but provides fresh avenues of inquiry through which state attitudes and policies towards Palestinian Arabs as a whole can be analysed. In so doing, it provides a unique opportunity not only to push the boundaries of research into state–minority relations in Israel, but also to challenge assumptions concerning the nature of the state itself and the status of Palestinian Christians within it.

In order to examine Israeli state policy and attitudes towards Palestinian Christians, this study applies a theoretical framework that borrows heavily from critical theories of state, society and minority policy. It is influenced by the contributions of Karl Mannheim's sociology of knowledge which emphasises the contingency of all ideas, value-systems, power relations and state institutions upon the bedrock of society. As both policy and attitudes are understood to originate in socially embedded mores and impulses, the ideological premises upon which Israeli society is founded are, therefore, given a central position in this study's analysis. The principles of political Zionism are central to the determination not only of social relations but of the boundaries within which the state is permitted to act on behalf of its Jewish majority. This has, however, led to a number of fundamental contradictions between the aspirations of the state to be both democratic and Jewish. Therefore, ethnocratic theory is used to overcome and reconcile these contradictions, providing a holistic understanding of the nature and structural limits not only of the state but of state–minority relations in Israel. As an ethnocratic state, this study then explores theories of systemic control which have been elaborated by others in their analyses of state policy towards the Palestinian Arab minority in Israel. A systemic approach is one that centralises the fundamental priorities and interests of the state over individual policies which, by themselves, may not sufficiently explain the manner in which the state perceives or engages with its minority. As this book's analysis of state policy towards its Palestinian Christian population is located within and subsumed by a broader systemic approach to the state's minority policy, the notion of a separate policy towards Palestinian Christians is considered to be both theoretically superfluous and ideologically redundant. Instead, this study identifies and examines a number of prevalent state attitudes towards Palestinian Christians in Israel and aims to locate these within the broader context of the state's systemic minority policy.

The theoretical framework outlined above has determined not only the manner in which the literature is assessed in this book but also the selection and interpretation of data. The methodology applied here combines a mixture of quantitative and qualitative research methods. The significance of demographic and territorial considerations to the maintenance of a given political order and the formulation of state policy, particularly within the context of deeply divided and plural societies, has resulted in the necessity to include an empirical profile of Palestinian Christians in Israel that is sensitive to these considerations. This profile draws heavily on data provided by the Israeli Central Bureau of Statistics (CBS) and, to a lesser extent, on statistical databases and reports produced by governmental and non-governmental organisations such as the Arab Centre for Alternative Planning (ACAP) in Israel, the Institute for International Strategic Studies (IIS) and the National Insurance Institute (NII) of Israel. However, given that statistics are, by their nature, malleable and subject to diverse interpretations, they cannot, in the context of their political functionality, be entirely relied upon or trusted.

While offering obvious benefits, the limits and dangers of statistical enquiry can never be fully overcome or neutralised. This does not mean that they cannot be contained. By integrating a qualitative basis to this research, the benefits of quantitative research can be more fully embraced. As such, a series of semi-structured interviews was conducted with 36 respondents from four different segments of society who are, in various capacities, expert on, or familiar with, matters relating to Palestinian Christians in Israel. The four segments were: academics, church leaders, NGO representatives and, finally, political and governmental representatives. These four respondent segments were chosen in order to acknowledge the potential diversity of views that can arise from differences in occupational and social statuses.

The nine academics who kindly shared their expertise for this study were: Amalia Sa'ar (Department of Sociology and Anthropology, Haifa University);

As'ad Ghanem, (School of Political Sciences, Haifa University); Dan Rabinowitz (Department of Sociology and Anthropology, Tel-Aviv University); Gabriel Ben-Dor (School of Political Sciences, Haifa University); Majid al-Hajj (Centre for Multiculturalism and Educational Research, Haifa University); Sammy Smooha (Faculty of Social Sciences, Haifa University); Raphael Israeli (Department of Middle Eastern and Chinese History, Hebrew University of Jerusalem); Michael Karayanni (Faculty of Law, Hebrew University of Jerusalem) and Fuad Farah (retired academic and Chairman of the Greek Orthodox National Council in Israel).

The church leaders and representatives who gave generously of their time were: the Greek Orthodox Patriarch of Jerusalem, Theofilos III; the Greek Catholic Archbishop of the Galilee, Elias Chacour; the Maronite Archbishop of Haifa and the Holy Land, Paul Sayyah; the Greek Catholic (Melkite) Patriarchal Vicar of Jerusalem, Joseph Saghbini; the Rector of the Latin (Roman Catholic) Seminary of Beit Jala, William Shomali; the Franciscan Custos of the Holy Land, Pierbattista Pizzaballa; the Court Registrar of the Anglican Church in Jerusalem, Nabil Zumot; as well as the Greek Catholic parish priest of Mailiya, Nadim Shakour and the Greek Orthodox parish priest of Rameh, George Hanna.

The political and government figures who contributed their views to this study were: the Director of the Department of Christian Affairs within the Ministry of the Interior, Cesar Marjieh; Palestinian Arab MK for Hadash/DFPE and Director of the Arab Centre for Alternative Planning, Hanna Sweid; former mayor of Yaffa an-Nasariyya and Head of the National Committee for Arab Local Councils and the Arab High Follow-Up Committee, Shawqi Khatib; Mayor of Nazareth for Hadash/DFPE, Ramiz Jeraisi; former Palestinian Arab MK for the Labour Party, Nadia Hilou; Legal Consultant to the Non-Jewish Committee in the Holy Land within the Ministry of the Interior, Yossi Hershler; Druze MK for the Kadima Party and former Deputy Minister for Foreign Affairs, Majalli Whbee; Senior Director of the Civil Service Commission in the Office of the Prime Minister, Henia Markovic; and the Head of the Authority for National Civic Service in the Office of the Prime Minister, Reuven Gal.

Finally, the representatives from the non-governmental sector whose views were sought out for this study were: the Director of the Jerusalem Centre for Jewish-Christian Relations, Daniel Rossing; Director of Baladna: The Association for Arab Youth, Nadim Nashef; Assistant Director of Mada al-Carmel: The Arab Centre for Applied Social Research, Einas Odeh-Hajj; Director of the International Centre for Consultations, Wadi Abu-Nasser; Director of the Palestinian Forum for Israeli Studies and Dean of the Mar Elias Educational Institutions, Johnny Mansour; Co-Director for Policy for Sikkuy: The Association for the Advancement of Civic Equality, Gubran Gubran; Director of HRA: The Arab Association for Human Rights, Mohammad Zeidane; Advocate for Adalah: The Arab Centre for Arab Minority Rights, Suhad Bishara; and, lastly, the Director of Mossawa: The Advocacy Centre for Arab Citizens of Israel, Jafar Farah.

This book is structured as follows: Chapter Two outlines the theoretical framework upon which this study is based. Theories of society, state and minority policy are discussed within the context of ethnocratic control theories. Chapter Three provides an empirical profile of the Palestinian Christian population of Israel which covers, amongst other things, their particular demographic, geographic and socio-economic features. This chapter is particularly useful in that it provides a basis through which both the state's national priorities (revolving around the twin pillars of land and demography) as well as various sociological claims regarding Palestinian Christians in particular can be compared and judged. Chapter Four reviews the available literature on the Palestinian Christian population in Israel and isolates a number of the most common themes which have occurred and recurred in these analyses and which, together, provide the basis through which an initial estimation of state attitudes towards Palestinian Christians can be made. Chapter Five presents the first set of independent findings and analyses the various respondents' impressions of Israeli state attitudes towards Palestinian Christians within the context of the prevailing theoretical assumptions outlined in the previous chapters. Chapter Six provides a case-study of one instance of intra-communal conflict in Israel which provides insights into Israeli state attitudes towards Palestinian Christians in Israel. The Nazareth 2000 affair, also referred to as the Shihab ad-Din crisis, emerged in 1997 between Nazareth city municipality and the local Islamic movement over the proposed development of the city centre in time for the 2000 millennium celebrations. Finally, Chapter Seven examines four additional instances of intra-communal conflict in Israel, all of which have taken place in the relatively recent past in various Arab mixed villages in the north of Israel. Unlike the case in Nazareth, each of these four conflicts occurred between local Palestinian Christian and Druze communities.

The roots of these different intra-communal conflicts, the response of the state and its authorities to them and the reaction of the Palestinian Christian communities themselves suggest a clear pattern in state–minority relations. While some instances of 'positive discrimination' in favour of Palestinian Christian institutions are found which support the notion of a differential state policy towards the minority, the general attitude of the state towards individual Palestinian Christian citizens tells a very different story. Not only are state attitudes towards the Palestinian Christian community comparable with state attitudes towards Palestinian Muslims and Druze, but, due to its small size and particular communal structures, state attitudes are often more ambivalent and reserved than has been hitherto been assumed. The significance of this finding extends beyond our understanding of the nature of the Israeli state and the general situation of state–minority relations in Israel, but has critically important consequences for the nature of intra-communal relations and the future status of Palestinian Christians in Israel.

2 Society, state and minority policy in Israel

On 14 May 1948, the State of Israel was born and the Declaration of Independence which accompanied it proclaimed that Jews had finally become 'masters of their own fate, like all other nations, in their own sovereign State' (MFA 2010a). It was expected that the creation of a Jewish state would 'normalise' the status of the Jewish people and 'restore' to them their individual and collective dignity as a people (Avishai 1985). However, the creation of the State of Israel in 1948 also introduced important new challenges to the Zionist concept of a Jewish state and to its fundamental principles of transformative and normative justice. The site chosen for the new Jewish state was already home to a culturally rich and diverse indigenous Palestinian Arab society and the creation of the State of Israel, together with the political and military actions which accompanied its creation, devastated the fabric of local Palestinian Arab society, ushering in a new majority–minority dynamic in society which has since come to dominate the public discourse and dictate the future political ambitions and development of the state.

This chapter aims to provide a theoretical basis through which the relationship of the Israeli state with a particular segment of the Palestinian Arab minority in Israel – the Palestinian Christians – can best be analysed in later chapters. In order to do this, a broader understanding of Israeli society, the Israeli state and its minority policy is first necessary. As such, this chapter is divided into several sections which address these topics in turn. The first section explores the nature of Israeli society and the structural or ideological foundations upon which it is based. The structure of Israeli society is understood to influence not only the range of possible social interactions between groups within it but also the relationship between state and society as a whole. This approach is inspired by Mannheim's sociology of knowledge which accounts for the socially embedded nature of power and the critical role of social relationships in the production of ideas and other normative value-systems in society. The second section of this chapter builds on this notion by investigating the particular nature of the Israeli state and the social and ideological parameters within which it operates. Out of a range of possible state definitions, this study isolates ethnocracy as the most comprehensive description of the nature of the Israeli state. Finally, the third section of this chapter addresses the particular nature of state–minority relations in Israel through an analysis of Israeli state policy towards the Palestinian Arab minority as a whole. Representing the typical format through which states formally engage with their citizenry, policy is understood to reflect the social values, attitudes and priorities of the state. As such, this section addresses several different approaches to the subject of Israeli minority policy and finds that, given the wider structural limits of society and the state, a systemic approach based on a revitalised theory of control offers the most holistic approach to later analyses of state attitudes towards the Palestinian Christian population in Israel.

Israel as a deeply divided society

Israel is a multi-ethnic, plural and deeply divided society. That Israeli society consists of a number of diverse ethnic communities is evident. However, the plural and deeply divided nature of Israeli society requires further examination. The literature on plural and deeply divided societies shares a number of characteristics. Both assume the existence of diverse groups possessing competing collective identities and normative value systems. However, in order for a society to be considered plural or deeply divided, these differences must extend beyond the mere existence of diversity into the realm of power divisions and inequalities, as manifested in the existence of particular majority–minority dynamics, as well as with regard to the political sustainability and stability of given social orders. Ian Lustick defines a deeply divided society as follows:

> I shall consider a society as deeply divided if ascriptive ties generate an antagonistic segmentation of society, based on terminal identities with high political salience, sustained over a substantial period of time and a wide variety of issues. As a minimum condition, boundaries between rival groups must be sharp enough so that membership is clear and, with few exceptions, unchangeable.
>
> (Lustick 1979: 325)

Group antagonism or conflict is, therefore, a defining feature of plural and deeply divided societies. Consequently, not only is the correlation between difference and conflict especially strong within the context of deeply divided societies, but the likelihood of conflict to emerge is particularly strong given the correlation of differences with issues which are deemed to be of particular political salience or relevance to the ruling establishment. As such, not all forms of difference are accorded the same level of political salience in any given society.

The Jewish–Arab divide represents the single most politically salient division in Israeli society (Shafir and Peled 2002: 31). This division is particularly emphasised as several lines of separation, encompassing national, ethnic, religious, linguistic, cultural and socio-economic differences, divide Jews and Arabs, while few cross-cutting cleavages unite them (Lustick 1980: 5). The political salience that is given to the Jewish–Arab national divide is compounded by three main factors. To begin with, decades of political conflict, encompassing seven wars, between Israel and its Arab neighbours have underscored the degree to which the

Israeli state has felt threatened or besieged by an enemy which is defined in ethnic terms as Arab (Rouhana 1997: 7). This, in turn, is aggravated by continued Israeli military, territorial and settlement expansion in the OPTs which have inflamed tensions and increased gaps between both Jews and Arabs domestically as well (Smooha 1989: 77).

However, the main factor which has contributed to the heightened political salience of the national divide in Israel is the fundamentally antagonistic nature of both the state and the Palestinian Arab minority in Israel. On the one hand, Israel was created not only as a Jewish state for the Jewish people but as a state in which the future maintenance of a Jewish majority was conceived. As such, the ideological boundaries of Israeli society, which are ethno-nationally defined, and its potential for future development remain exclusively within the hands of Israel's Jewish majority to the exclusion of its Palestinian Arab minority. While few would characterise Israeli society as a typical colonial or settler society, the vast majority of scholars agree that Israeli society demonstrates a basic level of ambivalence and political intransigence towards the rights and status of Palestinian Arabs as citizens of the state (Smooha 1989: 17–24). On the other hand, the Palestinian Arab minority, which is a sizable, territorially concentrated, indigenous, non-assimilating national minority, represents – both ideologically and demographically – a permanent source of threat, if not an implicit source of political destabilisation, to the exclusively Jewish character of the state (Yiftachel 2006: 99).

A further distinguishing characteristic of plural and deeply divided societies is the prevalence of unequal and asymmetrical power relations in society. The theoretical perspective provided by structural pluralism, for example, centralises the twin notions of dominance and subordination in inter-group relations as well as the monopolisation of power by the dominant group in society. As such, social differences are understood to become stratified and institutionalised in an attempt to maintain the hegemonic status of one group in society. An attachment to social continuity, rather than to social change, is a central component of structurally pluralistic societies. Moreover, subordination, prejudice, discrimination and ethnocentrism are considered to be fundamental elements in the creation and maintenance of a particular hegemonic order in society.

Sammy Smooha has contributed a great deal to understandings of structural pluralism within the Israeli context. Based on earlier international formulations of 'plural societies', which originally focused on the artificial social and economic structures imposed upon developing countries by European colonial powers, Smooha defines pluralism as 'a central structural feature of total societies' wherein two main features are centralised: cultural diversity and social separation (Smooha 1978: 13–14). Within the context of Israeli society, Smooha identifies three major social cleavages which demonstrate the plural nature of society: the Ashkenazi–Mizrahi divide; the religious–secular divide and the Arab–Jewish divide. Notwithstanding recent changes in intra-communal Jewish relations, the Jewish–Arab divide remains the most dominant social cleavage in society. As a result, this study accepts both the dominance and the political salience of the Jewish–Arab divide to its understanding of Israel as a deeply divided and pluralistic society.

Israel as an ethnocratic etate

The State of Israel is synonymously referred to as the Jewish state. But given the multi-ethnic and deeply divided nature of society, what does this designation signify? The roots of the Jewish state label lie in Zionist ideology and the idea of creating a permanent state for the Jewish people. State symbols (such as the flag and national anthem), institutions (such as the Knesset and the Israel Land Administration), laws (such as the Law of Return) and holidays (such as the Jewish Sabbath, Independence Day and Remembrance Day) all reflect the centrality of the particular values and imperatives of the dominant group in society, which is the ethno-nationally defined Jewish majority.

Israel was established not only on the Zionist principle of transforming Judaism 'from a religion or civilisation to a national movement, essentially modern and secular' but also on the selective basis of the Jewish biblical promise of 'return' to the 'promised land' (Kimmerling 1999: 342). This has led to some confusion as to whether Israel can legitimately be considered to be a secular state at all (Horowitz and Lissak 1989: 114). Given the close association between ethnic and religious Jewish identities, and the ideological equivalence that is proposed to exist between Judaism and the concept of the Jewish nation, the centrality of religious identity in Israeli society, as manifested in the Israeli Declaration of Independence, and particularly after 1967, has led some to consider Israel to be an ethno-religious state based on an uncomfortable admixture of democratic and theocratic principles (Kimmerling 1999: 340–2 and Shafir and Peled 1998: 413). The absence of civic alternatives in matters pertaining to the personal status of individual Israeli citizens and their relegation to the sole jurisdiction of religious authorities (particularly with regard to marriage and divorce); the increasing power of *haredi* (Jewish ultra-orthodox) religious parties and *halakhic* principles (Jewish religious law) in defining the boundaries of the territorial state, the Jewish national collective as well as of various governmental interests and priorities, have added to this scepticism suggesting – democratic 'checks' notwithstanding – that an increasing erosion of the boundaries separating religion from state, as well as the accentuation of the religious identity of all groups in society as a whole (Jewish and non-Jewish alike), is taking place (Horowitz and Lissak 1989: 142–4 and Rouhana 1997: 22).

While Israel is a Jewish state in ideological terms, the 'nation-state' label which is often proposed to describe it does not stand up to empirical analysis. This is because the 'nation' within Israeli Zionist discourse is defined according to particular ethno-national or primordial affiliations rather than on the basis of an inclusive and universal civic identity. Given that only 75 per cent of the Israeli population is – according to the CBS – defined as ethnically Jewish, with 20 per cent of the remaining non-Jewish population belonging to the Palestinian Arab ethno-national minority, Israel is clearly not a mono-ethnic state in a descriptive sense.[1]

Nonetheless, the nation-state label is frequently encountered even in critical analyses which see it as the best description of Jewish dominance in society.

Some, for example, consider the official ideology of the state to be none other than a nation-state-building ideology, referred to as *mamlachtiut* in Hebrew. *Mamlachtiut* refers to a highly centralised form of statist rule in which the dominant position of the Jewish nation is understood to be enshrined. While it owes its roots to the administrative transition of power from diverse and disconnected pre-state Jewish organisations typical of the *yishuv* period to a centralised state apparatus under the charismatic but authoritarian leadership of David Ben-Gurion, the particular etymology of the term reveals a further ideological component. Based on the term *mamlacha,* meaning 'kingdom' in Hebrew, *mamlachtiut* encapsulates the need not only to create a Jewish state in Israel, but also the need to create a new, single and unified Jewish nation out of culturally, ethnically and linguistically diverse groups of Jewish immigrants. Within this nation-state-building project, Orthodox Judaism and a selection of particular Jewish religious principles and symbols are understood to have become secularised by the state in its attempt to forge the new boundaries of the Jewish collective, thereby transforming it into the new 'civil religion' of the state (Cohen-Almagor 1995: 467–9, 481 and Kimmerling 2001: 101).

As the State of Israel is empirically speaking not a mono-ethnic nation-state, the next assertion that the state is both 'Jewish *and* democratic' – which is also often taken for granted in analyses of Israeli state and society – is equally problematic. This is particularly so given the ambiguous and overburdened nature of the term 'democracy' itself which lacks any clear theoretical definition or defining characteristics (Kimmerling 1999: 339). While democracy implies the basic notion of majority rule and consensus, several other social and political criteria are necessary in order for a state to be considered democratic, such as: the existence of 'an open regime based on free and fair parliamentary elections, protection of human rights, freedom of speech, autonomous judiciary, free choice of political affiliation, universal eligibility for public office, and the right to form and join organisations' (Yiftachel 1992: 17). Other commonly cited democratic features include: the provision of various civic rights and freedoms (such as freedom of religion, occupation and movement); gender equality; universal suffrage; political transparency and accountability; freedom of information; an open market economy and a vibrant civil society.

As the State of Israel embraces the vast majority of these democratic criteria and appears to satisfy the general conditions laid out by democratic theory it is often described as being a fully functioning democracy that is not only on a par with other democratic states but one that serves as a 'bastion of democracy' to authoritarian and undemocratic regimes in the Middle East as a whole.[2] However, despite the easy association and compatibility that is generally implied to exist between a democratic and an ethnic system of governance, these two philosophies are not easy or suggestible bedfellows. On the contrary, deep structural tensions exist between the basic normative values, practical requirements and ideological priorities of both systems which limit and erode the democratic character of the state. Such tensions, which are easily concealed within analyses of individual rights, immediately reveal themselves in analyses of majority–minority relations and collective rights, particularly minority rights, in society. This is particularly relevant given that the measure of democracy is also often judged according to whether the following four key additional principles are in place: (1) the existence of a secular and relatively neutral state; (2) the provision of comparable collective rights to groups in society; (3) full equality for all citizens before the law; and (4) the protection of minorities (Ghanem et al. 1998: 255 and Yiftachel 2006: 98). Therefore, the manner in which states relate to their minorities, the range of individual and group rights which they offer them and the level of individual and collective equality in society are important, if not fundamental, measures of any state's democratic claims.

The democratic characterisation of the Israeli state has been challenged on various structural and legal grounds. Beyond the centrality of exclusively Jewish symbols of identity and belonging, several Basic Laws legally enshrine the Jewish character of the state and affirm the right of the majority to maintain Jewish national and numerical superiority within society. According to the Basic Law of Return (1950), for example, any Jewish person in the world who wishes to immigrate to Israel has the right to do so. By contrast, hundreds of thousands of Palestinian Arabs who fled or were forced from their homes during the tumultuous years of 1948–9 have no such right to either re-enter Israel or return to their homes. Similarly, the Basic Law on Nationality (1952) provides any Jewish immigrant, or relative of a Jewish immigrant, with immediate citizenship. The same Law, however, stipulates several arduous and, with regard to spouses from the occupied Palestinian territories, quite impossible, conditions which non-citizen spouses of Palestinian Arabs must satisfy in order to become citizens of the state. Furthermore, the Basic Law on Israeli Lands declares that over 90 per cent of land in the country is 'state land' and a national resource of the Jewish people, despite the fact that the vast majority of this land was sourced through wide-scale government expropriations and confiscations of Palestinian Arab land. Similarly, amendment 7a to the Basic Law on The Knesset (1985) excludes any political party or list from running for office if they in any way negate or challenge the Jewish character of the state.

Beyond particular Basic Laws, the State of Israel provides international Zionist organisations such as the World Zionist Organisation (WZO), the Jewish Agency (JA) and the Jewish National Fund (JNF) with official status within the state. Furthermore, the provision of a wide range of social welfare and educational benefits are made contingent upon the performance of military service, a duty which Palestinian Arabs (with the exception of the Druze) are legally exempted from.

How can such obvious infringements of democratic principles be reconciled within pro-establishment discourses which identify Israel as a flourishing democratic state? Interestingly, the vast majority of pro-establishment analyses recognise and accept certain necessary but unavoidable limits to the democratic character of Israel. Such limits are generally understood to originate within the dual character of the Israeli state. The first layer of state identity concerns a commitment to the Jewish character of the state, with a corresponding set of ethno-national norms, values, priorities, procedures and institutions accorded a central and determining position. The second layer of state identity, however, is understood to be fundamentally democratic, whereby substantively democratic norms and values as well as formally democratic procedures and institutions are understood to underpin and guide state activity and policy, as well as to moderate and offset the ethnic priorities of the state. Within this dual characterisation of the state, each element is presented as having the strength and power to determine the direction of society. Yet while most analyses within this category treat both elements as mutually compatible, there is a paradoxical recognition that not only are there fundamental tensions and normative contradictions between both elements, but that a particular hierarchical order exists which prioritises Jewish national state interests in any instances where conflict between the two may arise. Such 'limits', 'tensions' or 'contradictions' are often explained away with regard to the exceptional thesis of 'national security' considerations. Despite a broad recognition that these limits are rooted in structural rather than security issues relating to the nature of the state, the fundamental characterisation of the state as democratic remains popular. In such accounts, democratic limits are usually justified and incorporated within the concept of 'defensive democracy', whereby the preservation of the dominance of the Jewish majority is considered to be 'democratically' legitimate both as a result of Jewish historical experience and the regional minority status of Jews in the Middle East. Furthermore, the Israeli Jewish majority is understood, according to this perspective, to be entitled or obliged to take proactive measures, even if they appear to be undemocratic, in order to protect the future of democracy from allegedly non-democratic forces both inside and outside the state (Jamal 2006: 7).

Considering these acknowledged structural tensions, the democratic claims of the Israeli state require further examination. The literature on democratic governance suggests that democratic states generally fall into one of the following two types: liberal democracies or consociational democracies. The characteristics of both, and the differences between them, are outlined succinctly by Smooha:

> In a *liberal democracy*, such as the United States, ethnicity is privatised. The state does not legislate or intervene in ethnic cleavages, but forges a homogenous nation-state by setting up uniform language, identity, nationalism, and national institutions for its citizens. It provides conditions for acculturation and assimilation, but also allows ethnic groups to remain socially separate and culturally distinct, insofar as they are prepared to pay the cost of separate existence. The cornerstone of society is the individual, personal skills, achievements, political and civil rights, and self-fulfilment.
>
> In a *consociational democracy*, such as Belgium, ethnicity is accepted as a major principle in the organisation of the state. Individuals are judged on merit and accorded civil and political rights, but ethnic groups are also officially recognised and granted certain rights, such as control over education and allocation of public posts on a proportional basis. The state is not identified with any of the constituent groups and tries to reconcile the differences between them. Ethnicity is thus institutionalised and ethnic identities and institutions are usually kept separate. Yet it is not illegal to assimilate or even

to intermarry. Each group has its own elite, and the state is managed by an elite-cartel that allocates resources according to the principle of proportionality and pursues compromises between the ethnic groups.

Liberal and consociational democracies share a set of democratic institutions, an extension of equality and citizenship for all, and an ethnically neutral state.

(Smooha 1997: 199)

For Smooha, it is clear that Israel does not fulfil any of the necessary requirements to be considered either a liberal or a consociational democracy.

[Israel] is not a liberal democracy, because the state recognises ethnic differences, accords some collective rights, and fails to treat all citizens and groups equally. It is not a consociational democracy, because the state is not ethnically neutral; rather it is owned and ruled by the majority, while the minorities do not enjoy autonomy and power-sharing.

(Smooha 1997: 200)

This basic contradiction between democratic and ethnic principles has led some to describe the Israeli state as a fundamentally undemocratic, authoritarian and dictatorial regime in which a 'tyranny of the majority' exists.[3] Maxime Rodinson (1973) and Elia Zureik (1974: 99–100; 1976: 40, 64–6) have, for instance, described Israel as a variant of a neo-colonial or settler state. Meron Benvenisti (1987: 199) and Baruch Kimmerling (2006: 39, 143) have proposed that the Israeli state, post-1967, belongs to the category of *Herrenvolk* democracies, while Uri Davis (2003: 37) has described it as an example of an apartheid state.[4] Despite this, theories which promote Israel as a type of 'partial' or 'limited' democracy that is susceptible to a number of unique structural problems and dilemmas remain more common. One of the first proponents of this middle-ground approach was Sammy Smooha who defined Israel as an 'ethnic democracy'. The ethnic democracy approach recognises the central role of Jewish ethnicity and the Jewish character of the state in determining certain limits to the democratic character of the state and the rights of the minority.

Ethnic democracy is a system that combines the extension of civil and political rights to individuals and some collective rights to minorities, with institutionalisation of majority control over the state. Driven by ethnic nationalism, the state is identified with a "core ethnic nation", not with its citizens. The state practices a policy of creating a homogenous nation-state, a state of and for a particular ethnic nation, and acts to promote the language, culture, numerical majority, economic well-being and political interests of this group. Although enjoying citizenship and voting rights, the minorities are treated as second-class citizens, feared as a threat, excluded from the national power structure, and placed under some control. At the same time, the minorities are allowed to conduct a democratic and peaceful struggle that yields incremental improvement to their status.

(Smooha 1997: 199–200)

While Smooha considers Israel, together with a small number of other states such as Estonia, Latvia, Slovakia, Poland (from 1918 to 1935), Canada (until the 1960s), Northern Ireland (until 1972) and Malaysia (from the 1970s), to be an ethnic democracy whereby the 'core ethnic nation' – in this case, the Jewish ethnic majority – dominates the state apparatus, he nonetheless maintains that Israel is basically more democratic than ethnic in nature, with the Palestinian Arab minority enjoying significant democratic rights on an individual and, to a lesser extent, on a collective basis as well. Thus, for him, 'ethnic democracy is located somewhere in the democratic section of the democracy-non-democracy continuum' of state types (Smooha 1997: 199).

Shafir and Peled echo this description of the Israeli state as an ethnic democracy (Peled and Shafir 1996 and Shafir and Peled 1998). In their analysis of the hierarchical and multiple nature of citizenship in Israel, they make a distinction between formal citizenship and full citizenship, whereby citizenship itself is understood not only as a measure of civic membership in a state, but also as a tool in its stratification. Within this approach, Israeli citizenship is said to consist of three separate components – liberal, republican and ethno-nationalist – each of which represents differential 'modes of incorporation' for groups in society (Shafir and Peled 1998: 412). The liberal element of Israeli citizenship accounts for the universal civic rights which are assured to every individual citizen of the state, regardless of ethnicity and in an unconditional manner. It is this form which is understood to be the most inclusive and democratic of all three citizenship types. The republican aspect of Israeli citizenship is identified on a collective basis as according special group rights exclusively to those who belong fully to the dominant community's particular conception of 'the common good'. This citizenship type is understood to be based on the '"pioneering" civic virtue' of Zionist ideology, particularly with regard to Israel's dominant male Ashkenazi community. Finally, the ethnonationalist dimension of Israeli citizenship is recognised as giving preference and priority to citizens of the state who are of Jewish descent. Palestinian Arab citizens are presented as enjoying the minimal form of Israeli citizenship – liberal citizenship – which provides individual Palestinians with full rights, but only so long as these rights do not conflict with the national priorities of the Jewish majority, in which case those rights are also restricted. As such, the Jewish majority alone is understood to enjoy full democratic rights, while the Palestinian Arab minority receives only partial democratic rights. Given their exclusion from the maximal republican and ethno-national categories of Israeli citizenship, Palestinian Arab citizens are identified as 'third-class citizens' of the state (Shafir and Peled 2002: 73, 110). Yet while Shafir and Peled believe the republican dimension of Israeli citizenship to have diminished in relevance in recent decades as a result of globalisation and the progressive 'liberalisation' of society, the state is nonetheless understood to be committed to upholding the Jewish ethno-nationalist character of the state, and consequently of Israeli citizenship as well.

Although the partial or ethnic democracy model recognises important structural limitations to Israeli democracy (and the ideological origins of these limitations) and makes important distinctions between the type and extent of rights available, this model also normalises the discriminatory and illiberal aspect of the Israeli state by focusing on certain democratic criteria, or features, rather than on the cumulative impact of the system as a whole. As'ad Ghanem has argued that a partially democratic state, as advanced by the ethnic democracy model is, rationally and philosophically speaking, not a democratic state at all. While there is arguably no such thing as a perfect democracy, for a state to be considered democratic, in his view, would require a basic structural and normative commitment to the principle of universal equality as well as to the state's neutrality with regard to the ethnic affiliations of its citizens.

> As for the ethnic-democracy model, in my opinion an 'ethnic democracy' is not democratic at all, from a number of viewpoints. First, the term yoked two concepts that are logically, practically and historically contradictory as the basic foundation of deeply divided societies. Second, Israel does not preserve the fundamental principles of democracy, such as equality before the law and freedom for all citizens.
>
> (Ghanem 1998: 430–1)

Therefore, not only is the presence of democratic *features* an insufficient criterion for qualification as a democratic *state,* but the twin concepts of democracy, with its implied capacity for universal equality, and ethnicity, with its inherent collective bias, are fundamentally irreconcilable (Ghanem et al. 1998: 254). Instead, Ghanem suggests that Israel is better defined as an 'ethnic state'. While in an ethnic democracy the state is understood to be basically democratic in nature, in an ethnic state, the reverse is true, with exclusive ethnic concerns overshadowing any formally democratic features of the state.

> It is much more appropriate to classify Israel as an ethnic state, such as Turkey, Latvia, Lithuania, Estonia, Canada until thirty years ago, and even totalitarian states like Iraq and Iran. Of course, it differs from such intolerant ethnic states in that it does offer restricted rights to members of the minority group and integrates them to a limited degree in its politics, society, economy and media. Israel conducts sophisticated policies of exclusion allied with limited inclusion in all spheres of life. It permits its Arab Citizens to exercise basic rights, including the right to vote for and be elected to legislative bodies, freedom of expression, and freedom of movement and organisation. At the same time, however, it follows policies of domination and control that guarantee continued Jewish hegemony and Arab marginality in all fields.
>
> (Ghanem 1998: 430)

Another proponent of the ethnic state model, Nadim Rouhana, has argued that Israel is based on 'superstructural ethnic exclusivity' which precludes the possibility of full equality or full democracy for all its citizens (Rouhana 1997: 6). While democratic elements do exist, an important distinction is made between 'formal', or procedural, elements of democracy and 'structural' democracy itself, which is based on essential recognition of the normative value and importance of the basic right to full equality by all citizens and groups in society. As such, the 'essence' of democratic rule has not been sufficiently internalised by the Israeli state structure, thus rendering its designation as a democratic state illegitimate (Rouhana and Ghanem 2007: 337). Furthermore, Rouhana identifies in the dissonance between ethnic priorities and democratic features a 'self-serving national deception' which both legitimates discrimination and suspends objective internal inquiry, which if tackled would open up society to a fundamental ideological crisis (Rouhana 2006: 69–70). This attitude is reflected in the conditional nature of Israeli public attitudes towards democratic principles:

> On the declarative level, Israelis accord democracy a high level of support. Once asked about particular democratic values such as minority rights and equality for non-Jewish citizens, that support breaks down.
>
> (Rouhana 1997: 39)

Interestingly, more establishment analyses of Israeli society also accept this notion of the 'conditional acceptance of democracy'. Dan Horowitz and Moshe Lissak have, for example, argued that 'the ideological commitment to democracy has not always been unconditional among all political groups, and consensus has not always prevailed concerning the specific norms implied by the broad concept of democracy', particularly when democratic norms are understood to challenge or contradict ethno-national interests and commitments (Horowitz and Lissak 1989: 144). Thus, 'Israeli democracy', as they recognise it, 'has been anchored to a greater extent in arrangements of political convenience than in a fundamental commitment to the normative foundations of democracy' (Horowitz and Lissak 1989: 144).

As adherents to the ethnic state model, both Ghanem and Rouhana have also supported Oren Yiftachel's definition of the State of Israel as a Jewish 'ethnocracy'. While ethnic and ethnocratic states share a number of assumptions, ethnocratic theory has provided a broader theoretical understanding of the nature of the Israeli state and the resolution of the persistence of democratic features within it, which is particularly useful to this study.

Ethnocratic theory identifies the same basic dissonance between the core concepts of ethnicity and democracy and recognises the sociological tendency towards 'conceptual stretching' and the 'inflationary use' of the term democracy within the Israeli context (Yiftachel 2006: 46–8). Yiftachel's analysis of the term 'democracy' itself underscores this contradiction. Correctly understood as a 'community of equal citizens within a given territory' and as appealing to 'inclusive association by origin', *demos* is considered fundamentally contradictory to the concept of *ethnos* which determines group membership according to 'selective association by origin' (Ghanem et al. 1998: 255, 264).

Yiftachel's approach draws attention to one of the key concerns of ethnocratic theory, which is the importance of territory and the land question to analyses of democracy. A commonly held requirement of statehood, as well as of democracy, is the existence of clearly demarcated and internationally recognised territorial state borders which, on the one hand, limit state sovereignty and jurisdiction to a particular territory and, on the other hand, demarcate the maximum boundaries of citizenship. The lack of consensus regarding the pivotal question of 'where is Israel?' and the deep disparities and incongruities which currently exist between the competing terminologies and territorial associations of 'the Jewish state', 'the State of Israel' (Medinat Israel) and 'Greater Israel' (Eretz Israel) have caused great confusion not only on the level of Israeli–Palestinian peace negotiations but equally on the domestic level of Israeli identity and citizenship. While observers may assume that the location of the State of Israel is limited to the area inside the Green Line, or the pre-1967 borders of the state, otherwise commonly referred to as 'Israel proper', growing Israeli military, political and settlement expansion within the OPTs and the gradual integration and normalisation of these territories within the broader political consensus of the state indicate the growing significance of the Greater Israel concept and the increasing erosion of both the boundaries of 'Israel proper' and of regular Israeli citizenship. In one work, for example, Yiftachel describes 'Israel proper' as an imaginary unit (Yiftachel 1999b: 383), and in another as 'a polity without borders' (Yiftachel 2006: 97). As such, the inclusion of Israeli Jewish settler-citizens living outside 'Israel proper' within CBS data, together with the fuzziness of the state's own understanding of the extent and limits of its territorial borders, weakens and undermines the concept of *demos* within the Israeli case. As the Greek origins of the term 'democracy' suggest, a civic understanding of rule, or government, by (all) the people for (all) the people, is clearly absent within the Israeli case, which is defined as a Jewish state for the Jewish people, wherever they may reside. Given these realities, the following definition of an 'ethnocracy' is more appropriate to the Israeli case.

> An ethnocracy is a non-democratic regime which attempts to extend or preserve disproportional ethnic control over a contested multi-ethnic territory. Ethnocracy develops chiefly when control over territory is challenged, and when a dominant group is powerful enough to determine unilaterally the nature of the state.
>
> (Yiftachel 1999b: 367–8)

Beyond the issue of land and territorial citizenship, Yiftachel provides a detailed elaboration of the key features and principles which characterise an ethnocratic state and which distinguish it from other forms of governance.

An ethnocratic regime is characterised by several key principles:

- Despite several democratic features, mainly ethnicity (and not territorial citizenship) determines the allocation of rights and privileges; a constant democratic-ethnocratic tension characterises politics.
- State borders and political boundaries are fuzzy: there is no identifiable *demos,* mainly due to the role of ethnic diasporas inside the polity and the inferior position of ethnic minorities.

- A dominant 'charter' ethnic group appropriates the state apparatus, determines most public policies, and segregates itself from other groups.
- Political, residential, and economic segregation and stratification occur on two main levels: ethno-nations and ethno-classes.
- The constitutive logic of ethno-national segregation is diffused, enhancing a process of political ethnicisation among sub-groups within each ethno-nation.
- Significant (though partial) civil and political rights are extended to members of the minority ethno-nation, distinguishing ethnocracies from *Herrenvolk* democracies or authoritarian regimes.

Ethnocratic regimes are usually supported by a cultural and ideological apparatus which legitimises and reinforces the uneven reality. This is achieved by constructing a historical narrative which proclaims the dominant ethno-nation as the rightful owner of the territory in question. Such a narrative degrades all other contenders as historically not entitled, or culturally unworthy, to control the land or achieve political equality.

A further legitimising apparatus is the maintenance of *selective openness*. Internally, the introduction of democratic institutions is common, especially in settling societies, as it adds legitimacy to the entire settling project, to the leadership of the charter ethno-class, and to the incorporation of groups of later immigrants. But these democratic institutions commonly exclude indigenous or rival minorities. [. . .] Externally, selective openness is established as a principle of foreign relations and membership in international organisations.

(Yiftachel 1999b: 367–8)

Thus, while the Israeli state does possess partial democratic features, 'most notably political competition, free media and significant civil rights', it is not, for Yiftachel, a democratic state (Yiftachel and Ghanem 2004: 649). Within the limited, selective, contingent, hierarchical and malleable nature of democratic features in Israel, Yiftachel suggests similarities between ethnocracy and 'façade democracy' (Yiftachel 2006: 3, 19). S.E. Finer defined a façade democracy as any political system which appears to adhere to certain formal procedures associated with democratic standards, such as periodic elections or the rule of law, but which selectively distorts, exploits or ignores such procedures in order to preserve and strengthen the political hegemony of a particular, and usually authoritarian, ruling elite (Finer 1970: 57, 124). Normally used to describe the selective use of democratic standards in other Middle Eastern states, such as Algeria or the political oligarchy of the Hashemite Kingdom of Jordan (Milton-Edwards 1993), a façade democracy is also one which uses the existence of open democratic features of the state both to promote a positive image of itself in the world and to legitimise the continuation of discrimination and inequality internally by appearing to offer avenues for political mobility, participation and change to its citizens while simultaneously reinforcing barriers to change.

Unlike Smooha's ethnic democracy model, Yiftachel suggests that an ethno-cratic state is a fundamentally unstable political regime, bounded as it is between 'opposite forces of expansionism and resistance [which are] in constant conflict' (Yiftachel 1999b: 368). However, this instability is not necessarily due to the definition of the state as a Jewish state. Other democratic states have enshrined a particular religious order (such as the Church of England in the UK), while simul-taneously maintaining high levels of neutrality of the state and its legal code with regard to particular ethnic identities. It is the illiberal manner in which the legal and political codes, as well as the territory of the state itself, have become 'Juda-ised' and 'de-Arabised' which renders it progressively more unstable, artificial and illegitimate (Yiftachel 1999b: 371). This study finds that ethnocratic theory best describes the nature of the Israeli state, and provides the most convincing account of the complex and uneven interaction between democratic and ethnic interests and priorities.

Minority policy in an ethnocratic state

The previous section has addressed the tension that exists between democratic and ethnic priorities and suggests that ethnocracy remains the best description of the nature of the Israeli state. That important democratic elements exist in Israel is undisputed by ethnocratic theory. However, given the more powerful structural commitment of the state to the maintenance of its Jewish character, the ability of such democratic elements to affect the necessary normative and structural changes in order for the state structure as a whole to be characterised as a democracy is limited and weak.

Bearing in mind the distinction between procedural and structural democracy, and the subordinate role of procedurally or formally democratic elements in non-democratic regimes, this section addresses the subject of how state policy towards the Palestinian Arab minority in Israel can best be described. However, this immediately raises the difficult question as to how state policy in general can be defined. Policy is usually understood to refer to a deliberate plan of action which is designed by state-appointed authorities with clear and rational outcomes in mind. However, policy can also have aims which are unstated as well as official, employ strategies which are indirect as well as direct, and bring about consequences which are both intended and unintended. This has posed a number of problems in defin-ing a practical and accurate conceptual framework within which Israeli policy towards its Palestinian Arab minority can be analysed, leading some to avoid the subject altogether; others to describe it as consisting of a range of separate or multifaceted policy directions or approaches; and yet more to suggest a broader systemic approach to policy analysis.

Typical of early, pro-establishment analyses, for example, is the tendency to describe state policy towards the Palestinian Arab minority in Israel as non-exis-tent or undefined. Don Peretz, for example, argued that no defined or particular policy existed towards the Palestinian Arab minority whatsoever (Peretz 1958: 95, 131–5). Instead, individual policy choices are understood to reflect the democratic character and universal principles of the state, while exceptions to this normatively defined democratic policy that are found to discriminate against the minority are presented as being the spontaneous, indirect and unfortunate consequences of the emergency situation and Israel's security matrix. Such exceptions are identified as unavoidable shortcomings of an otherwise democratic and egalitarian policy rather than as a deliberately planned set of measures aimed against the minority. Peretz does, however, cite policy choices that have differentiated between sectors of the minority but attributes this to the fragmentary nature of the state's bureau-cratic infrastructure and the internal machinations of various government depart-ments that struggle for control within it.

Walter Schwarz also reiterated this 'dilemma' mentality in his analysis of state policy towards the minority. State policy is identified as 'neither a defined goal nor a cynical scheme of neglect' (Schwarz 1959: 65). Instead, Schwarz argues that during the first ten years of the state, no policy at all can be said to have existed towards the minority outside the universal application of certain progressive laws, such as female suffrage, compulsory education, and legal prohibitions concern-ing polygamy and underage marriage. However, while conceding some failures concerning the treatment of internal refugees and the lack of full equality for the Palestinian Arab minority, military rule is nonetheless presented as being 'wrong, but justifiable' (Schwarz 1959: 78). In quoting what he presents as being the *real-politik* of Samuel Divon, the then Adviser to the Prime Minister on Arab Affairs, he agrees that the Arabs 'must be persuaded, and coaxed, and even bullied – for their own obvious good' (Schwarz 1959: 142).

Writing a number of years later, Zarhi and Achziera (1966) similarly identified state policy as universal and progressive, believing that it was aimed at advanc-ing the march of the minority towards the reputable goal of modernisation. Ori Stendel also lauded Israeli policy for what he observed to be its concerted effort to integrate the Palestinian Arab minority into Israeli society and to reduce what he perceived to be the cultural gap between Jews and Arabs 'without offending the national heritage and age-old traditions' of the minority (Stendel 1968: 8). Thus, the state is conceived of as both a facilitator and arbiter of progress and change. Equally relevant in this dynamic is the stress given to the state's role as protector and guarantor of cultural diversity in society.

Similar to the aforementioned views, S.N. Eisenstadt also presented Israel as a benevolent welfare state which provides for all of its citizens, including its Pales-tinian Arab minority (Eisenstadt 1967b: 394). The exceptional thesis surrounding the security argument continues to hold great sway in his analysis, and the legal exclusion of the bulk of the minority from military service is presented as an 'insti-tutional innovation' which protects the minority from the dilemma of their own conflicting loyalties and identity (Eisenstadt 1967b: 396). So, too, the creation of 'the special advisory office for minorities' in the Prime Minister's Office is described as resulting from the state's sensitivity and concern for the feelings of the minority rather than as a result of any dark or ill-intentioned motives (Eisenstadt 1967b: 399). While Eisenstadt does not recognise any formal differential policy towards the minority, he does concede that particular benefits and favours (such as travel permits, job opportunities, licence grants and land leases) are bestowed upon particular, but unidentified, elements within the minority in return for their support, particularly come election time, of certain political parties and figures. This attitude points to the rather 'equivocal' nature of official policy in his eyes (Eisenstadt 1967b: 402–5).

Another central pro-establishment academic, Jacob Landau, acknowledged the state's efforts to convert the Galilee into a Jewish region as a planned policy, thus indicating a slight shift away from the earlier tendency of viewing Israeli policy as being simply reflexive and spontaneous to one which has begun to concede that some deliberate, action-oriented and programmatic content is involved in the formulation of policy (Landau 1969: 6). Landau, however, maintains that the autonomy given to various religious minorities represents not only a central element of the state's formal policy towards its minority, but a symbol of its deep respect for their historical traditions and continuity in the region (Landau 1969: 7–10).

At around the same time, a neo-Marxist critical perspective of Israeli state policy emerged, as typified by Henry Rosenfeld's analysis of the changing nature of the Arab village and family structure. In this, government policy is described as deliberately maintaining and supporting the patriarchal leadership structure of the Arab village and of manipulating factionalism between the various *hamules* (extended families) so as to ensure the underdevelopment and dependence of the Arab village which thereby remains easy to contain, control and exploit for the state's own purposes (Rosenfeld 1968: 732). In a later study, Rosenfeld also argued that the state deliberately sought to create distinctions and deepen divisions between Muslims, Christians and Druze (Rosenfeld 1978: 389–92). This aim is understood to have become legally formalised through the provision of autonomous institutional structures under the pretext of pluralism and respect for diversity. However, the autonomy offered is identified as being restricted to a limited range of personal status matters, with no segment of the minority commanding either full or consequential autonomy over their community in any area that might overlap with state interests (particularly with regards to land, land planning, agriculture and economic investment). Furthermore, he charges that not only did the state pursue a policy of deliberate under-development and containment of the Palestinian Arab economy, it also pursued a policy of de-territorialising and de-classing the Arab minority as a whole; a policy that indiscriminately affected Arab life across all religious sectors in both village and city.

The 1970s also witnessed the emergence of a new generation of Israeli Palestinian academics who began to challenge typical understandings of the role of government policy. Elia Zureik, for example, described policy at the time as a concerted effort by the state to pursue a project of social engineering and the re-socialisation of the Palestinian Arab minority as dependent subjects of the state (Zureik 1974: 98–9). While he identifies the existence of a pluralistic, differential policy, this type of pluralism is understood as a deliberate strategy aimed at the 'structural differentiation', or the institutional separation of the various minority communities from each other, under the guise of affirmative action, which, in turn, is understood to facilitate the subordination and continued underdevelopment of the minority in economic, cultural and political terms (Zureik 1974: 104). In a later study, Zureik describes the discriminatory nature of Israeli state policy towards the minority as being rooted in a comprehensive legal framework, citing a range of laws which discriminate equally against all segments of the Palestinian Arab minority, regardless of their religious affiliation (including various Basic Laws and emergency regulations, and particularly the 1950 Absentees' Property Law, the 1950 Law of Return, the 1952 Israeli Nationality Law and the 1953 National Insurance Law) (Zureik 1976: 40–7). During the same period, Sharif Kanaana published an article which considered the decision made by the state to preserve the Ottoman *millet* system, which provides separate recognition and a degree of communal autonomy to each religious group, as being 'easily adapted to standard colonial divide and rule procedure' of the Israeli state (Kanaana 1975: 3). In addition to separate recognition and status, separate religious institutions and education systems are understood to be used in such a manner as to ghettoise the minority and disband political and cultural organisations that operate on a cross-sectional basis within the minority. Tawfiq Zayyad, a former long-serving and influential mayor of Nazareth, in an article entitled 'The Fate of the Arabs in Israel', described the state as 'adventuristic, chauvinistic and expansionist', and its policy towards the Palestinian Arab minority as being one based on 'oppression and discrimination' which aimed at weakening 'the ties of national identity' between members of the minority (Zayyad 1976: 101–3). As such, he considers the views expressed by former Advisor to the Prime Minister on Arab Affairs, cited below, to be unsurprising:

> Our policy towards the Arabs is to keep them illiterate by preventing the Arab students from reaching the universities. If they were educated, it would be difficult to rule them. We should make them wood-cutters and water-carriers.
>
> (Zayyad 1976: 100)

Within his analysis, the Israeli academic establishment is charged for what he views as their complicity with the government's political agenda. One of the 'absurd "theories"' which he claims the politically affiliated Israeli academic establishment popularised is the concept of a separate non-Arab Druze identity (Zayyad 1976: 93). He also makes reference to attempts from within official Israeli circles to deliberately 'stir religious strife' within the Palestinian Arab minority by exploiting the unfolding civil war in neighbouring Lebanon (Zayyad 1976: 102).

The increasingly vocal criticisms raised by both Israeli Jewish and Palestinian Israeli academics challenged the dominance and monopoly of the pro-establishment academic perspective. So too did the 1976 disclosure of an internal ministerial memorandum authored by Yisrael Koenig, a member of the ruling Alignment and the Northern District Commissioner for over 25 years.[5] In light of such criticisms of, and challenges to, traditional Israeli scholarship, a growth in the number of analyses providing a more nuanced, albeit compartmentalised, understanding of Israeli state policy can be observed. In discussing ethnic relations in Israel, for example, Yochanan Peres argued that Israeli policy towards its Palestinian Arab minority could best be understood as a duality of intentional and unintentional policies which led to state interference in the affairs of the minority as a whole (Peres 1971: 1029). Alfred Friendly identified a similar compound policy approach by the state towards the Palestinian Arab minority, particularly with regard to the Druze. While policy towards the 'Oriental' Jewish minority is understood to have been a combination of governmental neglect in key areas – which he refers to as 'sins of omission' – together with undefined instances of 'positive discrimination', policy towards the Druze is, by contrast, seen to have been largely positivistic and affirmative (Friendly 1972: 5, 10). Any perceived limitation to this state aim

> owes less to a determined or even subconscious discrimination or settled policy of keeping down a minority, than it does to the circumstance that the members of an essentially medieval culture have had much too little time in sharing a highly advanced Western environment to have achieved equivalent educational and professional status with the more sophisticated majority.
>
> (Friendly 1972: 26)

However, notwithstanding the responsibility that Friendly attributes to the minority for its own discrimination, he goes on to assert that:

> However fairly, decently and compassionately Israel may treat its minorities, however sincerely it subscribes to democratic principles, egalitarianism, justice and fair play, *political* discrimination is built into the system. A Druze, not to mention an Arab, must limit his ambitions. [. . .] They must remain politically limited not merely because of their small numbers but because they are, *a priori*, not of the group which founded a nation on the basic premise that it was to be a Jewish state ruled by Jews.
>
> (Friendly 1972: 26)

Despite growing awareness of the structural determinants of Israeli state policy towards the Palestinian Arab minority, fragmented traditional discourses stressing the essentially democratic nature of state policy remained popular. Nonetheless, the clear tensions between democratic and ethnic priorities, as manifested on the level of minority policy, raised the need to address or rationalise these tensions. One early Israeli academic response to these tensions was by Sammy Smooha who laid the basis for an integrated and systemic approach to the analysis of state policy in Israel. In his 1978 study, *Israel: Pluralism and Conflict,* Smooha argued that while the Israeli authorities remain more liberal in their attitude towards the Palestinian Arab minority than the general Israeli Jewish public, they are nonetheless interested in engineering the 'pacification' of the minority through a combination of carrot-and-stick initiatives, primarily involving the 'carrot' of voluntary 'compliance' based on recognition of the obvious benefits, incentives and rewards pertaining to them as citizens of the state, and the 'stick' of their forced 'economic dependence' on, and 'political subordination' to, the Jewish majority. Together, these strategies are understood to minimise 'the potential costs of the presence of an Arab minority to the core national goals of the Jewish character of the state, Israeli national security and democratic pluralism' (Smooha 1978: 45–6). Critically, Smooha made a radical departure from earlier and more traditional analyses by suggesting that Israel's policy towards its Palestinian Arab minority could, cumulatively speaking, be understood as 'an effective machinery of control-exclusion, dependence and subordination' (Smooha 1978: 45).

In his 1989 study, *Arabs and Jews in Israel,* Smooha identified the lack of a clearly defined state policy towards the Palestinian Arab minority in Israel. However, while arguing that the state is 'basically' democratic, he does not observe this to be incidental proof of the dominant position of a universally understood democratic policy in Israel. Instead, he sees the collection of 'long-standing "policies by default"' as a testament of the unresolved tension that exists between the democratic and ethnic priorities of the state and the dichotomisation of Jewish attitudes between accommodation and rejection of the minority (Smooha 1989: 22, 199–200). Moreover, Smooha's study highlights the limited nature of policy choices open to the state. The policy options which are generally available to states with regards to their minorities are understood to range between the two opposite extremes of assimilation and ethnic cleansing, with various other policy options, such as integration, binationalism and autonomy, intersecting this continuum (Smooha 1989: 107). Ethnic cleansing, involving such policies as 'population transfer' and genocide, is considered, within Smooha's analysis, to be outside the permissible boundaries of Israeli state policy. The assimilation of the Palestinian Arab minority is equally not considered to be a viable policy option for the state 'since the undesirability and improbability of cultural assimilation between Arabs and Jews are agreed upon' (Smooha 1989: 45). Similarly, true binational, bicultural or bilingual arrangements are equally deemed to be impossible given the structural definition of the state as the Jewish state and the hegemonic status of the Jewish majority within it (Smooha 1989: 45–6). Even the full integration of the Palestinian Arab minority is not considered to be a realistic state policy for the same structural reasons and biases:

> Arab integration presents a dilemma for Jews and Arabs. For the Jews, to permit integration is to demonstrate goodwill. It is also a device calculated to coopt and contain the Arab minority. Yet it runs counter to Israel's Jewish-Zionist mission of preventing Jewish assimilation by positive and negative reinforcements. For the Arabs, integration is a forceful means to achieve equality of opportunities and resources, but also a threat to their separate existence and identity.
>
> (Smooha 1989: 94)

Instead, integration, where is exists, is generally understood to imply the one-sided adaptation of individual members or segments of the minority to the standards and expectations of the dominant Jewish majority, rather than any serious government-led initiative towards the minority as a whole. Given the impossibility of assimilation and binational arrangements as well as the real limits of integration, policies promoting the autonomy of the Palestinian Arab minority are considered to be even more problematic.

> Israeli authorities have always considered Arab national autonomy a threat to Jewish domination and to the state's political stability and have adopted diverse countermeasures to avert it. These include depriving Arabs of control over their own institutions, preventing them from forming independent organisations, endeavouring to dismantle their majority status in certain regions, coopting their leaders, encouraging traditional internal divisions, and treating them as an ethnic rather than national group. These policies coupled with other restraints comprise the machinery of political control over the Arab minority.
>
> (Smooha 1989: 98)

As none of these typical policy responses are considered to be realistic or viable policy options for the Israeli state, the dominant policy matrix within which the state is understood to operate is one that is based primarily on exclusion and control (Smooha 1989: 55). While acknowledging the centrality of control to Israeli state policy, and providing the basis for a systemic approach, Smooha nonetheless fails to provide a clear analytical framework through which the control of the Palestinian Arab minority in Israel can be routinely addressed.

The greatest single contribution to the development of a unified theory of control with respect to state–minority relations in Israel was made by political scientist Ian Lustick in his ground-breaking work, *Arabs in the Jewish State: Israel's Control of a National Minority*. Lustick's analysis was concerned with the question of stability, and the regulation of ethnicity, in deeply divided societies. Writing in 1980, Lustick observed that, despite the existence of 'an open and democratic society' in Israel, there remained wide gaps between Jews and Arabs. In particular, there had been no independent Arab political parties or significant Arab social, economic, cultural, or professional organisations during the first thirty years of Israeli statehood, which cast significant doubt over Israeli democratic claims (Lustick 1980: 4). Instead, Lustick identified the Zionist project of transforming Jewish society in Israel, based on 'mass Jewish immigration or "the ingathering of the exiles" (*kibbutz galuiot*), "redemption of the land" through intensive Jewish agricultural settlement (*geulat haaretz*), the "Judaisation of the Galilee" (*Yehud ha-Galil*), the consolidation of a Jewish proletariat (*avoda ivrit*), and so forth', as the fundamental cause of these gaps, which initiated the 'regime's fundamental distrust of the Arab minority' and its designation of it as 'the Arab problem'; military rule (until 1966); massive expropriation of Arab lands; economic and political discrimination; and the relative deprivation of the Palestinian Arab population in society (Lustick 1980: 6–7, 66). As such, Lustick was interested in exploring why obvious 'Arab discontent' had not let to either an outbreak of ethnic conflict in society or to the political mobilisation of the Palestinian Arab minority in order to improve or affect radical change to their status and why, instead, the minority demonstrated a high level of 'political quiescence' and 'seeming docility' (Lustick 1980: 8, 15, 24). Following his investigation, he observed that the political quiescence and seeming docility of the Palestinian Arab minority were ultimately due 'to the presence of a highly effective system of control which, since 1948, has operated over Israeli Arabs' (Lustick 1980: 25).

Situating himself within international theories of structural pluralism, Lustick used the concept of control as 'an analytical framework for explaining the anomaly of political stability in deeply divided societies' (Lustick 1980: 69). Within the Israeli 'system of control', 'regime goals' together with certain 'techniques of control' are attributed more importance than official Israeli policy itself as, 'unlike apartheid, for example, the system of control over Arabs in Israel is not explicitly recognised in the legal framework of the state' (Lustick 1980: 25, 52). Thus, a highly sophisticated and predominantly extra-legal system of control is understood to exist parallel, but not subordinate, to official proclamations, declarations, laws and policies of the state, and to consist of three main, but interlinking, components on three separate levels of analysis. The three separate components of Israel's system of control, which Lustick also refers to as the 'functional requisites' of control (Lustick 1980: 250), are: segmentation, dependence and cooptation.

> "Segmentation" refers to the isolation of the Arab minority from the Jewish population and the Arab minority's internal fragmentation. "Dependence" refers to the enforced reliance of Arabs on the Jewish majority for important economic and political resources. "Cooptation" refers to the use of side payments to Arab elites or potential elites for purposes of surveillance and resource extraction.
>
> (Lustick 1980: 77)

The three separate levels of analysis are: the structural, institutional and programmatic. The structural level relates to basic historical, cultural, religious, ecological and economic identities and circumstances, as well as various attitudes and stereotypes. The institutional level relates to three different categories of institutions: governmental institutions, such as government ministries and agencies, the IDF and the Histadrut; Jewish national institutions, such as the JA, the JNF or the WZO; and Zionist political parties, primarily the Labour and Likud parties. Finally, the programmatic level concerns various policies, political acts and decisions (Lustick 1980: 77).

One of the central elements of Israel's system of control is, according to Lustick, the state's tendency to capitalise on internal differences within the minority. While such differences are understood to be historically present, it is the particular manner in which the state is understood to have operationalised these differences in its effort to weaken the national unity and territorial integrity of the minority and strengthen its control which is relevant here.

> On the structural level of analysis, attention is focused on basic ecological, social structural, religious, cultural and historical circumstances, as well as on

deep-seated attitudes which themselves constitute divisions within the Arab sector and between the Arab and Jewish sectors. These factors are significant for the way in which they have made the Arab population susceptible to effective control (1) by inhibiting the formation of political alliances within the Arab population or between Arabs and dissident Jewish groups and (2) by providing the regime with an array of primordial identities and divisions which can be reinforced and exploited by appropriate 'segmentalist' policies.

(Lustick 1980: 82)

As a result, differences between patterns of Bedouin and non-Bedouin as well as between Arab urban-rural settlement patterns; different Arab regional distribution patterns in the Galilee, the Negev or the Triangle; religious differences between Muslims, Christians and Druze; internal political factionalism with tribal, or *hamule* politics, on the one hand, and modern urban-based party politics, on the other; socio-economic differences between different segments of the minority; as well as so-called 'national' and allegedly ethnic-based differences between Arabs and Druze, all acquire new significance in the authorities' dealings with the minority (Lustick 1980: 82–3).

For Lustick, therefore, internal differences within the minority have become, in and of themselves, 'meaningful political categories' in Israel (Lustick 1980: 133). Such differences are institutionalised and exploited in a number of different ways. In the first instance, the language and terminology used by the state to identify the minority, particularly with regard to the registration of nationality on Israeli identification cards, formalises differences between groups, while the recognition that is given to the religious communal structures of each group institutionalises them (Lustick 1980: 133). The role of military service in the IDF, which is one of the major institutions of the state and a powerful tool of socialisation, and its differential approach to conscription within the minority, is singled out as a particular method through which such differences have also become institutionalised (Lustick 1980: 92–4). Also, the role of Zionist parties' 'affiliated lists' in promoting sectarian and traditional elites is another such method of segmentation and cooptation (Lustick 1980: 112–13, 136–7, 208–9).

Seen cumulatively, Israel's system of control is according to Lustick based on the network of mutually reinforcing relations which has emerged from these structural, institutional and programmatic patterns' and the 'reciprocal interdependencies' which have been forged between them based on each separate level of analysis (Lustick 1980: 77–8). While Lustick's systemic approach highlights the complex, dialectical and evolving nature of these interweaving components and relations of control, and the capacity for the overall system of control to change and adapt itself over time as well as to provide unanticipated and undesired consequences for the state itself, his approach is weakened by the temporal limits of his research and how he anticipated various 'challenges to the system' would be reconciled within it. Lustick's study, as with Smooha and Rosenfeld before him, was, to some extent, primarily focused on the period of military rule (1948–66). With the end of military rule in 1966 and the relaxation of the bulk of emergency regulations which had hitherto contained and repressed the Palestinian Arab minority, a new period of self-confidence and awareness, together with renewed contact with Palestinians in the occupied territories, brought about a growth in Palestinian Arab national identity, which has been referred to as the 'Palestinianisation' of the minority. This brought to an end the notion of a 'quiescent' and 'docile' Palestinian Arab minority (Lustick 1980: 232–50). Faced with growing challenges to its control system, Lustick forecast three different possible regime responses: 'system adaptation, breakdown or transformation'. Lustick considered these trends, together with the growth of internal Jewish voices of dissent and opposition, as indications of the weakening grip of Israel's system of control over the Palestinian Arab minority and of the concomitant strengthening of democratic forces within and upon the state (Lustick 1980: 252–65). In one study, he rather optimistically cited the 1984 elections, whereby Palestinian Arabs are understood to have new 'political clout' in Israeli electoral politics, as indicative of this general trend away from a system of control towards 'integration and effective binationalism' (Lustick 1989: 97–119). Despite a certain retreat from his earlier understanding of the dialectical and dynamic nature of control in maintaining stability in deeply divided societies, and his inability to sufficiently recognise the structural potential for a sophistication of the system of control, rather than an abandonment of it, Lustick's approach remains fundamental to analyses of state–minority relations in ethnocratic regimes today.

Control theories, however, continued to develop in the decades subsequent to Lustick's study. The 1990s saw the emergence of political geography as a popular research discipline within which critical control theories were centralised. The first to address control within a territorial framework was sociologist Baruch Kimmerling. Like Lustick, Kimmerling identified the existence of an Israeli control system over the Palestinian Arab minority. However, his analysis differed from Lustick's in that territory is centralised as the main agency and mechanism of control. Within this, the porous boundaries of Jewish society and the Israeli territorial state are addressed. For Kimmerling, Israel's control system is 'a territorial entity comprising several sub-collectivities, held together by purely military and police forces and their civil extensions (e.g. bureaucracies and settlers)' and based upon a combination of selective incorporation and exclusion of 'controlled collectivities' (Kimmerling 1989: 266–7). Within this territorially defined Israeli control system, which includes the territory both of Israel and the occupied Palestinian territories, control is conceived not only as affecting Palestinian Arab citizens of the state but also those Palestinian Arabs who reside in the occupied Palestinian territories and are subject to military rule.

The first to address state territorial control of its Palestinian Arab minority in a focused and systemic manner was Yiftachel, who documented an 'elaborate system of Jewish territorial control' in Israel as arising from the general national and political salience of land and constituting a fundamental technique in the maintenance of asymmetrical power relations in society (Yiftachel 1992: 25 and Yiftachel 1999a: 293). Jewish territorial control is understood to have been secured and maintained by the state through various 'regulative' measures, such as: urban and regional planning; the categorisation of land types, permissible land uses as well as differential land ownership and accessibility rights; the zoning, and re-zoning, of urban and municipal boundaries; and the unequal distribution of state resources and budgets to Arab municipalities.

For Yiftachel, Israel's system of control is an integrated and inseparable element of Israeli ethnocracy. Put another way, ethnocracy is, fundamentally and in and of itself, a system of control. The previous section has already outlined the broad theoretical assumptions of ethnocratic rule. Following on from ethnocratic theory, this study suggests that treating particular policy choices as separate, or independent, from the structural priorities and nature of the state represents a false sociological dichotomy which serves only to confuse and restrict analyses of what is, essentially, the functional and instrumental nature of policy to serve the system which formulates it. Furthermore, delimiting certain components of control, whether it is Lustick's segmentation-dependence-cooptation model or even Yiftachel's primary focus on territorial control, to the exclusion or denial of other factors and techniques serves only to reify individual policy choices and areas which runs the risk of over-looking the fluid, dynamic, responsive and, at times, spontaneous nature of policy in fulfilling the changing demands of an ethnocratic regime. Instead, policy in an ethnocratic regime should be understood primarily as a functional or instrumental mechanism of the state which it serves, reflects but is, ultimately, subordinate to.

Despite the growing popularity of systemic control theories in analyses of state policy towards the Palestinian Arab minority in Israel, the notion of a spontaneous, circumstantial and largely positive, albeit poorly defined, minority policy has remained popular within pro-establishment discourses. One interesting example of the exceptional thesis surrounding minority policy in Israel is provided within Alisa Rubin Peled's study of state policy towards its Islamic institutions. While identifying a differential and differentiating state policy, Peled attributes this not to a deliberate or single-minded policy of control, but rather to the very fragmentary and confused nature of Israeli policy itself. At its source she identifies the competing agendas of various government ministries and personalities struggling for jurisdictional control over the minority (Peled 2001a). Various ministries are identified in particular within this inter-ministerial battlefield. The first was the short-lived Ministry of Minority Affairs which was created in 1948 but lasted for only one year until it was replaced by the Office of the Advisor to the Prime Minister on Arab Affairs. To the Office of the Prime Minister were added the competing jurisdictional claims of several other ministries, particularly the Ministry for Religious Affairs, Foreign Affairs and Education. As a result of these bureaucratic and political inter-ministerial struggles, rather than any overriding ideological dissension over the importance of democratic or ethnic priorities, policy is understood as having 'developed in fits and starts, mainly as temporary measures which eventually became permanent' and which 'took shape through an informal system of checks and balances' (Peled 2001a: 2).

Peled rejects the grand vision or meta-narrative approach of both system-supportive and critical control analyses. Instead, Israeli state policy is described as bipolar or even schizophrenic, swinging inconsistently back and forth between benevolence and rigidity, between good intentions and wilful manipulations, between humanitarian and security considerations. Trapped within this unresolved dynamic, minority policy is, as a result, understood to be naturally fraught with internal contradictions. On the one hand, Peled observes a genuine governmental tendency towards supporting a more positive approach to the minority, as typified by the extent of religious autonomy enjoyed by religious minorities in Israel. However, 'an intrinsic link between Islam and Arab political nationalism, its greatest concern' is identified on the other hand, which severely limits and conditions that support (Peled 2001a: 3). In addition to bureaucratic struggles, the relevance of political personalities represents an important aspect of Peled's analysis. Her dichotomy between a benevolent and a security-oriented minority policy is demonstrated by her analysis of the personal and ideological disagreements between Bechor-Shalom Sheetrit and Yoshua Palmon, who both served as Advisors to the Prime Minister's Office on Arab Affairs during the early decades of the state. Within this 'mosaic of motives and ministries', Sheetrit is presented as having basically 'good intentions' towards the minority and as advocating a more liberal-minded view of them, while Palmon is presented as having a much more pragmatic, interventionist and Machiavellian approach to the minority based on security concerns. Thus, it is the personality of Palmon, rather than the state itself, that is singled out for having promoted a divide-and-rule approach to the minority. While Peled's analysis is weakened by her avoidance of a systemic analysis of state policy, including the important role of factional politics within it, her analysis of the complex interplay of personalities and ministries, and the competition and rivalry which existed, and continue to exist, between them, provides important insights into the formulation and application of minority policy in Israel.

Despite its weaknesses, Peled's contribution can be incorporated within this study. In outlining a more fluid conceptual framework through which Israel's system of control can be analysed, this study also finds the contribution made by multicultural theorist Majid al-Haj particularly useful in this regard. But before an analysis of his particular contribution can be addressed, a brief commentary on multicultural theory is required. Multiculturalism is a sociological term which, like democracy, suffers from the paradox of being both ambiguous and over-used. Difference, diversity, pluralism and interculturalism have all too often been used interchangeably with multiculturalism, compounding the confusion between them even further. However, in general, three different forms of multiculturalism have been observed, which are: *descriptive*, *ideological* and *programmatic* multiculturalism (Wieviorka 1998: 882–3). Descriptive multiculturalism refers to the basic acknowledgement of the existence of diversity in society, but is devoid of any associated ideological content or normative judgement call on the value or order of such diversity in society. Ideological multiculturalism, by contrast, implies a particular and normatively positive position with regard to the value of diversity in society. It understands the expression of collective identity as a central component of individual human identity and as a basic human right. Not only does ideological multiculturalism advocate that states should recognise, promote and protect such diversity, it believes that groups themselves should be empowered with various autonomous powers by a decentralised state that arbitrates between different groups in an impartial manner. Finally, programmatic multiculturalism refers to the practical dimension of multiculturalism in practice, whereby it is expected that the normative assumptions of ideological multiculturalism become reflected in government policy and institutions.

Given the earlier analysis concerning the realistic and viable policy options open to the state with regard to its Palestinian Arab minority, it may appear unusual to discuss multiculturalism within the Israeli context. While Israel may be considered to be a prime example of multiculturalism in the descriptive sense, this label breaks down immediately upon investigation of the ideological assumptions and priorities of multiculturalism which are deeply antagonistic to the central ethnonational priorities and structural demands of an ethnocratic state. However, the relevance of multicultural theory to the Israeli case surfaces with regard to the programmatic dimension of multiculturalism. The basis for this renewed association lies in recognition of the limits of multiculturalism in practice in any country in which it has been applied. This association is based, in particular, on the critical awareness of the structural and practical limitations of states, even those which are categorised as liberal democracies, to act as neutral arbiters of diversity in society and to be sufficiently 'difference blind' as to fulfil multicultural requirements (Joppke 2004: 238). Given the socially and culturally embedded nature of all states, and the intersection between national identity, whether civic or ethnically defined, and the state, the degree to which states can, practically or ideologically speaking, be considered impartial is highly questionable.

Despite this difficulty, several states have nonetheless adopted multicultural policies towards their minorities. However, given the ideological limits of states, the range and types of multicultural policies which have been applied by states – such as Canada, Australia, Sweden and the United States – are equally limited. Wieviorka conducted a comparative study of the type of multicultural rights which are in place in each of these four countries. Multicultural policy in Canada, for example, is described as one which is primarily concerned with the linguistic and educational rights of the two dominant groups in society. In dealing with the claims of the sizable Francophone minority, and reconciling their claims against those of the Anglophone majority, Wieviorka suggests that multiculturalism has been employed 'as a way of avoiding bipolarisation of Canada'; normalising the nationalist claims of both groups; pacifying a powerful minority and returning political order to society (Wieviorka 1998: 884–5). Critically, multiculturalism, within the Canadian context, excludes the cultural or linguistic claims of other, smaller minorities. In the case of Australia, multicultural policy is understood to be limited to immigrant groups, thereby excluding the indigenous aboriginal population from the potential benefits of multiculturalism. Moreover, its focus is economically conceived as it attempts to redress economic disadvantages experienced by immigrant groups and to create national 'economic cohesion' between them and the 'established society'. However, the ideological limits of multiculturalism are quite clearly outlined in the Australian context, given the accepted primacy of 'the culture of the established society' on the public level (Wieviorka 1998: 885). While multicultural policy in Sweden is similarly conceived of in economic terms with a singular focus on immigrant groups, multicultural policy in the United States is bound up with education on the one hand and 'affirmative action' on the other. With regard to 'affirmative action', Wieviorka criticises this as being 'not so much one of cultural recognition, but more one of action against social inequality based on, or reinforced by, racial discrimination'. In other words, affirmative action is far removed from the basic multicultural tenet of cultural recognition; it is solely concerned with social equality, and can in fact play a role in reproducing and intensifying discrimination and inequality in society.

Wieviorka's comparative investigation highlights the *particular, limited, selective and functional* nature of multicultural policies in each country in which it has been applied. Given the absence of a total ideological commitment to the normative premises of multiculturalism, or rather the practical inability of states to fulfil these premises, the persistence of programmatic multiculturalism alongside other ideological norms and value-systems is clearly possible. Moreover, programmatic multiculturalism has been shown to possess a functional and instrumental dimension in the manner in which it is used to control, pacify and stabilise divisions in society.

Majid al-Haj has conducted a number of studies investigating multiculturalism in Israel with particular respect to minority education. Addressing the tension between the democratic and ethnic priorities of the state within the context of a deeply divided society, he has documented the affects this has had on the formulation of a separate but unequal Arab educational policy and school curriculum. He finds that elements of multicultural education, stripped of its ideological multicultural content, have been unilaterally imposed upon the Palestinian Arab minority by the dominant group in society thereby increasing the dependency of the minority on the state, but also increasing the cultural gaps as well as the degree of alienation between groups in society (al-Haj 2002: 182). As such, he argues that 'the education system has been used by the Israeli establishment as a mechanism of control over the Arab population', with multicultural conceptions of difference cloaking the asymmetrical segregation of education in Israel (al-Haj 2005: 52). As such, programmatic multiculturalism as it is applied to the Palestinian Arab minority in Israel is redefined by al-Haj as 'ethnocratic multiculturalism' (al-Haj 2004: 681). This he elaborates as follows:

> Despite the veneer of deep cultural pluralism, no multicultural ideology has developed in Israel, whether at the level of Jewish-Arab relations or of intergroup relations within the Jewish sector of the population. The ethno-national structure of Israel has retarded the nourishing of an all-inclusive civil circle. Indeed ethnic stratification in Israel is evident in all spheres.
>
> (al-Haj 2004: 684)

This study does not suggest that instrumental or programmatic multiculturalism can, in isolation, explain all of the nuances of minority policy in an ethnocratic state such as Israel. However, what it does illustrate is the capacity for any given policy to be partially incorporated, instrumentally adapted and selectively used in order to reflect or serve particular state agendas. This selective incorporation may occur as an indirect consequence of the structural limits of the state. However, such selective incorporation may also be the result of calculated decisions to promote one policy under the guise of another more normatively positive and acceptable one. This latter capacity of democratic policies to become, themselves, coopted within a broader system of control borrows somewhat from the literature on façade democracy. However, as the previous section on ethnocratic theory demonstrates, democratic features of the Israeli state are not limited to their function as a façade, or 'cover', for non-democratic policies, and cannot solely be reduced to the level of pretence. Instead, ethnocratic theory suggests that while the marketing potential of such features is not lost on ethnocratic regimes, a real tension between democratic and non-democratic ethnic forces exists. Ultimately, however, it is the non-democratic and ethnic forces which are understood to predominate in the formulation of policy in an ethnocratic regime.

Conclusion

This chapter presents a general theoretical framework through which Israeli state attitudes towards Palestinian Christians can best be addressed in later chapters of this study. The first section describes the particular dilemmas facing Israeli society as a multi-ethnic, plural and deeply divided society and discusses the political salience of its most important social cleavage, the Jewish–Arab national divide. This approach lays an important foundation through which the definition of the state as an ethnocratic regime can best be understood in the second section. On the one hand, Israel is a Jewish, Zionist and quasi-religious state which aspires to the status of a Jewish 'nation-state' and which prioritises the interests, priorities and identity of the dominant Jewish majority group within Israeli society as a whole. On the other hand, real democratic forces and features exist which provide important structural challenges to the exclusive ethnic characterisation of the state. However, given the stratified and hierarchical relationship between the democratic and ethnic character of the state, it is ultimately the Jewish ethnic component which retains a dominant and hegemonic status.

The third section of this chapter provides a theoretical framework through which minority policy in an ethnocratic state can best be understood. Identifying the discursive weakness of separate analyses of democratic and non-democratic policy approaches, this study argues that a systemic approach provides the best measure through which the cumulative impact of policy in an ethnocratic state can be addressed. Building on the contributions of Smooha and Lustick, this systemic approach centralises control as an integral component of this system. However, integrating the theoretical assumptions of ethnocratic theory with those of instrumental multiculturalism, this study also recognises the nuances of Israel's control system, in which real democratic features and apparently democratic and even multicultural policies also have a formally significant role in the overall system of control. As such, this study proposes an adapted systemic control theory which is liberated from the strictures of particular control strategies or policy areas (such as Lustick's three components of control or Yiftachel's exclusive focus on land policy) and which provides space for the evolving, fluctuating, changeable and, at times, seemingly contradictory nature of state policy towards the Palestinian Arab minority in Israel.

3   Profile of the Palestinian Christians in Israel

Before an analysis of state attitudes towards Palestinian Christians in Israel can be conducted, it is first necessary to address who the Palestinian Christians in Israel are, what distinguishes them, as a community, from other segments of the Palestinian Arab minority and what features they share with the wider Palestinian and Jewish societies. This chapter addresses key issues concerning the ethnicity, nationality, religious make-up, demographic size, regional distribution, urban concentration, vital statistics, economic indicators and political representation of this community which are presented in order to facilitate a deeper understanding of this small community. The relevance of this profile cannot be understated. In the first instance, it provides the reader with an empirical basis through which a number of assumptions which will be encountered in the next chapter can be cross-referenced and thereby either confirmed or dispelled. It also provides a solid basis through which the state's national priorities and attitudes towards its Palestinian Christian population can be juxtaposed and examined.

Ethnicity

As the previous chapter has indicated, the Jewish-Arab ethno-national divide represents the single most dominant cleavage in Israeli society today. It is hardly surprising therefore that ethnicity itself has become a highly political, and politicised, concept. Despite the rigid political associations of ethnic identity in a society that is deeply divided along ethno-national lines, ethnicity is, by definition, a rather loose and elastic concept. While generally defined as representing the particular intersection of one or more distinguishing group traits or characteristics (such as a shared language, culture, geography, religious outlook, a common historical experience, or even an imputed genetic or biological connection), the practical definition of ethnicity often varies from country to country and according to the particular historical circumstances and political needs of the ethnic groups in question (Horowitz 1985: 51–4; Esman and Rabinovich 1988: 3; Smith 1988: 21–41).

Given the subjective boundaries of identity that often separate real from presumed shared characteristics, ethnicity remains a very malleable concept that is as much conditioned by human will and prejudice as it is by objective factors. In certain extreme cases, the term 'ethnicity' can be charged with re-processing the now outdated, unscientific and sinister concept of 'race' in softer and more acceptable tones. Despite the increasingly flippant usage of this inexact and seemingly scientific catch-all term, ethnicity nonetheless represents a key element in modern political and sociological discourses, particularly with regard to Middle Eastern societies, and can, therefore, not be disregarded.

Today, there are almost one and a half million citizens of the State of Israel who are defined by the CBS as ethnically Arab. This number excludes the substantial number of Arab Jews (both indigenous Jews who lived continuously in the area now known as Israel and those Jews who immigrated to Israel from Arab countries from the 1950s onwards) who were, for political and Jewish nation-building reasons, not recognised as Arab, but instead as 'Oriental Jews', then Sephardim and, most recently, as Mizrahim (Shohat 1999). Of the recognised Arab population of Israel, the majority – almost 84 per cent – is Muslim, with the remaining 16 per cent split evenly between smaller Druze and Christian communities.

The Arab ethnicity of Palestinian Christians is widely accepted as a given. The Palestinian Christians have, as a community, lived continuously on the land that is today known as Israel (formerly as Palestine) for at least two millennia. They have witnessed the passage of time which brought with it the emergence of Islam and the decline of several empires (Roman, Byzantine, Umayyad, Abbasid, Crusader, Mamluk, Ottoman and British) and, despite their religious difference from the Muslim majority, they speak the same language, have been shaped by the same cultural influences and contributed to the same historical processes which have united and distinguished Palestinians, irrespective of religion, from other groups of people in the region (Mansour 2004: 43–5).

Not all Christians living in Israel today are Arab, however. According to the CBS, 20 per cent of the total Christian population living in Israel at the end of 2009 – numbering approximately 30,000 Christians – were not Arab. The non-Arab Christian population of Israel is, in part, accounted for by small numbers of Armenians and Messianic Jews (also referred to as Hebrew Christians); however, the vast majority of the non-Arab Christian population consists of individuals who came to Israel from the former USSR during the early 1990s. These immigrants applied for Israeli citizenship under the Law of Return which gave individuals with Jewish ancestry (a Jewish mother or grandmother) the right to Israeli citizenship. While it is beyond the remit of this study to critique the Zionist concept of a single Jewish ethnicity or to elaborate on the work of those who see it as a social and political construct, it is relevant to note that it is quite possible within these parameters for an immigrant to be a practising Christian and an ethnic Jew at the same time (despite the internal controversy that this seeming paradox has created for certain political circles inside Israel).

Nationality

Like ethnicity, nationality is a particularly fluid and ambiguous concept with high political salience in Israeli society. Subscribers to the French school of nationalism – which also predominates in the US and several European countries – understand nationality to be a form of open and voluntary civic citizenship that supersedes considerations of ethnic or religious affiliation. Followers of the German romantic school of nationalism, by contrast, affix to their understanding of nationality qualifications based on perceived ethnic or even racial determinants.[1] As the previous chapter has indicated, the concept of nationalism followed in Israel is based on the latter German romantic tradition which gives centrality to the notion of a single Jewish *Volk* or ethnic group.

Rather than serving as a unifying concept, nationality remains an important differentiator of the Israeli population. The Ministry of the Interior today recognises approximately 137 different 'nationalities' in Israel, although 'Israeli' is not one of them (Nathan 2005: 268). This system of national classification reflects the political ideology of the state. While all of the internal diversity of the Jewish population in Israel is categorised as belonging to a single Jewish nationality, the Palestinian Arab minority is denied similar recognition as a single Palestinian nationality, and, by extension, as a distinct Palestinian national minority. Instead, the Ministry of the Interior classifies all Palestinians living in Israel according to one of two possible 'nationalities': Arab or Druze. As such, even the common ethnicity of Druze, Muslims and Christians does not warrant their designation according to a single, common nationality. While all Muslim and Christian Arab citizens are categorised as Arab nationals, the Druze population (which is nonetheless recognised as being ethnically Arab) is categorised according to a separate Druze nationality.

It is within this context that the state's identification of Israel's Palestinian Christian population as 'Christian Arabs' must be understood as a central component of a wider political struggle over the national identity and national rights of the Palestinian Arab minority in Israel. The insistence on the Jewish nature of the state, combined with the state's assertion of differential nationality for its Palestinian Arab citizens and the absence of an inclusive Israeli civic nationality that could potentially provide an integrated civic identity for Israeli citizens as a whole has led the Palestinian Arab minority in Israel to reject the state's labelling system and to redefine their national identity in a manner which is more meaningful and legitimate to them. According to surveys conducted by As'ad Ghanem, the preferred national self-identification of the minority today is Palestinian Arab (Ghanem 2002: 139), a trend which is reflected in the language of several important future vision documents published by Palestinian Israeli NGOs over the last decade[2] as well as in the language of this study.

Population size

As with ethnicity and nationality, demography is a highly sensitive and contentious issue in Israel. The maintenance of a Jewish majority in a Jewish state has been the stated priority and explicit raison d'être of the State of Israel since its establishment in 1948. The sense of demographic threat and encroachment associated with a large and expanding non-Jewish minority – as can be inferred from such political rhetoric as the 'numbers game' and the 'battle of the cradles' – should not be minimised.

Table 2.1 Population by group and religion (end of 2009)

	Total	Jews	Arabs	Palestinian Arabs		
				Christians	Muslims	Druze
CBS population figures						
Total pop'n (in thousands)	7,552	5,703	1,535	122	1,286	125
% of the total pop'n	*100%*	*75.5%*	*20.3%*	*1.6%*	*17%*	*1.7%*
% of the Arab pop'n	—	—	*100%*	*7.9%*	*83.8%*	*8.2%*

Note

The information presented here is based on CBS *Statistical Abstract of Israel 2010 (No. 61)*.

According to the CBS, Israel had a total population of just over 7.5 million people at the end of 2009, of which only 75 per cent was Jewish. Approximately 1.5 million people, representing 20 per cent of all Israeli citizens, were Arab, with the remaining 4 per cent or so of the population 'not classified by religion'.[3] As Table 2.1 shows, there were 122,000 Palestinian Christians living inside Israel at the end of 2009, representing just under 8 per cent of all Arabs and 1.6 per cent of the total Israeli population. The CBS data is slightly problematic as it includes individuals living outside the boundaries of Israel proper. In addition to approximately half a million Jewish settlers living throughout the OPTs who are listed as permanent residents of the state, the CBS data also includes approximately 280,000 Arab permanent residents who are not Israeli citizens, including roughly 10,000 Palestinian Christians who are listed as permanent residents of East Jerusalem. Taking into account these discrepancies, the correct number of Palestinian Christian citizens living inside Israel proper is closer to 110,000. This figure is consistent with other available sources. The Sabeel Survey on Palestinian Christians in the West Bank and Israel, for instance, estimates that of the 162,000 Palestinian Christians living in the combined area of Israel and Palestine in 2006, the majority (110,000) live inside Israel (excluding East Jerusalem) with the remaining 52,000 distributed throughout East Jerusalem (10,000), the West Bank (40,000) and the Gaza Strip (2,000) (Sabeel 2006: 48).

Internal religious divisions

Religion represents another central component of individual and collective identity in Israel. Home to five officially recognised religious communities – Jewish, Christian, Muslim, Druze and Baha'i – the significance of religion and of religious affiliation in Israel is accentuated not only by the ongoing Israeli–Palestinian conflict but by the Jewish character of the state. Of the many Jewish religious denominations which exist and are represented in Israel (Reform, Conservative, Orthodox, Ultra-Orthodox), only Orthodox Judaism receives official recognition by the state. As the previous chapter has shown, the high status accorded to Judaism and Jewish religious authorities in Israeli public life and government circles has meant that (Orthodox) Judaism has, over time, become the civil religion of the state.

The next largest religious group in Israel, the Muslim community – which accounts for 17 per cent of the entire population of the state – is distinguished by its high level of homogeneity. Unlike the majority of countries in the Middle East which have both Sunni and Shi'a communities, the Muslim community of Israel is almost entirely Sunni in its make-up. Based on the results of the latest official population census which was conducted at the end of 2008 (which were integrated within CBS data from 2010), the Druze minority has overtaken the Palestinian Christian community and is now, with just over 125,000 members (representing 1.7 per cent of all Israelis), the third-largest religious community in Israel after the Muslims. Originally an Ismaili sect which split from Islam in the eleventh century, the Druze follow a religious belief system which is distinct from Islam and other monotheistic faiths.

With 110,000 members, the Palestinian Christian minority in Israel is, with the exception of the Baha'i faith, the smallest officially recognised religious group in Israel. It is also the religion which demonstrates the highest level of internal diversity, with around 20 different Christian denominations active throughout the country as a whole. Of these, 10 receive official recognition from the state: the Greek Orthodox, the Greek Catholic (Melkite), the Latin, the Armenian Orthodox, the Armenian Catholic, the Syrian Orthodox, the Syrian Catholic, the Chaldean Catholic, the Maronite and the Anglican (Evangelical Episcopal).

With approximately 70,000 followers, the vast majority (two thirds) of Palestinian Christians in Israel today are Greek Catholic or Melkite (Ateek 2006: 3). The largest Christian denomination, they are also the most widely distributed of all the Christian denominations with their strongest concentrations found in the villages and towns of the Galilee region. The Greek Catholic (or Greek Melkite) Church is a 'uniate' church, signifying its split from the Greek Orthodox Church and subsequent union with Rome in 1724. This church is also typified by the fact that its clergy are predominantly Arab and its laity completely Palestinian Arab. The Greek Catholic Archdiocese of the Galilee is based in Haifa, and the current head of the church in Israel is Archbishop Elias Chacour.

The majority denomination in the OPTs, the Greek Orthodox community is the second-largest Christian denomination in Israel after the Greek Catholic Church. It also represents the largest Christian denomination in the city of Nazareth with 17,000 followers there (Ateek 2006: 3), in addition to smaller concentrations throughout the Northern Region as a whole. Unlike the Greek Catholic church, the leadership of the Greek Orthodox in Israel is entirely Greek while the laity is predominantly Palestinian Arab. The Greek Orthodox Church in Israel is distinguished by its significant land assets being second only to the state in terms of its land holdings in Jerusalem. The Greek Orthodox Patriarchate is based in Jerusalem and the head of the Greek Orthodox Church in Israel is Patriarch Theofilos III who was elected in November 2005, but only recognised by the State of Israel in December 2007.

The third-largest Christian denomination in Israel, the Latin (or Roman Catholics) community is mainly concentrated in the larger urban localities of Nazareth and Haifa, with a negligible presence in the smaller rural or mixed localities of the north. While the ranks of the Latin leadership consist of a mixture of Arab and non-Arab clergy, the laity is primarily Palestinian Arab. The Latin Patriarchate is based in Jerusalem, and the head of the Latin Church in Israel is Patriarch Fuad Twal who was appointed in June 2008. The Franciscan Custody of the Holy Land falls under the umbrella of the Latin Church and is relevant to this study as it is a major land-owner and service provider, controlling many of the Christian-run schools and hospitals that serve the Palestinian Arab minority in Israel. The ranks of the Franciscan order in Israel are predominantly made up of non-Arabs, and the head of the Franciscan Custody of the Holy Land, the Custos Pierbattista Pizzaballa, is Italian.

With only 8,000 members, the Maronite community in Israel is another uniate church. Concentrated in the northernmost part of the Galilee, primarily in villages close to the Lebanese border, they are also present in a few other towns in the north. Haifa represents the single largest Maronite parish in Israel but smaller congregations are also present in Nazareth, Akka and Jaffa. The ranks of the Maronite leadership in Israel are made up almost entirely of Lebanese Arabs, while the laity consists of a combination of Lebanese and Palestinian Arabs. The head of the Maronite community in Israel is Lebanese Archbishop Paul Sayyah and his headquarters are in Haifa.

Finally, the Anglican community is the smallest of the four main Christian denominations in Israel. Concentrated in urban localities such as Nazareth, Haifa, Ramla, Kfar Yasif, Shfar'amr and Reine, the leadership ranks of the Anglican Church in Israel are made up of a mixture of Arabs and Britons, while the laity is predominantly Palestinian Arab. Although they represent a relatively new Christian sect in the Middle East, their membership originates from disaffected members of the indigenous Greek Orthodox community. The head of the Anglican community in Israel is Bishop Suheil Dawani and his seat is in Jerusalem.

Regional distribution

As has previously been shown, demography and land represent two of the central priorities of the Jewish ethnocratic state of Israel. As such, an analysis of the regional distribution and concentration of Palestinian Christians in Israel vis-à-vis Israeli Jews and the remainder of the Palestinian Arab minority is essential.

Just under half of the Palestinian Arab minority in Israel live in Israel's Northern District, compared with only 10 per cent of Israel's Jewish population. Not only is the Northern District the only district in Israel where Palestinian Arabs represent the overall demographic majority vis-à-vis the country's Jewish population, but it is also the only district where the highest concentrations of each separate Palestinian Arab sub-group are to be found. 37 per cent of all Israel's Muslims live in the Northern District, compared with 72 per cent of all Palestinian Christians and 81 per cent of all Druze. Table 2.2 indicates the regional distribution of each community in greater detail. Next to the Northern District, the second most important district for Palestinian Christian settlement is the Haifa District where a further 13 per cent of all Palestinian Christians live. The Palestinian Muslim population

Table 2.2 Population by district, group and religion (end of 2009)

District		Total	Jews	Arabs	Palestinian Arabs		
					Christians	Muslims	Druze
Northern District	Thousands	1,257	553	667	87	478	101
	%	17	10	44	72	37	81
(Jerusalem District)	Thousands	924	623	286	12	274	—
	%	12	11	19	10	21	—
Haifa District	Thousands	898	626	223	16	184	24
	%	12	11	15	13	14	19
Central District	Thousands	1,814	1,596	148	4	144	—
	%	24	28	10	3	11	—
Tel Aviv District	Thousands	1,277	1,196	17	3	14	—
	%	17	21	1.1	2.6	1.1	—
Southern District	Thousands	1,084	821	194	0.5	193	—
	%	14	14	13	0.4	15	—
(Judea & Samaria)	Thousands	290	284	—	—	—	—
	%	4	5	—	—	—	—

Notes

The data presented here is based on the CBS Statistical Abstract of Israel 2010 (No. 61).

The percentage figures provided above are calculated as percentages of each population group.

demonstrates a much more evenly distributed presence in Israel while the pattern of regional distribution of the Druze population shows a clustering in the Northern and Haifa districts.

As the next chapter will show, much attention has traditionally been given in the literature to various assumed cultural, social and political by-products of geographic distribution patterns of the Palestinian Arab minority in Israel. The concentration of Palestinian Christians in Israeli urban centres is often singled out as a unique and differentiating characteristic of that community vis-à-vis the other Palestinian Arab communities in Israel. As Table 2.3 shows, just under 100 per cent (99.6 per cent) of all Palestinian Christians living in Israel at the end of 2009 live in urban localities. While this figure is higher than the average percentage of Israeli Jews listed as living in urban localities (92 per cent), so too are the percentages of Muslims and Druze living in urban localities significantly higher than that of Israeli Jews (94 and 97 per cent each respectively).

These surprisingly high figures result, in part, from the particular definitions used by the CBS, whereby an 'urban' locality is defined as any locality with a population in excess of 2,000 people. If the figures for all urban localities in Israel of over 100,000 people are combined, it can be furthermore observed that 44 per cent of Jews fall into this category, compared with approximately 23 per cent of Muslims and Christians respectively. This indicates a similar pattern of settlement in large cities for both Muslims and Christians, undermining the notion of unique Palestinian Christian urban settlement patterns. Significantly, Israel's largest urban localities have no significant Druze population whatsoever. Equally relevant is that the bulk of the Palestinian Christian population in Israel (76 per cent) is concentrated in urban localities of less than 50,000 people, a trend which is also

Table 2.3 Population by type and size of locality (end of 2009)

		Total	Jews	Arabs	Palestinian Arabs		
					Christians	Muslims	Druze
All localities	Thousands	7,552	5,703	1,535	122	1,286	125
Urban localities	Thousands	6,992	5,162	1,458	121.5	1,212	122
	%	92	91	95	99.6	94	97
200,000+	Thousands	2,087	1,665	319	28	290	—
	%	28	29	21	23	23	—
100,000–199,999	Thousands	1,216	1,124	5	0.4	5	—
	%	16	20	0.3	0.3	0.4	—
50,000–99,999	Thousands	883	693	158	26	131	—
	%	12	12	10	21	10	—
20,000–49,999	Thousands	1,502	1,134	304	20	277	6
	%	20	20	20	16	22	5
10,000–19,999	Thousands	696	272	413	25	326	63
	%	9	5	27	20	25	50
2,000–9,999	Thousands	538	273	258	23	183	52
	%	7	5	17	19	14	42
Rural localities	Thousands	630	542	77	0.5	74	3
	%	8	9	5	0.4	6	3

Notes

The information presented is based on the CBS *Statistical Abstract of Israel 2010 (No. 61)*, with the following modifications:

Localities of between 200,000–499,999 and of 500,000+ have been merged into one category (200,000+).

Localities of between 2,000–4,999 and 5,000–9,999 have been merged into one category (2,000–9,999)

The percentage figures provided above are calculated as percentages of each population group.

in line with the general distribution patterns of the Palestinian Arab minority as a whole. The relatively elevated presence of Palestinian Christians in urban localities of between 50 and 100,000 inhabitants compared with the lower figure for Muslims in this category is entirely due to the unique significance of Nazareth. This city of over 72,000 Palestinian Arabs – approximately one third of whom are Palestinian Christians – accounts for the entirety of the Palestinian Christian population making up this segment.

Beyond the importance of regional distribution patterns and varying levels of urbanisation, the concentration of Palestinian Christians living in individual urban localities is also relevant. By the end of 2009, there were, according to CBS figures, 1,186 localities (excluding approximately 106 unrecognised Arab villages[4]) in Israel. Of the (recognised) localities, 134 are listed as non-Jewish localities. The vast majority of these non-Jewish localities are, in fact, Arab.[5] Of these non-Jewish or Arab localities, 98 are urban and the remaining 36 are rural localities. Table 2.4 provides information on the 23 urban localities in Israel which have a significant number of Palestinian Christians and details their demographic presence in each locality relative to other segments of the population.

Table 2.4 provides useful information on patterns of communal living within the Palestinian Arab minority. With regard to the Palestinian Christian population

Table 2.4 Localities with significant Palestinian Christian populations (end of 2009)

Locality	Total	Jews	Arabs	Palestinian Arabs		
				Christians	Muslims	Druze
Christian-only villages						
Mailiya	2,800	—	100%	100%	—	—
Fassouta	2,942	—	100%	100%	—	—
Mixed Arab localities with a Christian majority						
Jish (Gush Halav)	2,700	—	100%			—
Eilaboun	4,676	—	100%	*70%*	*30%*	—
Rameh	7,200	—	100%	*53%*	*17%*	*30%*
Kfar Yasif	8,700	—	100%	*55%*	*40%*	*5%*
Mixed Arab localities with a significant Christian minority						
Hurfeish	5,500	—	100%			
Deir Hanna	8,900	—	100%	*20%*	*80%*	—
Ibillin	11,500	—	100%	*49%*	*51%*	—
Abu Snan	12,400	—	100%	*19%*	*55%*	*26%*
Reine	17,300	—	100%	*20%*	*80%*	—
Yaffa an-Nasariyya	16,500	—	100%	*30%*	*70%*	—
Kfar Kanna	18,800	—	100%	*17%*	*83%*	—
Mughar	19,900	—	100%	*20%*	*20%*	*60%*
"Arab Cities" with a significant Christian population						
Sakhnin	25,700	—	100%			—
Shfar'amr	36,200	—	100%	*28%*	*57%*	*15%*
Nazareth	72,200	—	100%	*30%*	*70%*	—
"Mixed Cities" with a significant Christian population						
Maalot-Tarshiha	20,600	70%	22%	*12%*	*9%*	*1%*
Natzeret Illit	40,800	72%	14%	9%	5%	—
Ramle	65,800	75%	23%	*5%*	*18%*	—
Lod	69,800	67%	24%	*2%*	*22%*	—
Haifa	265,600	81%	10%	5%	5%	—
Tel Aviv-Yaffa	403,700	92%	4.4%	0.9%	3.5%	—

Notes

Total figures in the first column are taken from the CBS *Statistical Abstract (2010) No. 61* (for locali-ties >5,000) and the ACAP Database on Local Arab Municipalities (2008) (for localities <5,000).

Percentage figures for Jewish presence in mixed cities are taken from the CBS and for Arab cities from ACAP.

The symbol "—" means "no presence".

A religious breakdown of the Arab population of each locality is not provided by either the CBS or ACAP, resulting in a number of gaps in the above table. Where possible, these gaps have been filled using latest estimates available (in italics).

it is possible to observe, for example, that with the exception of the two Christian-only villages of Mailiya and Fassouta, Palestinian Christians live alongside Muslims in every single other locality in which they are found. By contrast, Palestinian Christians live alongside Druze in only 7 of the 23 major localities mentioned,

Profile of the Palestinian Christians in Israel 47

suggesting that patterns of Palestinian Christian settlement in Israel are, in fact, far more closely aligned with those of the Muslim community than with those of the Druze community.

Vital statistics

A common theme in the coverage of Palestinian Christians in the literature which will be encountered in the next chapter is the positive significance attributed to Palestinian Christians in terms of their differential age distribution, life expectancy, fertility rates, marriage age rates etc. when compared with the rest of the Palestinian Arab minority. Given that the notion that Palestinian Christians pose less of a demographic 'threat' to the Israeli state as a result of these indicators is so popular and prevalent, it is important that it is addressed here also.

Table 2.5 confirms that the Palestinian Christian population in Israel is a relatively old population group when compared with the rest of the Palestinian Arab minority. Despite being a year younger than the average Jewish citizen, the average Palestinian Christian is ten years older than the average Palestinian Muslim and five years older than the average Druze. In terms of gender distribution, the ratio of men to women in the Palestinian Christian population is more closely aligned to that of the Israeli Jewish population than with either that of the Muslim or Druze population. While the CBS does not provide information on the average life expectancy of each segment of the minority, it does tell us that the average life expectancy for a member of the Palestinian Arab minority is a full four years less than that of Jewish citizens. The figures also indicate that there is no significant difference in the mean age of marriage among members of the Palestinian Arab minority, and while the figures do indicate differences in the total fertility rates of Palestinian Christians, Muslims and Druze, the Jewish fertility rate remains higher than that of both Palestinian Christians and Druze.

Table 2.5 Vital statistics (end of 2009)

		Total	Jews	Arabs	Palestinian Arabs		
					Christians	Muslims	Druze
Median age		29	31	21	30	20	25
% of pop'n under 19		36	33	48	34	50	42
Gender distribution (%)	M	49.4	49.3	50.5	49.7	50.6	51.0
	F	50.6	50.7	49.5	50.3	49.4	49.0
Avg. life expectancy	M	80	81	76	No info	No info	No info
	F	84	84	81			
Mean marrying age	M	29	29	28	30	27	28
	F	26	27	23	22	25	23
Total fertility rate		2.96	2.90	2.79	2.15	3.73	2.49

Notes
The data presented here has been collected from the CBS *Statistical Abstract of Israel 2010 (No. 61)*.
The total fertility rate relates to the average number of children born to a woman over her lifetime.

Economic indicators

According to the National Insurance Institute (NII) poverty index for 2008, almost one quarter (23.7 per cent) of Israel's total population and over a third of all Israeli children (or 34 per cent), live under the poverty line in Israel (NII 2009: 1). Despite these high rates, there remain significant gaps between the poverty rates experienced by Israel's Jewish and Arab populations which have distorted these total figures. Only 15.3 per cent of Jewish families in Israel fall below the poverty line, compared with 49.4 per cent of Palestinian Arab families (NII 2009: 18). In other words, half of all Palestinian Arab families in Israel live in poverty today, a rate which is more than three times higher than that experienced by Jewish families.

The NII figures also illustrate a marked imbalance in government welfare injections and other policy measures designed to reduce poverty within different segments of the population. While such measures have reduced the Jewish poverty rate by 46.2 per cent, the Arab poverty rate has been reduced by only 13.5 per cent (NII 2009: 18). Moreover, the particular concentration of Palestinian Arabs throughout the country has led to the development of clearly identifiable ethnic 'poverty pockets'. With a total poverty rate of 33.7 per cent, the Northern District is, after Jerusalem, one of the poorest areas in the country. Reflecting the general gaps in standards of living and socio-economic opportunities between Jews and Arabs in society, the Jewish poverty rate in the Northern District is only 16.6 per cent, compared with 47.6 per cent for Palestinian Arabs (NII 2009: 22).

As neither the NII nor the CBS distinguishes its data on income or poverty according to religious groupings, it is not possible to determine the Palestinian Christian poverty rate compared with other population groups in Israel. There are, however, some other sources of information which exist and which can provide a better indication of the socio-economic status of Palestinian Christians in Israel. In 2008, for example, the Arab Centre for Alternative Planning (ACAP) compiled a database mapping a range of economic and demographic indicators particular to local Arab municipalities and towns in Israel which is, in part, based on CBS material. Table 2.6 draws on this information and provides a snapshot of the socio-economic status of the 23 localities in Israel which contain either a Palestinian Christian majority or a significant Palestinian Christian minority.

It is interesting to note that all of these localities fall, on average, between the third- and fourth-lowest possible socio-economic levels. Given that the average socio-economic standing of all Arab localities throughout the Northern District as a whole is 3, this indicates that the socio-economic reality of villages with Palestinian Christian populations is no different to that of other Arab villages and towns. Indeed, the Arab villages of Deir Hanna, Kfar Kanna and the Arab city of Sakhnin, all of which have significant Palestinian Christian minorities, are rated with a socio-economic level of 2, thereby suffering from some of the worst socio-economic conditions in Israel. One exception to the generally poor socio-economic standing of Arab localities with significant Palestinian Christian populations is the village of Mailiya. This village, which has a socio-economic ranking of 6, is both the richest Palestinian Christian locality in Israel and the

Table 2.6 Socio-economic ranking and average salary by locality (2008)

	Total	Pal'n Christian	Socio-economic level	Average monthly salary (NIS)
Christian-only villages				
Mailiya	2,800	100%	6	5,521
Fassouta	2,942	100%	4	4,356
Mixed Arab villages with a Christian majority				
Jish (Gush Halav)	2,700		5	4,811
Eilaboun	4,676	70%	4	4,411
Rameh	7,200	53%	4	4,494
Kfar Yasif	8,700	55%	4	4,029
Mixed Arab towns with a significant Christian minority				
Hurfeish	5,500		4	
Deir Hanna	8,900	20%	2	
Ibillin	11,500	49%	3	4,008
Abu Snan	12,400	19%	3	3,814
Reine	17,300	20%	3	3,818
Yaffa an-Nasariyye	16,500	30%	3	3,944
Kfar Kanna	18,800	17%	2	3,383
Mughar	19,900	20%	3	3,786
Arab Cities with a significant Christian minority				
Sakhnin	25,700		2	3,668
Shfar'amr	36,200	28%	3	4,127
Nazareth	72,200	30%	4	4,133
"Mixed Cities" with a significant Christian minority				
Maalot-Tarshiha	21,235	12%	4	5,135
Natzeret Illit	43,082	9%	5	4,727
Ramle	64,900	5%	4	4,656
Lod	67,033	2%	4	5,019
Haifa	264,942	5%	7	7,007
Tel Aviv-Yaffa	378,902	0.9%	8	7,700

Notes

Data on the socio-economic level of each locality has been retrieved from the 2008 Database on Local
Arab Municipalities and Towns in Israel compiled by ACAP.
The socio-economic level of localities ranges from 1 to 10, with 10 being the highest possible level.
NIS = New Israeli Shekel.

richest Arab locality in the entire Northern District. Similarly, the Arab village of
Jish (also known as Gush Halav), which has a Palestinian Christian majority, has
a higher socio-economic standing than the Arab average for this region. However,
Nazareth – the largest Arab city in Israel and the city with the largest Palestinian
Christian minority – has a socio-economic ranking of only 4. While this ranking
places Nazareth one level above the regional average for Arab localities, it falls
well below the national average for Jewish localities of similar size. Only one

other Arab city, Tire, which is an entirely Muslim city located in Israel's Central District, has a similar ranking.

Table 2.6 shows that the average salary of an individual from a locality possessing either a majority or a significant minority of Palestinian Christians was only 4,154 NIS (GB£700 or US$1,040) per month in 2008. This figure is only around 240 NIS (GB£40 or US $60) higher than the average recorded annual salary of all Arab localities in the Northern District as a whole. Moreover, if we compare this data with data which is available concerning the minimum wage in Israel, which was set at NIS 3,710 (GB £624 or US $928) in 2008, it can be observed that the average salary for an individual from a locality with either a majority or a significant minority of Palestinian Christians was only 444 NIS (GB £75 or US $111) higher than the minimum wage, suggesting that the socio-economic level of Palestinian Christians is not significantly different from that of other Palestinians who are struggling with greater levels of poverty and socio-economic disadvantage that the majority of Israeli Jews.

According to the 2008 Sikkuy Index, which measures equality between Jews and Arabs in Israel, it was found that inequality between Jews and Arabs has, in fact, increased rather than decreased in Israel (Haidar 2009: 10). The Index, which measures equality in five key areas (health, housing, education, employment and social welfare) finds that the roots of this growing inequality stem from disparities in 'government inputs' (investment, welfare injections etc.) and different levels of implementation of government policy over time (Haidar 2009: 13). With regards to employment, Palestinians were found to constitute only 11 per cent of the Israeli workforce in 2008 even though they represented 20 per cent of the overall population, with the majority of Palestinians concentrated in 'labor-intensive industries with low wages' (Haidar 2009: 49).

According to the CBS, 7.5 per cent of the total Jewish civilian labour force in Israel was registered as unemployed at the end of 2009 compared with 8.5 per cent of the Palestinian Arab labour force. While the CBS does not provide a further breakdown of this figure by religious group, the Sabeel Survey on Palestinian Christians in the West Bank and Israel indicates that the Palestinian Christian unemployment rate in Israel in 2006 was 6.3 per cent, a figure which, if unchanged, would suggest that fewer Palestinian Christians suffer from unemployment when compared even with Israeli Jews (Sabeel 2006: 22).

Information on the various sectors of the economy in which the Palestinian Arab workforce are occupied is also useful. Table 2.7 indicates that the most significant areas of employment for Palestinian Arabs as a whole are: the construction sector, followed by education and, then, by the areas of manufacturing, wholesale and retail trade. With the exception of construction, which employs only a minimal number of Jews, the figures indicate smaller gaps between Jews and Arabs in the areas of manufacturing, education and wholesale and retail trading. The number of Israeli Jews employed in the areas of business, health, public administration, however, is more than twice that registered for the Palestinian Arab workforce.

Although it was not possible to isolate statistical information relating to the particular employment patterns of Palestinian Christians in Israel from the CBS data,

Table 2.7 Employment by sector (end of 2009)

	% of Employees	
	Jews	Palestinian Arabs
Services for households by domestic personnel	2.1	0.6
Community, social and personal services	4.5	3.1
Health, welfare and social work services	11.0	7.4
Education	**13.9**	**16.5**
Public administration	5.9	2.6
Business activities	**14.5**	6.4
Banking, insurance and finance	4.7	1.0
Transport, storage and communications	6.7	5.5
Accommodation services and restaurants	4.4	6.2
Wholesale and retail trade, and repairs	**12.7**	**14.4**
Construction (building and civil engineering projects)	2.6	**17.8**
Electricity and water supply	0.8	0.4
Manufacturing	**15.4**	**15.0**
Agriculture	1.0	2.9

Notes
The data presented here has been collected from the CBS *Statistical Abstract of Israel 2010 (No. 61)*.
The four most important employment sectors for each population group are highlighted in bold.

the Sabeel survey does indicate that the majority of Christians in Israel (68.2 per cent) are employed in the service sector, i.e. banks, insurance companies, schools, tourism, hospitals etc., with the next most significant areas of employment being industry (11.2 per cent), commerce (10.5 per cent) and construction (9.5 per cent). The least relevant area of employment for Palestinian Christians is agriculture which accounts for only 0.6 per cent of all Palestinian Christians (Sabeel 2006: 22). This would suggest that while Palestinian Christians suffer from the same socio-economic gaps as the remainder of the Palestinian Arab population, their rate of socio-economic deprivation is, due to their higher concentration in the service industry, relatively lower than that of Muslims or Druze.

Political representation

Different rates of minority activity and representation within Israeli national politics is often held up as an indicator of different orientations and outlooks within the minority itself. As such, a brief glance at the political representation of Palestinian Christians in Israeli politics is necessary here.

There are, in all, 120 Members of Knesset (MKs) who sit in the Israeli Knesset. As Table 2.8 shows, 14 of the 120 MKs which were elected to the current (Eighteenth) Knesset on 10 February 2009 were Palestinian Arabs. This figure represents just over almost 12 per cent of the total number of MKs in parliament. While this is the highest number of Palestinian Arabs to be elected to any Knesset since 1949, their number remains significantly less that their proportional share (20 per cent) of the total Israeli population. Of the 14 currently serving Palestinian Arab MKs, nine are Muslim, four are Druze and only one is Christian, representing a share of 64, 29 and 7 per cent for Muslims, Druze and Christians respectively. If these figures are compared with the overall religious distribution of the Palestinian Arab minority in Israel, then it can be observed that Muslims are considerably underrepresented in the Knesset while the Druze have almost four times their ordinary representation. Only the Palestinian Christians with their single solitary MK are correctly represented should the rules of strict proportional representation be applied.

As can be seen from Table 2.8, Palestinian Christians held a dominant share of the number of seats allocated to Palestinian Arabs in Israeli parliament during the first two decades of the state. In the first Knesset, for example, two of the three elected Palestinian Arab MKs were Christian. This relatively inflated Christian presence is largely due to the important leadership role of a small number of Palestinian Christians in the non-sectarian Communist Party (formerly known as Maki, latterly as Hadash/DFPE). Of particular note is the role of Christian-born Tawfiq Toubi who, having served in every one of the first 12 Knessets until his retirement in 1990, is currently the second-longest serving parliamentarian in Israeli history. In all, 62 Palestinian Arabs have, from 1949 until today, held parliamentary positions in the Israeli Knesset. Of these, 14 have been Christian, giving this community an overall parliamentary representation of 23 per cent over the past sixty years. Despite this pronounced involvement, the number of parliamentary seats secured by Palestinian Christians began to significantly decline as early as

Table 2.8 Palestinian Arab MKs by religious group, 1949–present

Knesset	Total MKs	Arab MKs	Palestinian Arab (Israeli Arab) MKs		
			Christian	Muslim	Druze
First Knesset (25 January 1949)	120	3	2	1	0
Second Knesset (30 July 1951)	120	8	4	2	2
Third Knesset (26 July 1955)	120	9	4	3	2
Fourth Knesset (3 November 1959)	120	9	4	4	1
Fifth Knesset (15 August 1961)	120	8	4	3	1
Sixth Knesset (1 November 1965)	120	7	3	3	1
Seventh Knesset (28 October 1969)	120	7	3	3	1
Eight Knesset (31 December 1973)	120	7	1	4	2
Ninth Knesset (17 May 1977)	120	10	2	4	4
Tenth Knesset (30 June 1981)	120	5	1	2	2
Eleventh Knesset (23 July 1984)	120	7	1	3	3
Twelfth Knesset (1 November 1988)	120	9	1	6	2
Thirteenth Knesset (23 June 1992)	120	10	2	6	2
Fourteenth Knesset (29 May 1996)	120	12	2	9	1
Fifteenth Knesset (17 May 1999)	120	13	2	9	2
Sixteenth Knesset (28 January 2003)	120	12	2	7	3
Seventeenth Knesset (28 March 2006)	120	12	2	8	2
Eighteenth Knesset (10 February 2009)	120	14	1	8	4

Note
The information presented here has been collected from the Israeli Knesset website (www.knesset. gov.il).

the 1970s in line with the gradual increase in the number of Muslims and Druze who became involved in local and parliamentary politics. From that point on, the Palestinian Christian share in the Knesset has never exceeded two seats during any single parliamentary sitting.

In terms of political factions, the 14 Palestinian Arab MKs serving in the current Knesset are distributed across six different political parties which are, by descending order of their parliamentary size: Kadima, Likud, Yisrael Beitenu, the Labour Party, Hadash, Ra'am-Ta'al and Balad. Receiving the majority of the Arab vote in 2009, Ra-am-Ta'al took four seats; Hadash took three, as did Balad, while one Palestinian Arab was elected on behalf of Labour, Likud, Kadima and Yisrael Beitenu.

A number of clear religious patterns can be discerned from this spread. First, all four of the Palestinian Arab MKs representing the largest Arab party, Ra'am-Ta'al, are Muslim, reflecting the predominantly Muslim character and appeal of this party and the electoral power of the Muslim segment of the Palestinian Arab minority. Second, all three of the Palestinian Arab MKs representing the Israeli right-wing parties (Likud, Kadima and Yisrael Beitenu) are Druze, indicating the close relationship between certain segments of the Druze leadership and the Israeli establishment. Third, Palestinian Christians play an important role in the Hadash/DFPE party. While only one Palestinian Christian secured a seat in the current Knesset, the Christian affiliation with Hadash/DFPE is long-standing.

Table 2.9 confirms the historic patterns of Palestinian Christian, Muslim and Druze political representation in the Knesset while Table 2.10 elaborates on the particular political affiliations and party memberships of Palestinian Christians since the first Knesset sitting in 1949. What these tables show is that while Hadash

Table 2.9 Palestinian Arab MKs by political faction, 1949–present

Political faction/list	Total	Christian	Muslim	Druze
Arab lists	15	3	9	3
Labour/Alignment	13	2	8	3
Mapam	5	2	2	1
Likud	3	—	—	3
Meretz	2	—	2	—
Kadima	1	—	—	1
Yisrael Beitenu	1	—	—	1
ICP/Maki/Rakah/Hadash/DFPE	12	5	5	2
Progressive List for Peace	1	—	1	—
Balad/National Democratic Assembly	6	1	4	1
United Arab List/Ra'am-Ta'al	10	—	10	—

Notes

The information presented above is drawn from the Knesset website.

Only major political factions and lists are shown. Certain MKs represented more than one list and are mentioned more than once in the statistics. For example, one Muslim MK, who served on several Arab lists, before joining Alignment and then the United Arab List, is mentioned three times. This is done in order to get a clear conceptual picture of the religious distribution of MKs according to their particular political preferences.

Table 2.10 Palestinian Christian MKs, 1949–present

Name	Place of birth	Knesset	Parliamentary group/list
1. Tawfiq Toubi	Haifa	1st, 2nd, 3rd, 3rd, 4th, 5th, 6th, 7th, 8th, 9th, 10th, 11th, 12th	Maki/ Rakah/ Hadash
2. Amin-Salim Jarjora	Nazareth	1st	Democratic List of Nazareth
3. Rostam Bastuni	Haifa	2nd	Mapam
4. Emile Habibi	Haifa	2nd, 3rd, 5th, 6th, 7th	Maki/ Rakah
5. Masaad Kassis	Maaliya	2nd, 3rd	Democratic List for Israeli Arabs
6. Yusuf Hamis	Reine	3rd, 4th, 5th	Mapam
7. Elias Nakhleh	Rameh	4th, 5th, 6th, 7th	Progress and Development, Participation and Development, Jewish-Arab Brotherhood, Participation and Brotherhood
8. Hanna Mwais	Rameh	9th	Hadash
9. Hanna Haddad	Jish (Gush Halav)	13th	Labour
10. Saleh Salim	Ibillin	13th, 14th	Hadash
11. Azmi Bishara	Nazareth	14th, 15th, 16th, 17th	Hadash-Balad, Balad
12. Issam Makhoul	Haifa	15th, 16th	Hadash
13. Nadia Hilou	Tel-Aviv/Jaffa	17th	Labour
14. Hanna Sweid	Eilaboun	17th, 18th	Hadash

Notes
The information presented here is collected from the Israeli Knesset website.
The Democratic List of Nazareth was an Arab list affiliated with David Ben-Gurion's Mapai party. Bastuni became, in 1951, the first Arab MK to directly represent a Zionist party, rather than participating on one of its Arab-affiliated satellite lists. The Democratic List for Israeli Arabs was an Arab List affiliated with Mapai. Progress and Development (Kidma ve Pituah), Participation and Development, Jewish-Arab Brotherhood, Participation and Brotherhood were all Mapai-affiliated Arab lists. Elias Nakhleh founded Jewish-Arab Brotherhood after he left Progress and Development. This list did not survive beyond one term.

(and its predecessors, Maki and Rakah) was once the party of choice for Palestinian Christians in Israel, other parties such as Labour and Balad have begun to erode its monopolistic standing both within the Palestinian Christian community and within the Palestinian Arab minority as a whole.

Beyond parliamentary politics, the role and participation of Palestinian Christians in central government is also worth mentioning. Table 2.11 documents every Palestinian Arab who has ever served in a central government position in Israel.

As can be seen, no Palestinian Christian has ever been appointed to any central government position in the history of the State of Israel. Where appointments have been made, it is generally Muslim and Druze representatives affiliated with mainstream Jewish parties who have been chosen. Of the eight members of the Palestinian Arab minority who have been appointed to such positions in recent

Table 2.11 Palestinian Arabs in government positions, 1949–present

Name	Religion	Party/faction	Role	Government
1. Abd El-Aziz El-Zoubi	Muslim	Alignment	Deputy Minister of Health	Gov. 15 (15/12/1969–10/03/1974)
2. Jabr Moade	Druze	Alignment	Deputy Minister of Communications	Gov. 16 (10/03/1974–03/06/1974) and Gov. 17 (03/06/1974–24/03/1975)
3. Walid Sadik	Muslim	Meretz	Deputy Minister of Agriculture	Gov. 17 (24/03/1975–20/06/1977)
			Deputy Minister of Agriculture and Rural Development	Gov. 26 (22/11/1995–18/06/1996)
4. Nawaf Massalha	Muslim	Labour	Deputy Minister of Health	Gov. 26 (22/11/1995–18/06/1996)
		One Israel	Deputy Minister of Foreign Affairs	Gov. 28 (05/08/1999–07/03/2001)
5. Saleh Tarif	Druze	Labour	Deputy Minister of Internal Affairs	Gov. 26 (27/11/1996–18/06/1996)
		One Israel	Minister Without Portfolio	Gov. 29 (07/03/2001–29/01/2002)
6. Majalli Whbee	Druze	Likud	Deputy Minister in the PM's Office	Gov. 30 (30/03/2005–20/06/2005)
			Deputy Minister of Education, Culture and Sport	Gov. 30 (20/06/2005–04/05/2006)
		Kadima	Deputy Minister of Foreign Affairs	Gov. 31 (29/10/2007–31/03/2009)
7. Raleb Majadele	Muslim	Labour-Meimad	Minister Without Portfolio	Gov. 31 (2/01/2007–21/03/2007)
			Minister of Science, Culture and Sport	Gov. 31 (21/03/2007–31/03/2009)
8. Ayoob Kara	Druze	Likud	Deputy Minister of the Development of the Negev and Galilee	Gov. 32 (01/04/2009–present)

Note
The information here was collected from the Israeli Knesset website.

history, four were Muslim and the remaining four were Druze. Generally speaking, these positions remain on the margins of central government and the national priorities of the state. It is also noteworthy that with the exception of two individuals appointed during the 1970s, most of the appointments have taken place only in the last two decades.

Conclusion

This chapter has provided a profile of the particular features and characteristics of Palestinian Christians in Israel which provides important clues as to the possible shape and content of state attitudes towards them. Ethnically Arab, Palestinian Christians are clearly on the 'other' side of the Jewish-Arab divide in Israel, which is confirmed by their national designation by the state as Arab rather than Palestinian. Countering this, however, it can be inferred from the data that Palestinian Christians do not, as a result of their religious difference from the predominantly Muslim-defined Palestinian Arab minority, represent a serious demographic threat to the state and its particular national priorities. This view is supported by their relatively benign vital statistics vis-à-vis the Muslims and Jewish populations. However, their fairly wide geographic distribution in the predominantly Arab north, together with their concentration in a number of pivotal Arab localities, amplifies the political significance of this otherwise relatively inconsequential minority, which is confirmed by their strong standing in opposition parties on the parliamentary level.

4 Writing the Palestinian Christians in Israel

Karl Mannheim's critical work on the sociology of knowledge explores the relationship between society, ideology and power in the production of social values, truth systems and political orders. His work also describes the potentially transformative effect of society upon scholarship but, critically also, of scholarship upon society. The insights which he made, while universal, are particularly relevant with regard to Israeli scholarship. In recent decades, the attention given by Israeli sociologists to the social and political contingency of their own research has grown considerably. As a result of this new research focus, two approaches to the study of Israeli society have been identified and distinguished from each other. One has been generally referred to as a dominant or hegemonic 'establishment' discourse and the other has been loosely categorised as a 'critical' discourse. A number of studies already exist which elaborate on the particular research methodologies and framework decisions which characterise each approach or discourse.[1] Instead of reiterating the conclusions made by others, this chapter provides a particular analysis of academic scholarship on Palestinian Christians in Israel cognisant of the fact that such an endeavour may advance understandings not only of Israeli state attitudes towards Palestinian Christians, but of the location of this community within a broader sociology of Israeli scholarship on the Palestinian Arab minority.

In order to avoid the blind spots created by an adherence to either a critical or an establishment discourse, this chapter follows an integrated thematic approach in its coverage of Israeli scholarship on the Palestinian Christian community which has the potential to shed new light on the particular relationship between the Israeli state and its Palestinian Christian population. This decision was made for two main reasons. On the one hand, the views of so-called pro-establishment scholars are indispensable to this study's analysis of state attitudes. Given their national allegiances and political sympathies, these scholars are more likely to reflect the view of the prevailing political establishment (as their name would suggest) than their critical counterparts. On the other hand, this approach is supported by the recurrence of the themes selected here in both establishment and critical analyses suggesting that, notwithstanding different interpretations, a basic level of conformity concerning the issues affecting the state's approach to this community exists. Beyond theoretical boundaries of state–minority relations in Israel, which were outlined in Chapter Two, the factors and characteristics of the Palestinian Christian community which have been identified from the literature as affecting, or influencing, state attitudes towards them are: their Arab ethnicity; their small size; their non-Muslim minority status; their 'Westernised' outlook; their lack of a central communal leadership; their external links in the region; their international religious significance; their political behaviour; as well as a degree of Jewish religious antipathy. Although a certain degree of overlap between these themes is inevitable, each will be addressed separately for the sake of clarity. The empirical data outlined in Chapter Three underscores the practical relevance of these topics and can be used to test various sociological and ideological claims encountered.

A modern, westernised and secular community

The first commonly encountered feature of sociological analyses of Palestinian Christians in Israel is the frequent reference given to their distinctive social and cultural attitudes and orientations relative to the rest of the minority. Described as being more 'modern', 'Westernised', 'liberal', 'progressive' and 'secular', Palestinian Christians have been identified in several studies as being closer to, and more compatible with, mainstream Israeli Jewish society than the remainder of the Palestinian Arab minority, with the Muslim and Druze communities being described, on the whole, as remaining more 'backward', traditional, conservative and patriarchal in nature (Ashkenazi 1988: 10).

This attitude towards Palestinian Christians was popularised by proponents of the modernisation thesis. The modernisation thesis, which dominated the Israeli academic scene until the late 1960s and which continues to exert an important (but decreased) level of influence on Israeli scholarship today, is a discourse which centralises various cultural, social and psychological characteristics of the Palestinian Arab minority and presents them as instinctive and primordial group tendencies which are conceived of as measures of that group's ability (or inability) to adapt to and integrate within 'modern' Israeli society (Nakhleh 1977: 41–70; Zureik 1977: 3–16). Within this analysis, particular aspects of collective identity are singled out and connected to what are presented as being either positive or negative political and cultural attributes of the group in question. In particular, 'modern' attitudes are equated with the presence of certain socio-economic features (such as high levels of education, professional qualification, personal wealth; urban residential patterns; a low fertility rate, low child mortality rates; smaller nuclear families; older marrying age; and increased contacts with Jews, etc.) (Landau 1993: 28–9). Situated within this logic of the anticipated social transformation of the Palestinian Arab minority, Palestinian Christians were frequently held up to be on the vanguard of this transformation.

Despite the relative decline of the modernisation thesis in recent years, the notion that Palestinian Christians are more 'modern' and, as a result, more akin to the values and culture of mainstream Israeli society remains popular. This is underscored by analyses which suggest that the alleged modernity of Palestinian Christians predates and, as such, is largely independent of the state's modernisation efforts with regards to the remainder of the Palestinian Arab minority. Citing as evidence of this the central role of a 'Western'-affiliated church school system, the Palestinian Christians are not only held up to be, by themselves, free-floating vectors of modernisation, but by virtue of their modern outlook, they are understood to preserve a degree of self-sufficiency and innovation which protects them from the worst excesses of the state's policy towards the Palestinian Arab minority.

Daphne Tsimhoni, who has written extensively on various Christian denominations in Israel and the OPTs, refers to the 'Western open lifestyle' of Palestinian Christians, their more liberal dress code and their more frequent social contacts with Jews as being both a source of hope for future Jewish–Arab reconciliation and indicative of their higher tendency towards 'integration' and 'Israelisation' (Tsimhoni 2002: 132).

> Due to their Western and higher education than that of the Muslims, their prominence in the white-collar professions and their forming a largely urban middle class group, they have been amalgamated within Israeli society to a greater extent than the Muslims.
>
> (Tsimhoni 2002: 149)

'Israelisation' is broadly considered to be a process whereby Palestinian Arabs change or adapt their social, cultural and political outlook sufficiently in order to absorb or internalise the 'modern' standards of Israeli society as well as its wide range of associated benefits. This process, however, is understood to be a wholly one-sided affair. It is the Palestinian Arab minority alone which must adjust if it wishes to integrate into Israeli society and enjoy the same levels of opportunity as the Israeli (Jewish) majority (Rouhana 1997: 116–20).

Given the perceived proximity between Palestinian Christians and Israeli Jews in cultural and social terms, and the implied higher expectation of Palestinian Christian compatibility with Israeli Jewish society, it would be anticipated that this factor would diminish the necessity of control over this community and improve the relationship between them and the state. However, given the structural limits of integration within Israel, as described in Chapter Two, this assumption is problematic. Critical anthropologist Amalia Sa'ar offers instead a more complex and layered understanding of Palestinian Christian identity which challenges this assumption of Palestinian Christian difference and state preference. Sa'ar studied the identity of Palestinian Christians in the mixed city of Haifa and observed that while Palestinian Christians are 'largely urban and better situated economically' their real identity is a shifting combination of seemingly contradictory tendencies, towards Palestinian self-identification on a national level and Christian Arab self-identification on a social and cultural level, which vary according to particular circumstances and needs and which, together, make up the complex arsenal of Palestinian Christian survival strategies in Israel (Sa'ar 1998: 215). This latter tendency, which she describes as Christian ethnocentric behaviour, is 'socially reproductive' in that 'it complies with the state's policy toward the Palestinian minority' of 'control, fragmentation and class discrimination' (Sa'ar 1998: 216).

By adopting a social-reproductive orientation – emphasising Christian cultural distinctiveness and drawing on the personal benefits that accompany
political conformism – many Christians cultivate the hope (or the illusion)
that they will be able to escape the class and civil subordination that they face
as Palestinians in Israel.

(Sa'ar 1998: 216)

Notwithstanding this, Sa'ar argues that the parallel tendency of Palestinian Christians to emphasise their national identity above and beyond their religious identity
represents the dominant tendency of the two. This national affiliation represents
Palestinian Christians' 'oppositional behaviour' to the state, thus pushing them
further away from the Israeli Jewish social orbit. That such system-supportive and
oppositional behaviour is understood by Sa'ar to co-exist even on the individual
level of Palestinian Christian identity challenges the assumption that a 'modern'
outlook necessarily renders Palestinian Christians natural allies of the state and
instead suggests a more complex relationship between the state and its Palestinian
Christian citizens.

Ethnically Arab

Given the deeply divided nature of Israeli society, and the particular political
salience of the Jewish-Arab ethno-national divide within in, Palestinian Christians
are, as a result of their Arab ethnicity, inextricably associated with the wider 'Arab
problem' (or *ha-baaya ha-aravit*, as it is frequently referred to in Hebrew). In his
seminal work on *Israeli Society*, Eisenstadt argued that 'the parallel development
of Zionist and Arab national movements' polarised the relations between Jewish
and Arab communities, narrowing or limiting the state's options with regard to its
minority which were, in turn, compounded by the 'continuous state of hostility'
between Israel and its Arab neighbours (Eisenstadt 1967b: 395). It is essentially
the 'ambivalence' of the Palestinian Arab minority to the state as a result of their
'ties of kinship, ethnicity, or incipient nationalistic orientation' which is understood to have introduced limits to state–minority relations in Israel (Eisenstadt
1967b: 396). The Palestinian Christians are, within this analysis, not differentiated
from this negative affiliation and associated ambivalence.

That the Arab identity of Palestinian Christians is an accepted and uncontested
given, even in pro-establishment sociological accounts of the minority, is particularly noteworthy given the much greater efforts which some scholars have made
in order to distinguish between 'Arab' and 'Druze' identities in society. While
the 'Arab' national affiliation of the Druze was re-categorised by the state into a
distinct non-Arab Druze nationality in 1957, the 'Arab' nationality of Palestinian
Christians has never been challenged. This is confirmed by the state's attitude
towards military service by the Palestinian Arab minority. While the Druze are
liable to perform compulsory military service, Palestinian Christians and Muslims
are exempted on the basis of their Arab ethno-national identity. This is not to suggest that the Druze are free from the restrictions of their Arab ethnicity when it

comes to the national priorities of the state, but rather to highlight the broad level of consensus surrounding the Arab ethnicity of Palestinian Christians in Israel.

The impact of being Arab in Israel has been directly felt by Palestinian Christians since 1948. Of the estimated 750–900,000 Palestinians who became refugees outside Israel, it is estimated that between 8 and 10 per cent, approximating 80,000 in all, were Palestinian Christian (Mansour 2004: 223–4). The Christian populations of several towns and cities were decimated as a result of the war and the new state's policies. According to Atallah Mansour, only two thousand of the 26,570 Christians who lived in Haifa in 1945 survived the upheavals of 1948, while the 15,000-strong Christian population of Jaffa was reduced to less than one thousand. Only a handful of Christians remained of Acre's 2,330 Christians, while the 20,000 strong Christian community living in West Jerusalem disappeared entirely, as did those of Safad, Tiberias, Beisan and Beer Sheba (Mansour 2004: 219–22).

The total number of Palestinian villages which were abandoned, evacuated or destroyed is a matter of much debate, with estimates varying considerably from 392 at the lower end to 531 at the higher end. While Benny Morris, who has put forward a more conservative estimate, has documented at least seven (destroyed) villages which contained significant Palestinian Christian populations (Al Bassa, al-Mansura, Birweh, Damoun, Suhmata, Mujeidil and Maa'lul), Mansour has argued that 80 out of all 425 abandoned or destroyed villages had contained Palestinian Christian communities of various sizes (Mansour 2004: 219–20). Thousands of Palestinian villagers – Muslims and Christians alike – were to become 'internal refugees' in other Arab localities inside Israel in this way, thus irrevocably changing the inter-communal dynamic of Arab settlement in Israel forever.

The state's discriminatory policy towards Arabs is also observable during the subsequent period of military rule clearly demonstrates the dominant role of ethnic affiliation in the determination of state policy towards them. While Eisenstadt defended the necessity of military rule within the context of security concerns arising from the concentration of Palestinian Arab citizens within sensitive border areas, it became apparent that a 'border area' was in fact designated to be any major area where Arabs were settled, regardless of their proximity to the territorial borders of the state (Eisenstadt 1967b: 396). As such, the entirety of the Galilee with its high concentration of Palestinian Christians came under strict military rule. In a study investigating the nature and practical administration of military rule on the Palestinian Arab population of Israel, Sabri Jiryis, a lawyer and Palestinian Christian from Israel, illustrates that within its tight territorial confinement of the Palestinian Arab minority, no exemption was made for Israel's Palestinian Christian population. The city of Nazareth, for example, which, at that time, was home to a Christian majority population, was designated a 'closed area' and experienced a strict level of control, military curfews and police surveillance (Jiryis 1968: 16, 20).

The impact of military rule, however, extended beyond the mere territorial containment of the Palestinian Arab minority. Jiryis observed three fundamental objectives of military rule: the expropriation of Arab land; the creation of Arab political dependence on the dominant Mapai Party; and the prevention of the development of an independent Arab party or national movement (Jiryis 1969: 44). Each of these objectives equally affected the Palestinian Christians in Israel. With regard to the expropriation of land, Jiryis notes that the selective use and zoning of 'closed areas' blocked Palestinian Arabs from entering their land for 'security reasons' which were contrived to free up the land for Jewish settlement and development purposes (Jiryis 1969: 44–5).

Testifying to the shared experience of land expropriation, expulsion and destruction, Jiryis mentions the famous case of two Palestinian Christian villages – Iqrit and Kfar Bir'am – which were destroyed by the state several years after the end of hostilities, in 1951 and 1953 respectively. Iqrit had a population of approximately 500 mostly Greek Catholic Palestinians when it surrendered to the IDF on 31 October 1948 during Operation Hiram. Six days after its surrender, the IDF ordered its residents to evacuate the village for two weeks on security grounds. However, they were never allowed to return. Following two years of internal displacement in neighbouring villages and towns, the residents appealed their case to the Israeli Supreme Court which they eventually won in July 1951. The military authorities were, however, opposed to the Supreme Court's decision and, on Christmas Day 1951, the IDF destroyed the village. Soon after, a *kibbutz* (similarly titled Yoqrat) was established on part of the land formerly belonging to the village, followed by a number of other Jewish settlements which sprung up nearby area (Mansour 2004: 220–36).

The Maronite village of Kfar Bir'am, with its 710 inhabitants, suffered a similar fate. Denied re-entry following their forced eviction in 1948 (in some cases across the border to neighbouring Jordan), the residents began submitting their appeals to the Israeli Supreme Court in 1953. Once again, the Supreme Court found in favour of the residents, leading the IDF to take the pre-emptive and unilateral decision to raze the village in its entirety (with the exception of the village church) on 16 September 1953. Today, a kibbutz (Bar'am) and a National Park stand where once this Palestinian Christian community lived (BADIL 2006).

Iqrit and Bir'am were not isolated cases. The Christian Maronite village of Eilaboun suffered a fate comparable to the now infamous village of Deir Yassin. Following the withdrawal of the Arab Liberation Army from the outskirts of the town in late October 1948, and its subsequent surrender to Israeli forces, twelve men were separated from the group of villagers who had been collected in the town square and shot. The remainder of the population was forced to leave the village and eventually were made to cross the border to Lebanon where they found temporary shelter in the Miyyeh Miyyeh refugee camp south of Sidon. The village itself was looted but not destroyed and, following international pressure, many of the village's refugees were subsequently allowed to return home (Pappe 2006: 182–3; Morris 2004: 479–80; Srour 2006: 7–8).

These incidents highlight the common experience of Palestinian Christians both during the period known to Palestinians as 'The Disaster' (an-Nakba) and the subsequent period of military rule in Israel. In fact, it can be argued that given the small size of the Palestinian Christian population, and the relatively small number of Christian-only villages in the territory that would become the State of Israel, Palestinian Christians have suffered disproportionately. Neither their small size nor their 'modern' outlook tempered or moderated the state's wider expropriation policy. Considering 'land expropriation [as] probably the most significant measure of deprivation' in society, Smooha argues that the government's policy of land expropriation affected every segment of the minority in Israel.

It is estimated that Arabs lost 40% to 60% of their land between 1948 and 1967. According to our survey, 52% of all Arab families were affected by land expropriation. (. . .) Of those affected, two thirds report their loss as being heavy. Among the landowners, 38% of the Druzes, *64% of the Christians*, 35% of Northern Bedouin, 81.5% of Negev Bedouin, and 70.5% of the non-Bedouin Moslems reportedly lost lands. [italics mine]

(Smooha 1989: 152)

Thus, Palestinian Christians suffered almost twice as much land losses than either of the Druze or northern Bedouin communities. This similar experience of land loss was not restricted to the period of military hostilities but extended into the post-war years and the state's initiative to 'Judaise the Galilee' (*Yehud ha-Galil*). This multi-faceted state policy aimed at creating Jewish territorial control over this predominantly Arab region as well as establishing Jewish demographic superiority within it through a system of land confiscations, Jewish settlement building and rezoning techniques. Falah has documented three separate stages in this 'Judaisation' policy.

In a *first stage* [from 1948 to 1974] the aim was to fill the 'vacuum' left by the demolition of Palestinian villages during the 1948 war and its aftermath (notably in border areas), and to create a belt of Jewish settlements surrounding the remaining Palestinian villages and lands. The *second stage* [1974 to 1982] involved penetrating the 'core' of greatest Palestinian population concentration through the implantation of new Jewish settlements, mainly small 'lookout settlements' (*mitzpim*). This served to create further spatial fragmentation and discontinuity of Palestinian lands and villages. Since these efforts did not succeed in altering the relative demographic composition, it appears that a *third stage* was initiated after 1982 involving an attempt, on a micro-geographical level, to intervene in the economy and spatial expansion of individual Palestinian villages. Among other things, this involved introducing new jurisdictional boundaries to control and hem in the economic development of these villages while strengthening new Jewish economic foci so as to dominate the economic life in the region.

(Falah 1991: 72)

Each of these three separate stages significantly affected each of the Palestinian Christian, Druze and Muslim communities. With regard to the first stage, for example, the 'vacuum' left by the destruction of the Christian villages of Iqrit and

Kfar Bir'am was filled by the construction of the Jewish settlements of Yoqrat and Baram. Nazareth – a city which not only housed a majority Christian population (until the late 1960s) but represented the centre of the Galilee – was also specifically targeted during this first stage by the construction of the Jewish 'development town' of Natzeret Illit in 1957 (primarily for Jewish immigrants from the former Soviet Union) on lands which had been confiscated from Nazareth itself as well as from a number of other predominantly Christian neighbouring villages, such as Reine and Ein Mahil (Falah 1992: 36). Designed as a Jewish 'buffer' town, the construction of Natzeret Illit aimed both to contain the physical expansion of the city and to curtail the political significance of Nazareth as Israel's unofficial 'Arab capital'. Another 'development town', Maalot, was built in the same year on the edge of the predominantly Christian village of Tarshiha. The second stage of the government's 'Judaisation' plan involved creating a 'territorial belt' of Jewish settlements in the area, thereby shoring up their infrastructural strength and providing better security and prospects for further Jewish settlement (Falah 1991: 76). While this stage provided for the economic control and the domination of the region's natural resources by and for its Jewish population, the third stage introduced a new era of direct intervention by the Jewish authorities in the affairs of Arab local authorities, particularly with regard to jurisdictional, development and zoning matters (Falah 1991: 79–81). Using the banner of economic efficiency and municipal reform, a number of Arab municipalities were merged with each other thereby reducing the total number of local Arab municipalities in Israel. The merger of a small number of Arab municipalities with larger neighbouring Jewish municipalities also took place which indirectly created Jewish political dominance over local Arab affairs in those areas. For example, Maalot-Tarshiha was the result of a merger between the Jewish municipality of Maalot and the Christian-majority municipality of Tarshiha. This policy significantly affected Palestinian Christian life in Israel as it reduced the number of localities in Israel possessing Palestinian Christian majorities thereby interrupting historic Palestinian Christian residence patterns in the region. Ultimately, it can be stated that, in these areas, the religious affiliation of the minority did not affect the ethnic determination of state policy.

Permanently trapped within competing national claims over the land, an intransigent Zionist discourse, and security concerns posed to the state by its Arab neighbours, the Palestinian Arab minority, including the Palestinian Christian segment of it, continues to be variously designated as a 'security risk', as an 'enemy-affiliated minority', as 'the enemy within', as 'potential fifth columnists', as a 'Trojan horse' and even as a 'second front' in Israel's wider struggle against both the Palestinians in the occupied territories and the Arab world, more generally.[2] Neither the different religious affiliation of Palestinian Christians nor their particular social outlook or orientations have protected them from the more general land policy of the state or resulted in a more lenient or preferential policy towards them. They are, in this respect, subject to the same measures of state control as the remainder of the Palestinian Arab minority.

A non-Muslim minority

However, ethnicity alone does not explain the complex nature of the relationship between the Israeli state and its Palestinian Arab minority. With a following of over one and a quarter million, Islam is the religion of 17 per cent of the total Israeli population and of 84 per cent of the Palestinian Arab minority, making it the single largest non-Jewish religious minority in Israel. The relative demographic strength of Palestinian Muslims has major consequences for state–minority relations in Israel. Muslims represent a minority in Israel; yet, the impact of their wider regional majority status together with their external links and affiliations with the Muslim world have significantly affected Israeli assessments of their real and potential strength and power. To this is added the internal demographic threat of a fast multiplying Muslim population which challenges the stated national priority of maintaining a permanent Jewish majority in Israel. Therefore, local and regional Muslim demographic factors together represent important reasons for the state's negative assessment of its Muslim population and relatively better view of its Palestinian Christian population. This is compounded by the coincidence between Muslim distribution patterns and the state's land priorities.

> Constituting the vast majority of rural Arab settlements in Israel, the majority of conflicts with the Jews and the government have occurred with the Muslims, be it land confiscation, disputes over popular holy sites, or confrontations regarding tax raising.
>
> (Tsimhoni 2002: 143)

It can, therefore, be observed that certain Jewish national priorities, such as the maintenance of a Jewish majority and Jewish control over the land, have become defined in primarily religious and anti-Muslim terms. The impact of regional hostilities and the persistence of political deadlock between Israel and its Arab neighbours have swamped or at least clouded Israeli assessments of the capabilities of its own predominantly Muslim Palestinian Arab minority (Karayanni 2006: 62). If, according to Horowitz and Lissak, 'the Muslim world sees Israel as an alien entity in the heart of a predominantly Moslem and Arab region' (Horowitz and Lissak 1989: 10), then the religious and demographic significance of Israel's own Muslim minority becomes accentuated and problematised to a degree which is well beyond the practical or political capacity of any other religious minority in Israel, whether Christian or Druze.

This close association between being Arab and Muslim in the Middle East has led to the two identities becoming fused in the minds of many. For Jacob Landau, for example, Arab nationalism and Islam are seen as largely interchangeable expressions of the same monolithic identity and Muslims are described as showing a far greater inclination towards 'radicalisation' and 'extremism' than other religious groups as a result of their imputed theological heritage (Landau 1993: 36–7). According to Raphael Israeli, the tendency of Palestinian Christians to follow secular and non-sectarian political options underscores the marginality of Palestinian Christians within the dominant religious-political framework of Arab-Islamic identity (Israeli 2002: 39).

One central determinant in the state's approach to its Palestinian Christian minority must, therefore, be its exceptional non-Muslim character. Religiously set apart from Palestinian Muslims, Palestinian Christians are 'outnumbered' by Muslim Arabs and are, thereby, disconnected, to a significant degree, from the default conceptual framework of a demographically and territorially 'threatening' Muslim Arab Middle East. Zureik considers one of the central features of Zionist thought to be the antagonistic and prejudicial view of Islam as a 'militant, vengeful and conquering religion' (Zureik 1979: 87). Within this analysis, it is Islam itself and the resulting 'Muslim mentality', not political circumstances, which are implied to be the root causes of the continued Arab hostility to the State of Israel.

> This one-sided explanation of Arab attitudes toward Israel, which is derived from an egocentric interpretation of Islam, and, as rightly pointed out by Said, has a pseudo-Gibbonian racist ring to it, fails to account for the well-known hostility displayed throughout this century by Christian Arabs in Palestine toward Zionist colonisation of the area.
>
> (Zureik 1979: 87)

The negative depiction of Muslims as tending more towards aggressive, intolerant, ignorant, intransigent, violent and, most recently, terrorist behaviour compares with the more benign stereotype of Palestinian Christians as being more peaceful, moderate and accommodating. While these stereotypes fail to address the politically problematic behaviour of important numbers of Palestinian Christians which will be detailed in a later section, the ideological and rhetorical power of these stereotypes to increase gaps and tensions within society is substantial. As a result, the depiction of Muslims in both Israeli and Palestinian Arab society as something of a school-ground bully is quite common. This is demonstrated with regard to analyses of village patterns of communal living amongst Arabs in Israel. In describing the regional distribution of the Druze in Israel, Landau, for example, described a history of 'long, cruel persecution' of the Druze by Muslims as motivating their particular residential patterns (Landau 1969: 12). In his study on the Druze in Israel, Gabriel Ben-Dor has also argued that as a result of greater levels of Muslim intransigence and intolerance towards other groups in society, the Druze have historically preferred to live, where possible, with Christians with whom they reputedly have greater mutual understanding and respect (Ben-Dor 1979: 97–8, 106).

The view that Muslims are unfamiliar with and, as such, are unwilling to accept their status as a minority in a non-Muslim society is relatively common (Landau 1993: 36). Accounting for their allegedly more pronounced feelings of hostility and resentment towards the state as a result of their historical memory of social and political dominance within the Middle East, the Muslim community in Israel is often described as an 'ex-majority minority' (Smooha 1978). Palestinian Christians, by contrast, are portrayed as being familiar with their minority status and, as a result, more willing to adapt to and accept their new minority status in Israel. One proponent of this argument linking historical group memory as a minority with a concept of political maturity, Ori Stendel suggests that the Muslims, lacking experience of being organised as a *millet*, have had a difficult transition to their new status as a minority in the Jewish state compared with other groups (Stendel 1973).

More recently, this characterisation is demonstrated by the increasingly common description of Palestinian Christians as a 'minority within a minority' in Israel, both as marginalised Arabs in the Jewish State and as a collection of threatened Christian communities in the Muslim Middle East. One proponent of this view of Palestinian Christians as a 'minority within a minority', Tsimhoni focuses her analysis on increasing patterns of Christian emigration from the Middle East and on the related 'loss' of traditionally Christian-majority urban centres (such as Nazareth and Shfar'amr) to a growing Muslim population and an increasingly dominant Islamic movement (Tsimhoni 2002: 124–5, 131). This characterisation is matched by her description of Palestinian Christians as the 'weaker party' in an allegedly growing number of Muslim-Christian conflicts brought about by the transformation of Palestinian Arab society into an increasingly violent and intolerant 'Muslim environment'.

> The major cause for their growing sense of insecurity and dependence on the Arab Muslim environment has been the rise of the Islamic movement in Israel. The official declarations of the movement in Israel are cautiously phrased, speaking of the common fate with 'our Christian brethren' as well as the need for cooperation with them in the common national struggle. However, no public discourse has taken place regarding the position of the Christians in the future Islamic state. But nobody is misled regarding the Christians' place in such a state bearing in mind the traditional *dhimmi* position of the Christians and Jews in Islam.
>
> Since the early 1990s, a growing number of verbal incitements against Christians and Jews have been heard in the mosque and printed in the newspapers of the Islamic movement. (. . .)
>
> The growing Islamic influence can be noticed in many Muslim neighbourhoods. The observance of the fast of Ramadan in public has become commonplace, more girls are clothed in Muslim dress, including head cover, even though this phenomenon is still less evident than in neighbouring Arab countries. Loudspeakers call for prayers and chapters of the Qur'an are broadcast for hours at a time, reminding the Christian neighbours that they live in a Muslim society. The general atmosphere in the Arab street denounces the Western open lifestyle as 'Israelisation' (Asralah) and the maintaining of social contacts with Jews as 'collaboration'. And many of those to be blamed for these 'faults' are Christians. Businessmen and professionals who cater for the Muslim majority need to adapt themselves to the general atmosphere lest they be boycotted economically and socially.
>
> (Tsimhoni 2002: 132)

The marginal status of Palestinian Christians within Palestinian Arab society is frequently understood to be caused by Muslim anti-Christian feeling, whether this is as a result of resentment or jealousy of the relative socio-economic advantage of Christians in society; religious antipathy or bigotry against Christianity; their association with the period of the Crusades or of European colonialism; or their more recent association with either Christian evangelicalism or US foreign policy in the region. Raphael Israeli has written extensively on the role of 'fundamentalist Islam' and the deterioration of Muslim–Christian relations in Israel. According to his analysis, Muslim attitudes towards Christians are heavily influenced by the latter's historical designation as a *dhimmi* people during the period of Muslim rule in the Middle East and their later status as a separate religious community, or *millet*, from Ottoman times, as well as their false association with the worst excesses of European intervention in the region (Israeli 2002: 6–10, 23). He also observes that Christians are singled out by 'Islamists' due to their more modern, secular, liberal and Westernised attitudes which they allegedly share with the Jewish majority.

> The outcome flows evidently from these hallowed assumptions shared by Muslim fundamentalists: not only are Jews and Christians detested in their own right, but being the long arms of the West in the Islamic world, they are considered as its agents in its endeavour to undermine Islam, corrupt it from within, alienate its youth by their permissiveness and immoral conduct, and penetrate its educational systems in order to destroy them, etc.
>
> (Israeli 2002: 67)

If this analysis of Palestinian Christians as a scared, threatened, insecure and vulnerable 'minority within a minority' is correct, the degree of threat which Palestinian Christians could pose to the Jewish state, or which is associated with this community, should be minimal. The non-threatening nature of Palestinian Christians is underlined by their practical disconnection from the regional demographic majority (of Muslims) and the absence of any political or religious links with political Islam. Furthermore, given the common experience which is suggested to exist between Christians and Jews in the region, a more sympathetic, empathetic and supportive policy towards Palestinian Christians would be expected to follow. It should, therefore, be anticipated that this reported Jewish affinity and solidarity with the plight of Palestinian Christians, together with these other pragmatic demographic and territorial concerns, should minimise, or eliminate altogether, the necessity of control over this community.

A small, insignificant community

At just 1.6 per cent of the total Israeli population and 7.9 per cent of the Palestinian Arab minority, Palestinian Christians represent a very small segment of both societies. Their small size has had two major consequences for the formulation of state policy towards them. The first of these has already been encountered.

Given their small number relative to both the Jewish majority and the predominantly Muslim Palestinian minority, Palestinian Christians do not constitute the same 'lurking demographic threat' (Kanaaneh 2009: 2) which is otherwise associated with the predominantly Muslim Palestinian Arab minority. Nor are they sufficiently plentiful in the region to constitute a serious (independent) territorial threat. The non-threatening nature of Palestinian Christian demography is underlined by their unchallenging and inconsequential socio-economic characteristics. Their wide regional distribution together with their low fertility rates and high rates of emigration, remove the sense of threat which is otherwise associated with the Palestinian Arab minority.

However, a second consequence of the small Palestinian Christian demographic is their negligible significance relative to the overall electoral weight of the Palestinian Arab minority in Israeli politics. The electoral significance of a minority which accounts for 20 per cent of the total population of the state cannot be overstated. During the period of military rule, the politically disorganised and weakened Palestinian Arab minority was quickly identified as a valuable resource to the state in that it constituted an accessible 'floating Arab vote' which could easily be harnessed to bolster the power and hegemonic status of the ruling Mapai party (Kaufman 1997: 83, 113–14). However, its primary function was one of control, particularly with regard to its use of affiliated Arab lists.

> The Zionist parties, and especially Mapai, unwilling to accept Arab members, encouraged leaders of clans, communities or religions to set up satellite lists that could attract Arab electoral support. This approach provided the Jewish parties with an instrument for controlling the Arabs and a means for mobilising their votes and support in Knesset.
>
> (Ghanem 2001: 41)

Another source clarifies the purpose of these lists even further:

> Arab affiliated lists were one of the most efficient instruments of channelling Arab votes, in particular in the late 1960s. These affiliated lists were initiated and backed by Zionist parties, mainly the Labour Party, which was the principal force in the Israeli establishment until 1977. The object of these lists was not the political mobilisation of the Arab population but rather the 'catching' of Arab votes through traditional means of persuasion. The structure of the Arab affiliated lists was tailored to fit the deep social territorialisation of the Arab population and the traditional character.
>
> (al-Haj 1995b: 142)

Therefore, dependent Arab lists such as 'Agriculture and Development', 'Progress and Work' and 'Cooperation and Brotherhood', etc., which remained popular well into the 1970s, were composed of various influential leaders within the traditional Arab elite who were willing and able to bring to the Israeli political table the voting power of their area, religious community or tribe in return for personal and family benefits and privileges. They demonstrated total subservience to the demands and ethnic priorities of the state, including, at one point, in 1961, voting in favour of a continuation of military rule (Ghanem 2001: 41–2).

One vote-catching tactic concerned the selection of Arab candidates who would run on these lists. As the authorities were interested in coopting those who could secure the widest revenue of votes possible, 'men who have commanded large religious, sectional or kinship followings' were deliberately sought out and coopted (Lustick 1980: 208–9). While several Christian representatives were included on Arab lists – most notably Amin-Salim Jarjora, Masaad Kassis, Yusuf Hamis and Elias Nakhleh – the potential number of votes which these representatives could furnish paled in comparison with their Muslim counterparts.

Mapai was not the only Zionist Party interested in 'collecting' the Arab vote. The National Religious Party, which was founded in 1956 as a Mizrahi religious party and which came to dominate several key government ministries for several years, also sought out the Arab vote. Not only did it control the budgets for Arab municipalities and become closely involved in their internal affairs, it mobilised religious differences within the minority for its own sake, inspiring what Landau describes as their 'horse-trading' electoral strategies within the Arab sector (Landau 1969: 143–4).

Thus, the insecure atmosphere of military rule and the political cooptation of traditional Arab leaders by the authorities proved very effective in capturing the Arab vote. In the seven parliamentary elections which took place between 1949 and 1969, for example, Zionist parties and their affiliated Arab lists secured an overwhelming majority (80 per cent) of the Palestinian Arab vote, compared with an average electoral return of only 20 per cent for the CP, the only opposition party operating in Israel at that time (Ghanem 2001: 201). In 1951 alone, 84 per cent of all Arab voters voted for Zionist parties and their affiliated lists (Smooha 1997: 215; Ghanem 2001: 201). The majority of these (55 per cent) voted for affiliated Arab lists. Despite the fact that Zionist parties and their affiliated lists together continued to secure the majority of the Arab electorate's vote until 1984, the appeal of Arab lists had already begun to decline by the early 1970s as a result of the termination of military rule and the increasing politicisation of the Arab electorate.

Changes in the political arena also changed the role of the Arab vote in Israeli politics. Previously, the purpose of Arab lists had been limited to the selective cooptation, containment and control of the Palestinian Arab minority in an uncontested, primarily one-party system of government. But with the territorial enlargement of the state in 1967, the state's focus expanded to include the Palestinians of the newly occupied territories thus reducing the centrality of Palestinian Arab citizens within the national security discourse of the state. Jewish and, in many cases, messianic religious politics also entered the fray with new vigour, deepening the significance of religious affiliation throughout society as a whole (Rouhana 1997: 11–23).

The victory of Likud in the 1977 elections introduced not only a new period of political competition, but a growing trend towards right-wing religious Jewish nationalism in Israeli politics. Owing its electoral success to the new national religious fervour which was gripping society; to the untapped electoral base of Jewish settlers in the occupied territories; and, internally, to the powerful protest vote of Israel's underprivileged Mizrahi population, Hanna Herzog has shown how Likud's electoral strategy towards the Palestinian Arab minority operation-alised religious, residential and so-called ethnic differences within the minority in order to win the Arab vote and to secure its own political future (Herzog 1985: 163, 166). By contrast, Labour's electoral strategy within the Arab sector focused on its apparently more 'dovish' and inclusive nature – in other words, its greater willingness to engage in a meaningful peace process with the PLO and its prom-ises for greater integration of Palestinian Arabs in society (Rouhana 1997: 102).

As a result, the role and function not only of the Arab vote but of internal dif-ferences within the Palestinian Arab minority, which had always played a factor in Israeli policy, became of greater importance from this period onwards. In several cases, they became decisive factors in determining the outcome of elections, and with the emergence of direct and competitive electoral strategies which increas-ingly recognised the numerical significance of religious cleavages and differences in society, the Arab vote itself became politicised.

The Labour Party has traditionally been the most popular Zionist party among the Arab electorate. When, in 1981, it cancelled its support for affiliated Arab lists and started running Arab candidates directly on its own list, Labour's popularity within the Arab sector jumped from 11 per cent in 1977 to 29 per cent four years later (Ghanem 2001: 201). The two Arab Labour candidates selected to repre-sent Labour (then running as The Alignment) in the 1981 elections were Hamad Khalaily from Sakhnin and Muhammad Wattad from Jatt. Neither candidate was Christian (one was Muslim and the other Druze). In fact, the first Christian to be elected to the Knesset on behalf of the Labour Party was only elected 14 years later in 1992 – 20 years after Arabs were first allowed to run for election on the Labour Party ballot. This anomaly highlights the issue of reserved seats for Arab candidates on the electoral lists of Zionist parties as a strategic component of Israeli electoral *realpolitik*. Majid Al Haj describes the decision by the Labour Party at that time to allocate its twentieth slot for a Muslim candidate (Nawwaf Mazalha); its thirtieth slot for a Druze (Saleh Tarif); and only a much lower and more marginal slot for the Christian candidate (Hanna Haddad).

> This decision has outraged Christian members of the Labour Party, since the Christian candidate was pushed into a marginal slot. Leaders of the Labour Party sought to prevent a crisis with the Christian community. Subsequently a Christian candidate was allotted to the forty-sixth place.
>
> (Al Haj 1995b: 148)

Clearly, the Christian slot was subsequently moved up the list as Labour only secured 44 seats in the 1992 parliamentary elections and Haddad was finally allot-ted one of them. Only one other Palestinian Christian has ever been elected to represent the Labour Party in the Israeli Knesset – Nadia Hilou – who was elected

14 years later and served only one term.

The electoral strategies of other Zionist parties are not dissimilar to those followed by Labour. The unusual appeal of the Arab vote to religious and right-wing Jewish parties continued after the end of military rule. Writing about the Druze community in Israel, Oppenheimer observes the role of these parties in politicising and manipulating the newly created Druze national identity for their own electoral purposes (Oppenheimer 1985: 276). Druze representation on these parties' electoral lists is common. In elections to the Tenth Knesset in 1981, for example, 22 per cent of the Arab electorate voted for 'other Zionist parties' which included the NRP and Likud, resulting in the election of only one Arab candidate – a Druze, who ran on behalf of the Likud Party (Ghanem 2001: 201). Moreover, in the five elections which took place between 1992 and 2006, non-Labour Zionist Parties attracted, on average, 21.3 per cent of the Arab vote, compared with 12.9 per cent electoral returns for the Labour Party itself. While no Arab has ever represented the NRP or Shas, a Druze was, for the first time, elected MK for the ultra-nationalist right-wing religious party of Avigdor Lieberman, Yisrael Beitenu, in the last, Eighteenth Knesset. Palestinian Christians, by contrast, have never been elected to the Israeli parliament for any Jewish religious or right-wing nationalist party. Therefore, it would appear that both the appeal and the electoral strategies of these parties are limited primarily to the Muslim and Druze communities.

As a result, it can be argued that the numbers game remains an important factor in the determination of Israel's electoral policy towards its Palestinian Arab minority. The political influence of traditional elites and sectarian leaders has declined as the power of practical numbers and demography has taken over. This is particularly so given the consistently high turnout rates of Arab voters in Israeli elections until recently. In the 15 parliamentary elections which took place between 1949 and 1999, for example, an average Arab turnout of 78 per cent was recorded (Ghanem 2001: 201). Until the 2001 elections, Arab voter turnout was usually as high as Jewish voter turnout, making the Arab vote not only important to the Labour Party in its attempt to unhinge the power of Likud, but 'an attractive pool of voters for several parties including Likud and the Orthodox Party' (Peretz and Doron 1997: 98). As such, the strategic importance of a numerically superior and 'predominantly Muslim and conservative electorate' (Frisch 2001: 160), together with the sectarian electoral policies of Zionist parties, becomes emphasised, while the relative importance of demographically smaller segments of the minority diminishes accordingly. By contrast, the electoral insignificance of Palestinian Christians is understood to be determined by 'the changing attitudes of the governments, which seek out votes for their parties among the Muslim majority of the Palestinian Arabs in Israel' (Tsimhoni 2002: 149). However, it is understood that the functionality of the Arab vote is limited to particular situations in which a tightly fought contest between Israeli Jewish political factions is anticipated and so long as Arab voter turnouts remain high. Thereafter, or otherwise, it is disposable.

Political behaviour and the issue of loyalty

Given their Arab ethnicity, the political behaviour of Palestinian Christians intro-
duces potential roadblocks to state attitude towards them. The question of the
loyalty and trustworthiness of the minority as a whole has dominated analyses of
even this small, 'Westernised', non-Muslim, 'minority within a minority'. Notwithstanding their popular description as a politically moderate and 'peace-lov-
ing' community (Peretz 1958: 5, 45), an alternative line of thinking emerged early
on which cautioned that while this perceived politically moderate behaviour is
desirable, it is also only a consequence of their relatively isolated and vulnerable
position as a small religious minority and that, ultimately, their allegiance to the
state cannot be given too much trust or credence. As early as 1959, Walter Schwarz
had quoted Samuel Divon, former Advisor to the Prime Minister on Arab Affairs,
as saying that only a few Palestinian Christians can be considered within the category of 'Arabs who really accept us' (Schwarz 1959: 140–1). Ten years later,
Yochaman Peres and Nira Yuval-Davis argued that loyalty shown by any segment
of the Arab minority to the state is as a reserved type of loyalty that is based upon
their pragmatic awareness of the new political realities which surround them, and
that the 'real' attitude of the minority towards the state is concealed by a 'mask'
of apparent political quiescence, pragmatism and indifference (Perez and Yuval
Davis 1969: 226–31).

Independent political activity within the Palestinian Arab minority has traditionally been viewed with a heavy dose of mistrust, understood as it is to ema-
nate from fundamentally 'radical', 'extremist' and 'ideological' motivations. This
is particularly true of the authorities' attitudes towards Palestinian Arab activity
within the ICP, known by the Hebrew acronym Maki before it split in 1965 to form
the first Arab-dominated party in Israeli politics, Rakah, which later merged with
other left-wing parties in the 1970s to form Hadash, also known as the Democratic
Front for Peace and Equality (DFPE).

Until the 1990s, the leadership structure of Rakah was dominated by secular Palestinian Christians (of predominantly Greek Orthodox background) from the key
urban centres of Haifa and Nazareth. Of the ten Palestinian Arabs who represented
the leadership cadre of Maki between 1948 and 1959, the majority were Christian.
Tawfiq Toubi, a Christian from Haifa, became the sole Palestinian Christian to represent Maki in the four seats which they took in Israel's First Knesset (1949–1951).
In the Second Knesset (1951–1955), when the number of seats controlled by Maki
increased to seven, Emile Habibi (also from Haifa) joined Maki as the second Palestinian Arab and Christian MK. Over the course of the next three Knessets (from
1955 to 1965) when Maki lost seats, dropping to just four seats during the Fourth
Knesset (1959–1961), Toubi retained his seat, indicating his centrality to the party.
Similarly, Israel's only Arabic daily newspaper, *al-Ittihad*, which is also the official
organ of the Arab Communist Party in Israel, was founded in Haifa by three Palestinian Christians (Emile Habibi, Fu'ad Nassar and Emile Touma).

One common explanation for the relatively inflated presence of Palestinian
Christians within the ICP/Rakah stems from the universal, inclusive, secular

and nationalist ideology which it espouses and the notion that it represented the best 'path to [their] inclusion in the national community' (Sa'ar 1998: 226). Some Israeli Jewish analyses have criticised this heavy Christian involvement as a form of political pragmatism which is ultimately delusionary and contrary to the 'real' long-term interests of Christians in Israel and the Middle East (Tsimhoni 2002: 133). Regardless of how their involvement has been interpreted, what is not disputed is the prominent position of a significant segment of the Christian population in the development and leadership of what has been viewed, by the state, as the 'threatening' or 'radical' political activity of this party. As one analysis puts it:

> [T]he fact that the Arab Christian elite was more intensely involved in political activity than the Muslims served to confirm the views of many sections of the Israeli establishment that they constituted a threat. The major role played by Christian Arabs in the development of the Communist movement in Israel and in Arab nationalist activity also influenced this official view.
>
> (Bialer 2005: 127)

Although defined as a sectarian party from the point of view of the Israeli authorities (whereby sectarian, in this instance, came to be defined, in part, to be both Arab and Christian), Rakah/DFPE was the first party to successfully mobilise the growing Arab protest vote in Israel on the basis of a universal, secular and non-traditional national platform. It promoted an integrated form of Arab identity stressing the common ethnicity and national destiny of all Palestinian Arabs in Israel; it demanded an end to military rule and called for equality and justice for Arab citizens in Israel; it opposed the government's land expropriation efforts and organised several conferences and strikes as well as public protests against them, most notably Land Day, 1976; it pushed for a just peace with the Palestinians and the recognition of Palestinians inside Israel as a national minority; it opposed military service for Arabs; and accused traditional Arab political leaders who served on Arab-affiliated lists of treason (Kaufman 1997: 60–7).

As such, Rakah came to both represent and spearhead the Arab cause in Israel, and while it remained marginal within Israeli national politics until the mid-1970s, it became a successful opposition party to the Israeli political establishment, leading to its designation by the authorities as a 'militant', 'radical' and 'ideological' organisation (Smooha 1978: 224; Ghanem 2001: 32). Given its vocal political position, both Rakah and its predecessor Maki experienced persistent harassment by the authorities who were extremely hostile to it. For example, Ghanem reports that a number of Arab teachers and civil servants were dismissed from their jobs during the 1950s, 1960s and 1970s for expressing sympathy with the CP and that the authorities also encouraged Arabs to spy on neighbours who were known for their Communist sympathies or party affiliations. Lustick also reports the designation of Rakah by government officials as a serious source of threat to the state and as a 'hostile element' which must be actively countered (Lustick 1980: 133, 243, 255, 332).

This designation as a 'hostile element' came primarily as a result of the incremental gains made by Rakah in successive Israeli national and municipal elections. In the five parliamentary elections before the Rakah–Maki split of 1965, for example, the CP had managed to secure an average of only 17 per cent of the Arab vote. However, by the parliamentary elections of 1965, this figure had already increased to 23 per cent, continuing thereafter to grow until 1977 when Rakah reached its highest ever recorded electoral returns of 50 per cent of the Arab vote (Ghanem 2001: 201). This impressive trend was mirrored in local municipal elections when, in 1975, Rakah/DFPE succeeded for the first time in taking control of an Arab local council in Israel (Rabinowitz 2001a: 104). That this local council happened to be located in Nazareth – the largest Arab city in Israel and the city with the highest number of Palestinian Christians – underscored both Rakah's victory and its connection with Palestinian Christian political activity in Israel.

Rakah's electoral victory became symptomatic of a wider trend which was negatively perceived as the 'radicalisation' and 'Palestinisation' of Arab society in Israel. It is no coincidence that this new sociological approach also emerged in the 1970s. Peres and Yuval Davis (1969) applied the radicalisation thesis to their analyses of Palestinian Arab political behaviour, arguing that the minority's so-called radicalisation was the consequence, or flip-side, of their modernisation in Israeli society. Within this rationale, modernisation provided the minority with new educational benefits and social opportunities, but was unable to affect their deeper and more 'radical' emotional attachments to Arab nationalism. The relationship between modernisation and nationalism, therefore, is understood to equip a hostile minority with the practical skills to manipulate and exploit the 'loop holes' created by the liberalisation of Israeli policy following the termination of military rule in 1966. And while Smooha countered the radicalisation perspective with his own 'politicisation' thesis which saw the political mobilisation of the Palestinian Arab minority as a natural consequence of their increased opportunities, the changes within society, and the growing level of Palestinian Arab dissatisfaction with their discriminated status in society, the radicalisation thesis proved more influential in government circles (Smooha 1989: 9–17, 169, 177).

The contents of the leaked 1976 Koenig Report, for example, made several direct references to the threat posed by both Rakah and the Nazareth municipality. It warned of 'the nationalist manifestations in the voting in the Nazareth municipal elections on 9 December 1975' and 'the devious and unexpected call-up of the inhabitants of the inhabitants of Nazareth to help the municipality pay off pressing debts, which at that stage eased Rakah's burden in running the town' (MERIP 1976: 11). These 'pressing debts' had accrued as a result of budget cuts placed by the central authorities on the Nazareth municipality in an attempt to weaken its ability to function effectively at this critical time. In addition to a system of 'rewards and punishments', the Report also recommends providing an alternative political 'valve for communities still sitting on the fence', whether through Mapai-affiliated lists or through the promotion of alternative political movements and parties among the minority in order to divide and weaken the strength of Rakah/DFPE/Hadash and the role of Nazareth in promoting Arab nationalism (MERIP

1976: 12). In this regard, a significant proportion of its energies at this time were spent in promoting the fledgling Islamic movement, a policy which would later backfire upon the state. As Lustick has noted, 'the coordination of a smear campaign against Rakah activists, and the harassment of "all negative personalities at all levels and all institutions"' was a central component of the Report's recommendations (Lustick 1980: 255–6).

Rakah/DFPE does not represent the only opposition movement within which Palestinian Christians have played a central role. The rise to prominence of Balad – also known as the National Democratic Assembly (NDA) or at-Tajamu'a in Arabic – which was founded in 1996 by Nazareth-born Azmi Bishara further undermined the political hegemony of Hadash/DFPE and its unique representative function among Palestinian Arabs. Unlike the Islamic movement, which offered a limited sectarian political path, Balad proposed a novel non-sectarian and ideological alternative to Hadash/DFPE (Peled 2001b: 384). In challenging the Jewish character of the state, it demanded that Israel become a fully democratic state by becoming 'a state for all its citizens'. It also led the drive for recognition of the collective rights of Palestinian Arabs as a national minority (Rekhess 2007: 12–14). Moreover, it exposed a number of weaknesses and shortcomings of the Hadash/DFPE platform. Seen as increasingly ineffective, rigid, traditionalist, old-fashioned and weak, Hadash/DFPE was criticised for not moving with the times and incorporating younger Palestinians, particularly Muslims, within its ranks (Kaufman 1997: 48–50). It was also criticised for concentrating on its international character as a communist party and its regional role as Palestinian representative to the detriment of local Palestinian interests and needs and for its ambiguous stance on the Jewish character of the state and the rights of Palestinian Arab citizens of Israel as a distinct national minority (Rekhess 2007: 8–9).

The issue of loyalty is clearly a deeply important and central aspect of the Israeli establishment's attitude towards the Palestinian Arab minority as a whole. In terms of their overall trustworthiness, the Palestinian Christians, while considered more trustworthy than Muslims, are not considered to fall into the same category of trust as the Druze who are held up to be 'model Arabs' in society (Schwarz 1959: 148). Thus, 'positive elements' within the minority are continually singled out from what were perceived to be 'negative elements', with the distinction between both categories often rooted in terms of religious affiliation. Thus, the Druze are generally observed to be the most loyal segment of the minority, followed by the Christians, with the Muslims relegated to the bottom of the scale (Lustick 1980: 78). Perceptions of loyalty are occasionally further differentiated according to religious sect or cultural grouping. Henry Rosenfeld, for example, suggested that the ranking which best describes Israeli establishment perceptions of the minority is, by descending order of trustworthiness: the Druze, the Maronites, the Bedouins, the Greek Catholics, the Greek Orthodox, followed by the Muslims, who are relegated to the lowest position (Rosenfeld 1978: 392). This suggests that although the Christians rank higher than the Muslims, perceptions of their political behaviour are themselves divided.

Regional links

The relevance of regional links in the determination of state policy has previously been encountered with regard to the state's determination of its Muslim population. As a religious minority in the region, Palestinian Christians do not suffer from this same negative association. This is mitigated by the common relevance of their Arab ethnicity which has contributed to their association with the wider 'Arab problem' and regional 'threat'. However, religion and demography do not represent the only areas of interest to the state in its orientation towards Palestinian Christians. Regional links and contacts also represent an important factor to the state, albeit in a functional sense.

While the Druze are – with the exception of the incorporated Druze population of the Golan Heights – cut off from their co-religionists in neighbouring Arab countries, Palestinian Christians continue to have important links with Christians not only in the West Bank and Jordan, but also in Lebanon and Syria (Ben-Dor 1979: 108). Given their small numbers, these links do not constitute a grave threat to the state. What they can offer the state, however, is a unique point of leverage or manoeuvrability. Referring to their 'consanguinity across the borders', Landau addresses historic patterns of Palestinian Christian migration and intermarriage, which have, in turn, been compounded by the historic location of much of the northern Galilee within the former territorial boundaries of Greater Syria (Landau 1969: 30).

While each of the Christian denominations in Israel share communal links with neighbouring communities in Lebanon, the Maronite community demonstrates the greatest communal solidarity with their co-religionists abroad, notably in Lebanon. Contributing to this accentuated affiliation is the fact that the Maronite population of Israel is very small, amounting to less than 8,000 individuals in all (Ateek 2006: 4). Furthermore, their weak demographic presence is underscored by their isolated regional distribution along Israel's border with Lebanon. All of these factors have enhanced the strong religious-based transnational identity of Maronites in Israel. Beyond the particular identity of the Maronite community in Israel, Lebanon itself represents a particular emotional significance to Palestinian Christians in Israel. As the only country in the Middle East with a sizeable Christian minority, Christians in Lebanon benefit from a range of personal and political freedoms and powers unknown to any other Christian minority in the region. However, the diversity of Lebanon's social and religious landscape, together with its flawed confessional system of governance, has simultaneously proven to be a major source of political instability and violence both in the country and the region, providing political opportunities which have not passed its neighbour and political adversary by unnoticed.

Discussing government strategies to quash the increasing power of Rakah in the 1970s, particularly in the run-up to the 1975 municipal elections, Oppenheimer observes the ultimately unsuccessful attempts made by Israeli government and party officials to use the civil war in Lebanon (1975–90) to stir up religious strife between Christians and Muslims in Israel.

In this election, the non-sectarian alliance of the Communist Party (RAQAH) and members of the local professional intelligentsia was successful in a town with a mixed Christian and Muslim population. This happened in spite of attempts by Government representatives to exploit the tragic events in Lebanon in order to persuade the electorate that the real issue in Nazareth was the religious division, in the hope of thereby splitting support for the radical list and attracting votes for Labour-sponsored candidates.

(Oppenheimer 1985: 265)

While the regional links of Palestinian Christians only represent a small factor in the determination of the state's attitude towards its Palestinian Christian population, they are nonetheless important as they demonstrate the subordinate and functional role of local Palestinian Christian needs to broader Israeli Jewish national priorities.

Absence of a central communal leadership

That religious affiliation represents a central organising principle both of Arab communities within the Middle East and of the Jewish state is well known. That Israel also extends separate legal recognition to its religious minorities is similarly well documented. However, the question of how structural differences between religious communities have affected the state's attitudes towards and interactions with Palestinian Christians in Israel is less well understood. The significance of communal organisation in determining state–minority relations in an ethnocratic state is often overlooked. The presence or absence of internal fragmentation within each religious segment of the minority has important consequences not only for the organisational and leadership structure of each community – whether on a religious, social or political level – but it also determines to a significant extent the manner in which the state can practically engage with it.

The Muslim population of Israel receives legal recognition from the state as a distinct religious community. As a result of the homogeneous nature of Islam in Israel, however, the communal organisation of Muslim affairs in Israel follows a highly centralised and singular pattern. Their religious authorities are responsible for all matters of 'personal status' affecting Muslims in Israel, such as marriage and divorce, and they are responsible for the administration of all Muslim religious lands and endowments (known as *waqf*, plural *awqaf*, in Arabic). As part of the system of separate religious accommodation in Israel, Muslims possess separate communal structures and a judicial court system based on the *shari'a* which is administered by a council of religious judges, known as *qadis*. While possessing the widest jurisdictional authority of any minority religious community in Israel, the Muslim authorities have, however, also suffered from the highest level of state interference in, and control over, their affairs which is in no small way connected to the high level of threat and suspicion that is associated with this community (Karayanni 2006: 59). Michael Karayanni details Israeli state interference in Muslim religious affairs as follows:

First of all, Muslim *qadis* to the *Shari'a* courts are appointed by a special statutory committee. Although the committee has representatives from the Moslem community, its agenda was controlled by the Minister of Religions, today the Minister of Justice. In addition, local *Imams* are appointed by the state and are in essence state officials. A substantial portion of Moslem religious endowments (*waqf*), regarded as absentee property, was transferred to the hands of the Israeli government.

(Karayanni 2006: 62)

The coopted Muslim religious authorities are tightly controlled by the Israeli state authorities and their range of powers is tightly restricted and constrained. The Druze community is also homogeneous in terms of its religious make-up and communal structure. Following their recognition by the state as a separate religious community in 1957, the Druze religious authorities were provided with their own separate and independent court system in 1962. However, unlike the Muslim community, the Druze are perceived as a non-threatening and, indeed, as the most favoured segment of the minority. As a result, their religious authorities and court system receives a far greater level of real autonomy with regard to the administration of their religious affairs, and with time, 'the Druze religious courts became important political institutions controlled entirely by the Druze community, including the process of selecting judges' (Karayanni 2006: 63).

However, despite their greater level of autonomy, the Druze communal structure is 'weak' in terms of its ability to act independently of the state. Jonathan Oppenheimer has argued that it was the homogeneous nature of Druze identity and their singular communal organisation which made the Druze community particularly prone to Israeli state manipulation and interference. By offering the Druze leadership the novel opportunity of administering to the personal affairs of their own community, the state was able to institutionalise the exclusive authority of these notables; politicise the Druze and separate them from their Arab identity through the extension of a separate Druze nationality; and to extract a number of added benefits from them (Oppenheimer 1985: 268–9). One of these added benefits for the state was compulsory military service for Druze. As the decision to make military service mandatory for all young Druze (men) was not a popular decision, the coopted Druze leadership were obliged to apply coercive measures against their own community in order to preserve the personal benefits which they had been awarded by the state.

This practice became compulsory for Druze males in 1956. According to official claims this followed the request of the Druze themselves. It is clear, however, that the community has never been united on this question, and those who made the demand (if demand it was) were the same traditional leaders who had previously become clients of the Israeli administration and, in particular, of the then dominant Labour Party, MAPAI. A popular account of this development among Druze who oppose the officially recognised leadership suggests that traditional leaders were pressed into making the request in exchange for specific favours, and in particular, the granting of religious autonomy which was finalised the following year.

(Oppenheimer 1985: 269)

Military service was not the only area which demonstrates the vulnerability of the Druze community caused by its particular form of centralised communal leadership. Voting patterns and Druze electoral politics have also been easily influenced by the wishes of the Druze leadership. The creation of Druze-only affiliated lists during the period of Mapai dominance and military rules as well as the more recent success of Zionist parties in 'catching' the Druze vote are, in no small way, connected to the influence of a central Druze communal leadership structure.

The benefits of this 'Druzification' process were, however, limited. For example, the Druze remained excluded, together with the remainder of the Arab population, from joining the Labour Party until 1972. They have suffered similar losses of land as a result of the government's expropriation efforts, particularly during its 'Judaisation of the Galilee' initiatives as has been previously shown. Furthermore, despite their commitment to military service, the relative deprivation of Druze villages, together with their general marginalisation from the broader workplace, continues, contributing to growing levels of frustration among all sectors of the community. Thus, while the power of the traditional Druze elite is slowly eroding, primarily as a result of the challenges posed to it by a new generation of more educated, secular and nationalist Druze who wish to reintegrate with the Palestinian Arab minority, the traditionally unified and hierarchical Druze leadership structure continues to be a significant source of weakness and vulnerability in this community's relations with the Israeli authorities (Firro 2001: 45–6).

The communal organisation of Palestinian Christians is markedly different to that of either the Muslim or Druze communities. It is a deeply heterogeneous community and is internally fragmented along several different and quite separate religious denominational lines. The State of Israel officially recognises ten different Christian communities, the largest of which are: the Greek Catholics, the Greek Orthodox, the Latins (Roman Catholics), the Maronites and (since 1970) the Anglicans. Each of these ten recognised Christian denominations possesses their own separate jurisdictional powers, religious courts and judges compared with the single jurisdictional power of each of the Muslim and Druze religious communities. They also experience a high level of autonomy over their affairs compared with, for instance, the Muslim religious authorities. The state, therefore, must engage separately with these ten different religious authorities. A single, blanket policy towards Christian religious authorities is, as a result, quite impossible.

This diversity is compounded by the fact that several of the Christian churches have extensive external links and are composed of a mixed ethnic clergy. This two-fold division of Christians in Israel between several different denominations and, within each church between its clergy and laity, has had major consequences for the nature of the engagement between church and state in Israel. As Michael Dumper has put it:

[T]hese churches often have different approaches to dealing with the Israeli government, partly owing to a situation in some of the churches wherein senior clergy are non-Palestinian or non-Arab, whereas the laity are either Palestinian Arab or identify politically and socially with Arab society.

(Dumper 2002: 52)

The absence of an indigenous Arab clergy which can not only communicate effectively with its flock but understand its local needs and priorities provides the state with a unique opportunity to affect decisions which serve its own interest. This is perhaps best demonstrated with regard to the Greek Orthodox Church, which is controlled by a non-Arab and non-indigenous clergy which, in many cases, can speak neither Arabic nor Hebrew. The former Patriarch of the Greek Orthodox Church became involved in a number of high-profile scandals involving the sale of communal properties (*awqaf*) to Jewish settler groups. Showing a lack of concern over the sensitive issue of the land issue, the Patriarch dissolved a number of communal church properties, primarily in Jerusalem's Old City, in order to pay off the church's mounting debts. In the face of his own congregation's outrage, however, his position became destabilised and ultimately untenable. A new Patriarch, Theofilos III, was elected in 2005. However, as Greek Orthodox Church tradition stipulates that all Patriarchs must receive the formal recognition of the state, the Israeli government was able to use this historical precedent as leverage against the patriarchate, withholding recognition for several years in the hope that their demands to restore these properties to the church would be abandoned or compromised.

The particular structure and organisation of the Greek Orthodox Church has rendered it relatively weak and more vulnerable to Israeli state pressure than other churches which have been able to maintain a greater degree of organisational independence from it. However, structural factors surrounding the internal fragmentation of the Christian community do not represent the only explanation for the lack of a central Christian communal authority in Israel. Of much greater significance is the division between the churches and the general Palestinian Christian 'street'. The literature has already pointed to the relevance of the small size and secular predisposition of this community. Being on the whole a more secular community, Palestinian Christians have demonstrated a greater degree of independence from their religious authorities than is true of other segments of the minority, as can be observed from the reaction of the Christian community to the scandals within the Greek Orthodox Church.

It can, as a result, be argued that the power of the churches to command the will of Palestinian Christians in Israel is weaker than that of either the Muslim or Druze religious authorities. Having said that, the political orientation of Palestinian Christians in Israel can occasionally differ according to denomination. Writing in the late 1970s, Rosenfeld described the Greek Orthodox as the most 'radical' of the Christian denominations, with the Greek Catholics and the Maronites deemed more 'moderate' in their political outlook (Rosenfeld 1978: 392). An elaboration of this denominational understanding of Palestinian Christian attitudes towards the state is provided by Landau.

Of the two largest Christian denominations in Israel, the Greek Catholics and the Greek Orthodox, the latter are more extreme in their political attitudes. Many of the children of this community are educated in Protestant schools, which usually emphasize Arab tradition and nationalism more than do the Greek Catholic educatíonal establishments. For generations, the Orthodox leaders were Greeks, while most members of the Church were local Arabs. In recent years, Arabs have succeeded in entering the top ranks, and their struggle for the Arabization of their community is well integrated with the trends of Arab nationalism. Perhaps because the Greek Orthodox are the largest Christian group in the Middle East, yet do not enjoy the support of any great power, the Arabs among them feel that they have to demonstrate political extremism, in order to maintain relations with the Muslims, together with a struggle for Arabization (or even Palestinization) of their community. In contrast, the leadership of the Greek Catholics, made up entirely of Arabs, presents a more moderate national stand, characterized in the first twenty years of the State of Israel as ready to cooperate with the state authorities.

(Landau 1993: 31)

Landau goes on to argue that, despite the differences between them, the relatively moderate position of Greek Catholics in Israel became increasingly 'radicalised' after 1967 and a change which took place on the level of the Greek Catholic church leadership. Therefore, not only is the Palestinian Christian community disunited according to their basic political outlooks, but their separate communal authorities are understood to have a significant impact on the political attitudes of each Christian community. This understanding of Greek Catholics as being a more politically moderate community in Israel is also found in Sa'ar's analysis of the role which church schools in Haifa have had in creating ethnocentric and 'socially reproductive' behaviour amongst Palestinian Christians in Israel. While the Greek Orthodox high school is understood to adhere to an 'explicitly secular orientation', the remainder of the Catholic-run schools are described as propagating an exclusively Christian atmosphere in their schools (Sa'ar 1998: 218). According to Sa'ar, the state allowed the predominantly Catholic church school system to have its current monopoly over education in the Arab sector not only because it relieved the state of its obligations to educate the minority, but because these schools possessed a 'highly conservative and explicitly apolitical agenda' which not only did not challenge the state, but secured, or 'reproduced', its power and control over the minority. The elite nature of these schools also has, however, also had the reverse effect of inculcating feelings of political resistance among its students over time, primarily as a result of its ability to attract the broadest catchment of students from all religious and political backgrounds. 'The Christian educational institutions, then, bear the dual potential of political obedience and opposition to the state or, in other words, of social reproduction and resistance' (Sa'ar 1998: 218).

In this context, it would be more accurate to describe the direction of influence between church and street in Israel as being 'bottom up' rather than 'top down'. The gradual 'politicisation' of the Christian churches in Israel over time is undoubtedly also connected with the growing 'Arabisation' and 'Palestinisation' of the various Christian clergies, which have not only changed traditional clergy–laity relations in Israel but also re-contextualised church–state relations within Israel's wider 'Arab problem' as a whole.

From the earliest years of the state, the political activity of Christian leaders had aroused the suspicion and criticism of the Israeli authorities. This was equally true of the more 'moderate' Greek Catholic Church as it was of other Christian denominations. The Capucci Affair of 1974 was one such famous instance which illustrated the difficulties faced by the authorities in controlling or trusting Christian leaders in Israel. Born in Aleppo, Syria, Hilarion Capucci was the Greek Catholic Archbishop of Caesarea when he was arrested by Israeli police in August 1974 for having illegally smuggled a large quantity of weapons and arms from Lebanon into Israel which he had concealed in his car. The weapons were destined for the Palestinian Liberation Army in the OPTs. Having used the unique privileges extended to a small number of Christian religious leaders to cross back and forth over the Lebanese border to administer to their flock, he was nonetheless found guilty of smuggling and sentenced to 12 years in prison.

The case of Egyptian-born George Hakim, Greek Catholic Patriarch and Archbishop of the Galilee from 1967 to 2000, demonstrated the ability of Christian religious leaders to extract the greatest advantage from the state's confessional policy while paying the minimum price in return. According to Uri Bialer, Hakim was particularly adept at taking advantage of the benefits provided to him by the state due to his status as a Christian leader. Describing him as a 'shrewd businessman', he profited well from the Christian tourism industry and accumulated substantial personal wealth. He was also involved in several corruption and smuggling charges which the state overlooked in their (failed) attempt to foster greater allegiance from him (Bialer 2005: 141–2).

Given the resilience of the majority of Christian church leaders to the traditional tactics employed by the state to coopt them, the former Director of the Department of Christian Affairs within the Ministry of Religions (now part of the Ministry of the Interior), could complain:

> That the great majority of Christians in Israel are Arabs is bound to colour Christian affairs: in the nature of things, 'political' problems of the Arab inhabitants, as such, can hardly fail to be linked at times with Church problems, if not deliberately confused with them.
>
> (Colbi 1969: 127)

Other church leaders have demonstrated either a similar level of political aloofness or opposition to the state. Nazareth-born Michel Sabbah, who served as the first ever Arab Latin Patriarch of Jerusalem for 21 years from 1987 to 2008, and another Nazarene, Naim Ateek, the Baptist director of Sabeel, have used their religious platform to capture a wide international audience on behalf of the Palestinian cause. These trends not only demonstrate the closing gaps between clergy and laity in Israel but also the chilly distance between some church leaders and the Israeli authorities.

While the fragmentation and differentiation of Christian communal authorities has, in the case of the Greek Orthodox Church, been a source of weakness and vulnerability, it has, in the case of other churches, proven to be a source of relative strength. The absence of a unified Palestinian Christian leadership structure has rendered this community outside the reach of typical cooptation strategies. With regards to the political arena, this is also demonstrated by the dismal failure of attempts to rally Christian voters along sectarian lines. An already small minority, their internal differentiation renders their electoral weight politically insignificant and irrelevant.

No Christian party or affiliated list has ever run for election during the Mapai period of rule when such sectarian lists were common within the broader minority. Later efforts to set up a Christian caucus within the dominant Zionist parties have also met with limited success. In the 1981 parliamentary elections, for example, the Labour Party attempted to run a Christian list under the leadership of a retired police officer, Hanna Haddad, to attract Christian voters. Having only received 8,300 votes, however, it failed not only in that objective but it also failed, by a substantial margin, to cross the electoral threshold required to secure representation in the Knesset. The list disappeared soon thereafter (Landau 1993: 44).

In conclusion, the static and disunited nature of the Palestinian Christian community together with the growing politicisation of the Christian churches and the increasing role of local Palestinian clergy in the decision-making process of their communities, have increased the negative association of these churches with the 'Arab problem' and 'radical' politics in Israel. While it is to be expected that control of the Christian religious communities remains a desired aim of the state in line with its broader confessional policy, this aim is obstructed and limited by the diffused and incongruous nature of the Palestinian Christian communities themselves.

International religious significance

One of the most commonly cited factors which are understood to affect state attitudes towards Palestinian Christians in Israel is the international significance of Christianity. Given their spiritual connection to the Holy Land, Christians worldwide and their representatives are interested in the satisfactory maintenance of Christian Holy Places in Israel. Of the multiplicity of Christian denominations and churches, a smaller number of churches have taken direct responsibility for the administration and guardianship not only of the Holy Sites but of extensive properties and land-holdings in the state, making them a significant contender in local politics as well. Eager to pursue their churches' interests with the state, they have relatively more power to interfere with the authorities or the political processes of the state than other interest groups, and frequently do.

Several of these churches carry political weight both as independent religious organisations and as a result of their close connection with powerful 'Western' states, such as the Anglican Church in England or the Evangelical movement in the US. However, perhaps the most historically powerful of all is the Vatican. Based in Rome and constituting its own sovereign city-state, it represents, through the papacy, the spiritual and administrative leadership of all Catholics (whether Latin, Greek Catholic or Maronite) in Israel. International Christian interest in Israel represents, as a result, a central element in Israel's foreign and diplomatic relations with countries which traditionally possess strong Christian religious and cultural traditions. Disagreements or conflicts with churches often have significant and deleterious effects both on Israel's foreign policy relations and its media image around the world. Therefore, the manner in which Israel deals with local Christian interests can significantly affect the nature of its engagement with the international community.

On the basis of their international connection with powerful 'Western' churches, the Palestinian Christians are often presented as a strong community which has the connections and negotiating power to extract more from the state than other sections of the minority. According to this argument, Palestinian Christians are considered to be relatively more protected and privileged in Israel than other segments of the Palestinian Arab minority. Daphne Tsimhoni has, for instance, observed that Palestinian Christians have, as a result of their proximity to Rome, generally received preferential treatment from the Israeli authorities. This, she notes, was particularly evident during and subsequent to the 1948 war and was reflected, amongst other things, in the state's attitude to the return of Christian refugees and the restitution of confiscated Christian communal properties (*awqaf*).

> Hence, the Catholic Arab inhabitants of the Galilee village of Ilabun [Eilaboun] were expelled from their homes in 1948 by Israeli soldiers who suspected that they had cooperated with the Syrian invading forces. But they were allowed to return following Vatican intervention on their behalf. The Israeli authorities demonstrated a greater openness toward the return of Christian refugees and family unification shortly after the war than they did regarding Muslims.
>
> (Tsimhoni 2002: 126)

While some have argued that the repatriation of a small number of Palestinian Christians to Israel proves the existence of a relatively more 'lenient' policy towards Palestinian Christians in Israel, Tsimhoni and others point to the central role of the international factor in the state's decision-making process.

> The Israeli Ministry of Foreign Affairs was well aware of the possible pressures that might be put on the state by the Christian church headquarters, in particular the Vatican, in case of what might appear as harassment of the churches. The Israeli authorities abstained therefore from confiscating church properties, particularly if they were registered in the name of the church or a European clergyman.
>
> (Tsimhoni 2002: 126)

In her analysis, Tsimhoni draws an important distinction between state policy towards the various churches and state policy towards individual Palestinian Christians themselves. This dual approach which echoes the church–laity division previously encountered absorbs an international–local dynamic with elements of an Arab-non Arab policy divide.

> Unlike the Christian churches, individual Christian Arabs have been treated by the Israeli authorities similarly to Muslim Arabs in matters such as confiscation of lands and the military administration.
>
> (Tsimhoni 2002: 127)

Writing about the deep impact of 'the Christian world' in Israeli politics, Uri Bialer has painted a more complex picture of how the state authorities perceived, and reacted to, external Christian intervention in its domestic affairs. In particular, Bialer describes the important political influence of the Vatican in discussions surrounding the recognition of the newly founded State of Israel and its acceptance into the international political community following its creation in 1948. Initially quite hostile to the idea of a Jewish state, both for theological, administrative and probably also anti-Semitic reasons, the Vatican vocally questioned the legitimacy of the new state's territorial gains and backed a plan calling for the internationalisation of Jerusalem and the Holy Places. Illustrating the close connection between religion and politics, the Security Council is described as adopting tougher stances towards Israel during the 1948–9 war as a result of Vatican pressure. Conscious of negative international attention, Ben-Gurion himself is described as having personally issued orders expressly prohibiting the looting or defilement of Holy Places which had been occurring at that time, and as countermanding an IDF plan to expel the inhabitants of Nazareth, the majority of whom were at that time Christian (Bialer 2005: 7–9). Despite this, several instances of Jewish vandalism of Christian Holy Places and destruction of Palestinian Christian villages were observed by the international press, leading to a 'wave of anti-Israel propaganda' around the world and calls to the UN to establish a commission of inquiry to examine the Israeli government's treatment of its Palestinian Christian minority (Bialer 2005: 10).

During this time, the Vatican's priorities remained essentially focused on Jerusalem and the continuation of its traditional rights and privileges under the new Israeli administration. Their recommendation that Jerusalem be internationalised was ratified by the UN in December 1949 demonstrating the power of the Vatican in the UN, and the Israeli government, outraged both at the Vatican's power and opposition, retaliated by moving its capital to Jerusalem (Bialer 2005: 14–23). Responding to what it saw as a clear threat to both its existence and its political ambitions, Israel employed three main strategies, described by Bialer as its political Machiavellianism, to undermine the position of the Vatican. First, it threatened that any continuation of what was perceived to be the Vatican's anti-Israeli policy would affect local Palestinian Christians and interests. This was mirrored by threats against local Catholic leaders that, if they did not disassociate themselves from the Vatican's position, it would be 'liable to alter the government's intentions with regard to Christian refugees and its attitude toward internal developments in local Christian communities' (Bialer 2005: 48). Second, it attempted to exploit the internal differences and discord between the various churches by promoting non-Catholic churches in Israel such as the Copts, Armenians and Greek Orthodox. Finally, it conducted a concerted propaganda (*hasbara*) campaign in the Christian world to nullify the internationalisation of Jerusalem as a non-feasible and impractical solution (Bialer 2005: 33–4, 46–8).

Notwithstanding the subsequent Israeli success in removing the internationalisation plan from the discussion table, relations between the state and the Vatican remained frosty. However, due to the practical necessity of engaging with the new state and Israel's awareness of the political clout of the Vatican, quiet and indirect diplomacy between both parties became standardised. Critically, the small Palestinian Christian community proved very useful to Israel's foreign policy relations and international media campaigns. By providing Christians with religious autonomy and freedom of worship, Bialer notes that Israel satisfied the major demands of the international churches, including those of the Vatican and helped the new state 'look good' abroad (Bialer 2005: 121–12). The central point of Bialer's argument here is that while international church considerations deeply affected the state's relationship with its Palestinian Christian population, this relationship was, to a large extent, orchestrated for the benefit of external audiences. Moreover, the situation couched a deeper ambivalence towards its Palestinian Christian citizens both as Arabs and, now, as an externally backed community within its borders. Observing that 'the prevailing attitude of the government towards Christian Arabs was not different from attitudes towards Muslim Arabs, especially in light of the general consensus which perceived every Israeli Arab as a potential enemy', Bialer notes that the international significance of Christianity and the political power of the churches are understood to have increased the level of potential threat associated with this community above all others (Bialer 2005: 125).

> Important elements of church activity in Israel, particularly among the Catholics, were perceived as a very real security threat by the authorities, which invested considerable efforts in countering them. (. . .)
>
> The fundamental political need to take the demands of the Church heads in Israel into account sharpened the perception of the Christians as an enemy, at least in the eyes of the highly influential security establishment.
>
> (Bialer 2005: 126)

This view echoes the opinion expressed in the late 1960s by Landau:

> These contacts with their churches abroad strengthen the position of the leaders of the Christian communities in Israel; they serve them as an important source of political power, both within their own community and in their relations with the Israeli Government. Sometimes these contacts are used

as a means of attack on the Israeli Government, and, in consequence, this strengthens their own political or personal standing.

(Landau 1969: 17)

This negative attitude of suspicion and resentment manifested itself in several ways. In the first instance, the Israeli military authorities and its security establishment were sorely opposed to the return of church properties which had been expropriated by the state in 1948 (Bialer 2005: 126). There were also strongly ambivalent towards the existing *status quo* arrangements. The *status quo* arrangements date back to Ottoman times and delineate the responsibilities and rights of access of the main Christian churches in the administration and use of the Christian holy places (Dumper 2002b: 52). Bialer cites the former Advisor to PM (Ben-Gurion) on Arab Affairs, Yehoshua Palmon, as describing the *status quo* arrangements as '[the Christians'] way of waging a struggle to restore and increase their power and influence among members of the community and of their community among the Arab public' (Bialer 2005: 126).

In 1993 – 45 years after the establishment of the State of Israel – a Fundamental Agreement between the Vatican and Israel paved the way for the extension of formal recognition and the establishment of formal diplomatic relations between the two.

This provided for the continuation of the religious *status quo* with regard to the Holy Places; the maintenance of the church school system; freedom of movement for clergy to administer to their religious functions; as well as providing other fringe benefits and privileges traditionally enjoyed by the churches since Ottoman times. However, the reluctance of the new state to recognise the communal authority of the Christian churches has become particularly apparent in the last two decades, as has its increasing independence from international opinion and pressure, with the result that the terms of the Fundamental Agreement have not in fact been met, leading to a serious diplomatic impasse between both parties which shows no immediate sign of becoming resolved.[3]

The growing confidence of the Israeli authorities in their diplomatic relations with the churches, and their increasing independence from, if not indifference to, the churches' stipulations and demands, suggests the dilution of the latter's negotiating power and influence on Israeli policy. It would, therefore, follow that, in line with the decreasing political weight of the Vatican, the relevance of local Palestinian Christians to Israeli diplomatic strategies is also declining. This changing relationship has two main consequences for Palestinian Christians. To begin with, it can be expected that Palestinian Christians would become increasingly invisible and irrelevant to the state. As their functionality to the state, whether as a diplomatic or a media tool, declines, the need to maintain a special relationship with this community also declines. As a result, the second consequence of declining international church influence on the State of Israel is the emergence of a state policy towards local Palestinian Christians that is increasingly uniform with its wider 'Arab' policy.

Jewish religious antipathy

Changing attitudes towards the international significance of Christianity are underlined by the growth of Jewish religious antipathy and anti-Christian feeling within important segments of Israeli Jewish society and government. While it is difficult to gauge the prevalence of religious-based hostility in any society, analyses which have mentioned this factor with regard to Christianity have usually distinguished between historical and local contributing factors.

The historical dimension of modern Jewish anti-Christian feeling is understood, first and foremost, to be a reaction to the tragic plight of Jews in Europe. Identifying the roots of modern anti-Semitism to be not just in European racist and nationalist thought but in the theological core of Christianity itself, there has been a tendency to associate, or blame, the historically disconnected local Palestinian Christians of these European sins (Mansour 2004: 217–18). Tsimhoni, for example, describes this attitude as being rooted in the minority complex of Israel's Jewish majority.

> The Jewish experience of hundreds of years of persecution in Christian Europe still reflects on the Jewish attitude towards the Christians in Israel despite the very different historic role of the Christians in the Middle East. Modern anti-Semitism, partially rooted in the medieval Christian church attitudes towards the Jews, and the extensive missionary activity during the nineteenth and early twentieth centuries to convert them, just added to the feeling among Jews that the Christians will always try to eliminate them.
>
> (Tsimhoni 2002: 142)

Within this historical perspective, the experience of Jews living in Christian Europe is compared with that of Jews in the Muslim Middle East, with the latter, quite reasonably, receiving better coverage.

> Jewish experience under Islam was much more favourable until the twentieth century. Despite the disabilities of their position as *Dhimmis*, they were allowed freedom of worship, vast measures of autonomy and security of life and worship. Hardly any pogroms or attempts to convert the Jews to Islam occurred.
>
> (Tsimhoni 2002: 142)

In a paradoxical shift from contemporary analyses of the two communities, Muslim treatment of Jews is, therefore, perceived in a far better light, while the historically disconnected local Christians, who also suffered substantially from European Christian bigotry, become permanent reminders of this past. This irrational transference of European guilt to Palestinian Christians is frequently encountered within the literature. Moroccan-born historian Shlomo Ben-Ami, who was later appointed Minister of Internal Security for the Labour Party, revealed the full extent of this antipathy in an interview he conducted in the run-up to the 1999 national elections.

No doubt, Christianity is the eternal enemy. With Islam it has been easier. It [Islam] did not emerge from us. Its relations with us have not been ideal or without hate. I do remember pogroms . . . on the other hand, Muslims and Jews visited together tombs of Jewish holy men.

(Tsimhoni 2002: 142)

Within this context, instances of Christian political activity, whether by individual Palestinian Christians or by their churches, as well as public demonstrations or expressions of the Christian faith, are often viewed with an undertone of scepticism and hostility. However, historical grounds alone do not explain modern Jewish anti-Christian sentiment in Israel today. The rise of Jewish fundamentalism and the increasing role of Jewish religious parties in Israeli politics also represents an important contributing factor.

Michael Dumper has observed a significant deterioration in Jewish-Christian relations in Israel parallel with the general drift towards right-wing religious politics which has taken place since 1977. He describes the appointment of 'officials patently less concerned about maintaining good relations with the Christian communities' as 'souring' relations not only between the state and the various churches, but also between the state and its Christian citizens as a whole (Dumper 2002b: 53). To this he notes an increasing number of arson attacks and incidents of vandalism against church property conducted by 'Israeli militants and Jewish fundamentalists'; as well as the open support provided by the government to Jewish settler groups, particularly in Jerusalem, which share a common desire to 'Judaise' Christian sectors of the city as well (Dumper 2002b: 53, 64 n. 4).

Even pro-establishment sources have acknowledged this growing Jewish religious antipathy towards Christians. Describing an emerging political consensus between Jewish and Islamic fundamentalist groups, Israeli observes how opposition to Christian interests has unified them even further. He mentions, in particular, their mutual distaste and rejection of the 2000 millennium celebrations in Israel as symbolic of Christian rather than of either Jewish or Muslim values.

For the non-nationalistic ultra-Orthodox Jews of Israel, whose record of loathing the Christians and acting violently against their missionaries is long-standing, would conceivably feel as threatened by the millennium as the Islamists do. They can envision the physical turmoil, the spiritual torment and individual unrest that would grip Israel under the pressure of the millions of tourists and pilgrims who would be literally flooding the country. Everything would be Christian, about Christianity, of Christianity, by Christianity, and the entire land would appear to yield to this orchestrated invasion by foreigners whose omnipresence, backed by the omnipotence of their Christian countries, would dictate an alien pace of life and a strange sequence of events to this land. The ghetto-minded ultra-Orthodox, just like their Islamist allies, are not equipped to deal with this reality, they are afraid of it and would do everything in their power to stifle it, thwart it or make sure it never happens. Thus, Islamists and ultra-Orthodox Jews, who see eye-to-eye on so many social and state affairs, and share a suspicion and fear of Christianity, find themselves to be ideal partners in this joint endeavour, strange bed-fellows as they may be.

(Israeli 2002: 81–2)

Thus, anti-Christian religious feeling hovers over both Israeli Jewish society's and the state's attitude towards, and relationship with, Palestinian Christians in Israel.

Conclusion

While the majority of sociological analyses of the Palestinian Arab minority in Israel have either overlooked or only briefly attended to issues relating to Palestinian Christians, this chapter has sought to isolate various accounts and descriptions of them in order to address what factors, if any, are deemed significant or relevant by Israeli academic scholars with regard to this community. This approach was guided by contributions made regarding the critically important role of scholarship and its relationship with both prevailing and countervailing political forces. A thematic approach was applied as it united analyses from across the ideological divide and provided a broader perspective on the role and importance of each theme. What can each of these themes, therefore, say about state–minority relations with regards to Palestinian Christians in an ethnocratic Jewish state? To begin with, all accounts accept the problematic nature of Palestinian Christians' Arab ethnicity with regards to the Jewish nature of the state and their competing national priorities, as confirmed by their common experience of exemption from military service in the IDF and patterns of land expropriation. This negative association is compounded by the important role of Palestinian Christians in Palestinian opposition parties and nationalist movements. The Arab Communist Party emerged as the first internal political threat to the Jewish establishment. That this party was traditionally dominated by Palestinian Christians is, therefore, deeply significant and indicative of the state's general attitudes toward this community. More recently, the political opposition of Balad, which was founded by a Palestinian Christian, upholds the association of internal Palestinian politics with political 'disloyalty' to the state.

By contrast, it has been shown that other factors, such as their small size, Westernised outlook and their significance as a non-Muslim minority, have reduced the degree of 'threat' associated with Palestinian Christians. This diminished sense of threat is primarily rooted in their small demographic weight relative to the rest of the Palestinian Arab minority, but is also based on their wider minority status in the region. It would be expected that these factors would diminish the distance between both groups and, thereby, also the necessity of state control over them. However, their small size has also increased their irrelevance to the political establishment, particularly during election campaigns when political courtship and allegiances with numerically stronger communities is sought, suggesting the hollow and functional nature of state attitudes towards the minority.

Other factors have also complicated the state's practical ability to either effectively control this community or to administer a preferential policy successfully.

On the one hand, the significance of the local churches, and their connection with powerful religious centres abroad, have increased the state's suspicions of the political capabilities and powers of its local Christian population. On the other hand, the absence of a single and centralised communal structure within the Christian community has seriously impeded the state's ability to successfully coopt a representative and malleable Christian leadership. In addition, elements of anti-Christian antipathy from within both the Jewish majority and the political authorities have increased the level of stigma associated with this community.

The picture formed from the literature reviewed in this chapter describes a complicated and uneasy relationship between the Israeli state and its Palestinian Christian citizens. In some senses, this relationship is much the same as that experienced by the remainder of the Palestinian Arab minority. However, in other senses it is quite different. While some analyses question the applicability of systemic control theories to this community, it is surprising is that, beyond the level of rhetoric, there is little sociological evidence to support the existence of a preferential state attitude towards this community. On the contrary, the literature suggests that Palestinian Christians pose something of a unique dilemma to the state. The manner in which the state has responded to this dilemma will form the subject of the following chapters.

5 Locating state attitudes

In order to investigate the accuracy of the viewpoints identified within the literature, this study has sought out the opinions of 36 different individuals who are either connected with the Palestinian Christian community or have first-hand experience of the particular issues affecting them today. The format of a semi-structured interview was followed in order to facilitate an open and fairly flexible framework for discussion. The respondents were initially asked to describe the situation of Palestinian Christians in Israel in a general manner, and where then asked to identify any similarities or differences which they could observe between their situation and that of other segments of the minority. They were then asked what represented, to their mind, the greatest issues or most pressing concerns affecting Palestinian Christians living in Israel today. As a final question, the respondents were asked to describe what role, if any, they saw state policies or attitudes as playing in the general situation and status of Palestinian Christians in Israel today. This pivotal question was left until the end of the interview so as not to crowd or guide the interviewee in his or her thought process.

Although it may be expected that the opinions expressed by the respondents would loosely reflect the dominant ethnic and political cleavages in society, this was often not the case. As a result, the presentation of different viewpoints along such lines was deemed to be both problematic and ineffective. This has resulted in the decision to present and review the opinions encountered anonymously and according to respondent sample (academics, church leaders, political figures and NGO representatives), rather than according to ethnic group or theme. While this approach renders generalisations more difficult, it allows for a more nuanced understanding of individual perceptions of state attitudes. This integrated approach is particularly important given the overall function of this chapter to identify in a more precise manner the attitudes of the Israeli state towards Palestinian Christians. It also provides a useful method through which the broader theoretical and sociological assumptions encountered in the previous chapters can be meaningfully compared and correlated. As the general trends identified in this chapter have motivated and supported the selection of case-studies which will be undertaken in the next two chapters, its importance cannot be understated.

The academics

Within the academic segment, a number of different perspectives arise. The first was a non-control view of state policy which was expressed by two Israeli academics who may be described as adhering to a 'pro-establishment' outlook. In the absence of control, however, neither of these two respondents could easily identify an alternative policy towards Palestinian Christians. For one, Israeli state policy towards the Palestinian Christians is best understood as a 'mixed bag' of different and, occasionally, conflicting policies reflecting the ambiguous nature of state attitudes towards this community. On the one hand, the lack of any coherent state policy towards the Palestinian Christians is, in this analysis, the result of the misguided tendency of Palestinian Christians to willingly involve themselves in Palestinian nationalism as well as other 'radical' or 'extremist' oppositional politics which are understood to have both antagonised the state against them and contributed to their policy neglect. Even with the development of political Islam in the 1980s and the alleged decline of secular Palestinian politics in Israel since that time, which are both understood to have increased the vulnerability of this community, 'the Israeli government made the mistake of not running to embrace them'. Implicit in this argument is the 'tit for tat' belief that the lack of a coherent policy towards Palestinian Christians is due to the political choices made by this community.

The state is, however, also understood to have extended some more generally positive measures towards the community which demonstrate the state's ultimate commitment to their welfare. The role of the state as protector of Palestinian Christians against the perceived onslaught of political Islam is mentioned. By way of an example, the appointment by the state of a bodyguard to protect the Mayor of Nazareth, Ramiz Jeraisi, during a particularly bad period of intra-communal tensions is cited, the context of which will be further elaborated in the next chapter. However, even these protective measures are tempered by what is referred to as the state's preferred strategy of non-intervention motivated by the desire not 'to rock the boat' in state–minority relations. This attitude is seen to have removed Palestinian Christians even further to the periphery of the state's priorities and concerns.

> [W]e know that the Christians are persecuted in the Holy Land and mistreated and what have you, but we don't want to rock the boat, because if we bring this whole thing into an open rift with the Muslims then the fate of the Christians would be even worse and therefore we mitigate the situation and make believe that everything is all right.

Thus, both the demographic size and political insignificance of Palestinian Christians as a non-Muslim minority represent major components in this respondent's understanding of state policy and attitudes. However, an additional factor which this respondent believes to have motivated the government's preferred policy of non-intervention into the affairs of the Palestinian Christians is a general misunderstanding of the state's intentions and the lack of positive returns for their efforts when it does intervene as a result of widespread cynicism and distrust on the part of the minority as a whole. Once again the case of Nazareth is mentioned, this time with respect to the role of the authorities and, especially, the Israeli police. Within this context, the international significance of Christianity is also understood to have loaded the dice against local Palestinian Christians with whom the state is unwilling to engage on any terms lest it be misunderstood or manipulated by foreign media.

Another Israeli academic who echoed this 'hands off' analysis of state policy towards the Palestinian Christians argued that the state would prefer to take a more protective stance towards the Palestinian Christians, but is limited or obstructed by several factors. Firstly, the lack of political differentiation between Muslims and Christians has negatively affected state attitudes towards Christians. It has also both undermined and deterred the state's ability to engage separately with each community in practical terms. Secondly, the political and electoral strength of Muslims compared with the demographically small size of Palestinian Christians has, in the eyes of this respondent, reduced the relevance of this small community to the state. Finally, state intervention, even when well-intentioned, has been misunderstood and rejected by the minority themselves, thus further compounding the situation. The case of Nazareth is once again cited to demonstrate each of these points.

> There is no coherent policy that I can see . . . [T]he Israeli government is interested in working out some kind of relationship with the leadership of the Israeli Arabs who tend to be Muslim. And even the Christians among them, speak the language of Muslims. They don't identify as Christian . . . And there is the Druze question. I don't think there is any equivalent policy towards the Christians. When problems come up such as the great feud over the mosque in Nazareth, the government is ambivalent. On the one hand, they would like to appease Muslims. They don't want to fight Islam. On the other hand, they would like to protect the Christians who are the weaker party and the party in the right apparently in that particular case. And they just try to navigate through the crashing waves with no great degree of success.

Despite these obstacles or setbacks, the government is presented as encouraging and promoting the integration of Palestinian Christians, despite the inherent limits of Palestinian Arab integration within Israeli Jewish society. Integration, according to this respondent, consists less of any particular or affirmative measures taken by the state than of an indirect policy of *not* obstructing self-motivated efforts on the part of individual Palestinian Christians who wish to integrate themselves within Israeli Jewish society. When asked whether this would render his description of Israeli state policy towards Palestinian Christians as multicultural, the respondent was more reticent. Suggesting that there is a 'reluctant, grudging kind' of multiculturalism in Israel, a number of practical dimensions of multicultural policy were mentioned, such as 'the independent cultural and educational institutions which cultivate a multiplicity of identities' and the status of Arabic as a second official

language of the state. However, the extent of multiculturalism is clearly understood to be limited by the nature of the state and the absence of normative multicultural attitudes. On the one hand, 'there is the ideology of the Jewish state. It's
a national state of the Jewish people and everybody else is a minority. That's part
of the game'. On the other hand, the Palestinian Arab minority is also described as
being uninterested in multicultural arrangements.

> The Palestinian Arabs in Israel basically object to the Jewish character of the
> state. They reject it. And the Israelis, the Jews, react accordingly, and see that
> minority as a hostile one which is to be controlled, to be dominated, kept in
> check so it doesn't become a very actively hostile group. That's not a good
> breathing ground for multiculturalism. Multiculturalism is one of two things.
> It's either the luxury of those who are well off, and are very tolerant and
> liberal, or else it's a mode of conflict resolution . . . And neither of these two
> prevails in Israel at this time.

While observing no evidence of a more affirmative and protective state policy
towards Palestinian Christians, this academic believed that one should be introduced on the basis of the close cultural and social affinity that was understood
to naturally exist between Christians and Jews in Israel. Firstly, Palestinian
Christians represent a valuable resource to the Israeli state in that they 'could be
a very important cultural bridge between Palestinian nationalism and the West
generally defined'. In this regard they are also described as being very similar to
Israeli Jews and 'could be a very functional bridge in trying to reduce the gap'
between Arabs and Jews as well. Secondly, 'they are valuable from the point of
view of skill and manpower. They are educated, they are skilled, they work hard,
they work in the modern sectors of the economy. They are very useful citizens'.
And, finally, both Jews and Christians share similar experiences of fear and insecurity as minorities against a common enemy, 'radical Islam'. Interestingly, while
this description reveals two factors which were encountered in the literature (that
Palestinian Christians represent both a 'western' and a non-Muslim community)
as a positive resource and a potential asset to the state, neither of these attitudes
are understood to affect the state's approach to them.

While these two accounts are largely consistent each other, the remainder
of the academic respondents, while reiterating some of the same factors, have
come to very different conclusions on the overall nature of state attitudes and
policy towards Palestinian Christians in Israel. One Israeli Jewish academic, for
instance, argued that the state has never tried to assert a differential policy towards
Palestinian Christians.

> Let's put it this way. Because the Christians . . . We have to bear in mind that
> the Christians were the leaders of Palestinian Arab nationalism. It would be
> hard to cut them off from the rest of the Arab community. (. . .) This was one
> factor. And I think the government, or the Jewish establishment, read the map
> rightly [sic] and correctly.

The political behaviour of Palestinian Christians, therefore, remains a central determining factor in state attitudes towards them. However, in a radical departure from the two previous analyses, this respondent pointed out that Palestinian Christians have, in fact, suffered relatively more than other segments of the Palestinian minority in terms of political and social discrimination as a direct result of their greater proximity to, and contacts with, Jews in society.

> But, the Christians in Israel, paradoxically, are more discriminated against than Muslims as Arabs. Because they live more in mixed towns - we say mixed, but they are Jewish towns – than any other group. If they live in Jewish towns, it means that they also compete with Jews more than other Arabs. They also suffer more from discrimination. It's another reason for them to leave. This is why they are quite ambivalent . . . more ambivalent than other Arabs about Jews, because they have more contacts than other Arabs with Jews.

It is, therefore, their greater experience of living side by side with Jews and, as a result, their first-hand experience of Jewish discriminatory attitudes which is understood to have increased the ambivalence of Palestinian Christians towards Israeli Jewish society and the state. This interpretation is markedly different from accounts which see Christian nationalist tendencies as resulting solely from Christian compensatory or survivalist tactics. Similarly, their higher rates of emigration are, to a large extent, understood to represent a political statement of Christian protest against the state, its policies and its attitudes.

Notwithstanding this experience of discrimination, this respondent did observe a number of instances where the state has attempted to differentiate Palestinian Christians from the wider Palestinian Arab minority. Education represented one such area, while the 'real autonomy' received by Christian religious communities with respect to the administration of their communal affairs represented another. Christian autonomy is considered to be above and beyond that which other religious groups receive from the state. However, these measures are not understood to be the result of more positive state attitudes towards this community. Instead, they are understood to be a consequence of Israel's foreign policy concerns and the international significance of Christianity in general. Rejecting any identification of Israel as a multicultural state 'in the ideological sense', this respondent nonetheless observed selective multicultural policies in practice, such as the symbolic status of Arabic as an official language and the apparent autonomy extended to all religious minorities. Given the ethnic priorities of the state, this form of selective or 'thin multiculturalism' is, as a result, more correctly defined as 'multi-sub-culturalism' whereby the subordinate role of the Palestinian Arab minority and other non-Jewish groups is guaranteed.

A number of other respondents also observed aspects of divide-and-rule in their analyses of the role of state attitudes and policy towards Palestinian Christians. For one Israeli Jewish academic, the state perspective 'was and remains the divide and rule approach'. However, this divide-and-rule approach is understood to be less concerned with creating divisions between religious minorities than it is in distinguishing between radical and non-radical elements within the minority, whereby 'radicalism is being anti-state' and anti-state attitudes are understood to be any claims or positions which oppose the Jewish definition of the state. As such, religious differences, while they may coincide with perceptions of radicalism and non-radicalism, do not necessarily represent the primary axis of differentiation of the minority by the state. Whatever lines of difference are used to differentiate the minority, divide-and-rule strategies are considered to directly target the cohesion and integrity of the Palestinian Arab minority as a whole. According to one Israeli Palestinian academic, state policy towards Palestinian Christians, as towards other segments of the Palestinian Arab minority, remains one that is ultimately based on control. This approach, which considers the unified Arab ethnicity of the minority to have unified state policy towards it, is based on an understanding of Israel as an ethnocratic state. The increasing academic tendency within pro-establishment circles to relate to Arabs as just Muslims and Christians (but not Druze) represents one example of the state's desire to create divisions within the Palestinian Arab minority. With particular respect to Palestinian Christians, control measures are evidenced by this respondent in such areas as the recent civic service initiative which was designed as an alternative to military service; the promotion of military service among Christians; and the more liberal approaches by the state to Christian education, or the church school system in general.

Another Israeli Palestinian academic who echoed the description of the Israeli state as an ethnocratic regime noted that, as a 'typical' Middle Eastern state, there is no real separation between religion and state in Israel, thus rendering the multicultural label void of any significant ideological value. In addition, this respondent observed that while the Israeli state is becoming more open to discussion about the external Israel–Palestinian conflict, it is simultaneously becoming more closed and intransigent about the nature of the state and internal dynamics within the state itself and between the state and its Palestinian minority. The shrinking space that is available to internal dissenters is matched with a parallel growth of Jewish religious parties in Israeli politics, a trend which, it is argued, does not bode well for any non-Jewish religious community in Israel. As a result, while it may appear that Christians have achieved a greater measure of autonomy than other groups within the minority, primarily through their separate church school system, this type of autonomy is, according to this respondent, fundamentally limited and controlled by the state. In addition, other strategies such as a 'silent process' of minority enlistment in the armed forces and the police, which Palestinian Christians are understood to be particularly susceptible to, are mentioned to illustrate the efficacy of the state's divide-and-rule policy. As a result, it was suggested that the gap between Palestinian Christians and Muslims in Israel is, in fact, widening rather than shrinking, a view which was not expressed by any other respondent.

Another Palestinian Israeli academic suggested that existing state policy towards Palestinian Christians was more negative to state policy towards Muslims as a result of what was considered to be the growth of Jewish religious antipathy and hostility towards Christians and Christianity in society. Discussing the lack of Israeli police intervention in a number of village conflicts which will be examined in further detail in the next two chapters, it is the religious factor which is understood to have determined their 'hands off' policy to a greater degree than the politically cautious or reticent tactics observed by others. Moreover, this respondent argued that 'Christian ideology' also represents a direct form of political challenge to exclusive Jewish national and religious claims over the land. Christian claims to the Holy Places are understood, from a religious point of view, as being stronger than those of 'Muslim ideology' and, therefore, as representing a greater threat to the exclusive religious authority of the Jewish state. This respondent also suggested that many Israeli Jews continue to view Christians as 'Crusaders', thus providing an added historical and emotional dimension to their hostility.

For another Palestinian Israeli academic, however, Israel's strategic interests and foreign policy commitments cannot be discounted in accounts of differential Israeli state policy. The strategically different application of state policy towards different groups and communities within the minority is understood to have been a permanent and continuous feature of state policy since the creation of the state in 1948. The role of Israel–Vatican relations during the formative years of the state and, particularly, during Israel's diplomatic efforts to secure international recognition of its statehood by the UN, is understood to have had a significant influence on Israel's apparently more open policy towards Palestinian Christians and the churches. Notwithstanding this international pressure on Israel to maintain a positive policy towards its local Christian community, the persistence of identifying Palestinian Christians as part of the wider 'Arab problem' is also clearly identified by this respondent. Palestinian Christians are understood to have experienced similar discrimination and suffering to their Muslim neighbours during the traumatic early years of the state. The expulsion of Christians outside the boundaries of the state and the destruction of Christian villages in the early years of the state are mentioned as examples of this unitary policy. Instances where Christians were allowed to return to their homes and villages are understood to have occurred solely as a result of international pressure and only on an individual and *ad hoc* basis. Citing from his own family's personal history of expulsion and repatriation, this respondent could not observe the existence of a preferential policy towards Palestinian Christians or towards a general return of Palestinian Christians.

Moreover, this respondent observed a clear policy by the Israeli establishment to divide the Palestinian minority along religious lines. In discussing what was referred to as the convenient historical precedent of the Ottoman *millet* system and how it was instrumentally applied by the new Israeli state the following was observed:

Historically, and that has been something that people wrote about, there was a kind of an establishment policy where if you fragment the Palestinian minority inside of Israel more, one factor being religion, the better able you are to control the community. So, in this sense, as I did write about also the historical millet system of the Ottomans that was in place here for so many years, it proved to be some kind of national treasure. I mean, it does work to fragment the community. And it has established this sense of being different and of being a separate nation and that did affect the reality of fragmentation and therefore the government was happy to find that reality in place because that way it could control better the Palestinian minority, and the idea of control was the dominant policy of the Israeli government since 1948 I would say until today, but it was very severe from 1948 until 1966 when the military government was in place.

Unlike other analyses, the view expressed by this respondent does not identify Israel's policy towards the Palestinian Christians as being one that is based simply on divide-and-rule. Israel's foreign policy interests and its need to secure international recognition and support is also identified as being 'a very important ingredient in why Israel also applied this differentiating policy'. Similarly, the role of internal politics within the Palestinian minority in which Palestinian Christians played a major part supplied an additional element in the dynamic underlying Israeli state policy. Furthermore, the reciprocal and interconnected relationship between official Israeli state policy and Israeli Jewish public attitudes is highlighted as an important factor in the determination of unofficial state policy towards Palestinian Christians. While concrete evidence of differential policy is generally lacking beyond the restitution of a few church properties and the appointed jurisdiction of churches over the religious affairs and personal status issues of their communities, the media is accorded a higher degree of agency in determining or reflecting the state's approach to Palestinian Christians in general.

Well, the media has this stereotype. I've been asked a number of times, are you an Arab or a Christian, as if there's a difference. I could be both. The Israeli media and the general public [are] very undereducated on these issues of how the Arab community is conceived and what [are] the internal divisions and the character of that community. They perceive it through the prism of a threat, and the threat issue is something that determines how they would relate to the Christians as historically not being a threat. So they are categorised as a threat from the Muslims who are regarded as a threat not only inside of Israel but because of being part of the regional threat for Israel. That's the prism, it's a prism of fear, and how the Jewish community feels threatened determines how that community perceives others, and because the Christian community has not been a threat I would suspect that in the media they would be differentiated and they would hint that it's a success of some kind . . .

Fear is, therefore, acknowledged to motivate to some extent the differential attitudes of the Jewish state and the Jewish public towards the Palestinian Arab minority. Within this prism of fear, the Palestinian Christians are not considered to represent the same level of security threat as Palestinian Muslims. Opportunism, however, is also understood to motivate state policy and attitudes, not only for the sake of increasing international credibility and engendering favourable public opinion but also for the sake of making significant internal gains. Creating dissension within the ranks of the minority aids and promotes the extension of state control over a feared minority, while facilitating increased Christian autonomy similarly removes a number of clear financial burdens and responsibilities from the shoulders of the state. By facilitating increased autonomy on the part of a handful of comparatively rich churches, the responsibility of the state to distribute adequate resources to the minority as a whole is diluted under the pretext of respect.

> I suspect that it was like a mutual kind of interest. Because the Christian communities have their own resources, I mean, they were left with a lot of their properties, so they rent a lot of places that they sell here and there and they also get a lot of money sometimes from abroad. So, they are established, and they don't need the government money to handle their own affairs and that's also convenient for them, because not having the government regulating them does not make them have to submit to any kind of standards or supervision or file certain documents, the government would not know what's happening, so that's kind of convenient. And the government, for its own purposes, also found that convenient. It does not have to fund it, and it can say to the whole world, look how well we're treating these Christian communities, giving them absolute autonomy to handle their own internal affairs.

Therefore, a degree of complicity between the churches and the state is identified by this respondent which has both facilitated the application of a differential state policy towards Palestinian Christians and supported a wider policy of state control over the minority as a whole.

Church leaders

Within the church leadership segment, attitudes concerning the nature of Israeli state attitudes and policies differ. One church respondent, for example, did not attribute a discriminatory aspect to state policy towards his church or its community. The fact that Palestinians in Israel are citizens of the state in possession of Israeli passports confirms their equality in society.

> [T]hey live regularly . . . they're not being discriminated against because they are Druze, or Muslim or Christian. They are living as minorities, but they have their own representatives in the Knesset. There are a lot of things that are common with the Israelis, with the Jews.

However, given that Israel, and the world in general, does not consider Palestinian Christians to be a 'tentative bomb', from either a demographic or political perspective, as they do Muslims, has, to his mind, significantly improved both their relations with the state and their situation in society at large.

From this perspective, the state's approach has been dictated and limited by the role of historical precedent as well as of various status quo agreements. At most, Israel is understood to have added to, or exacerbated, existing tensions and problems which predated the state's establishment. 'Israel added to the problem, but it was not the cause of it or its initiator.' In particular, the extension of official state recognition of the Anglican Church in 1970 was seen as a positive step towards mutual recognition and the practical administration of his church's affairs. With regard to the unresolved issues of church taxation (the *arnona* tax) he goes so far as to identify the state's attitudes towards the churches as being one of tolerance and respect. While this viewpoint makes reference to the international power of Christian churches, this respondent departs from previous analyses by suggesting that the main factor shaping state policy towards the churches is the role of different personalities within the Israeli government rather than any particular malicious intention towards them.

> Maybe one minister will issue a statement blaming the church for what they are doing or one of the employees will, you know, take a stand against this church because they have done so and so. It's a rather personal rather than a general policy.

Similarly, in discussing the changeover of ministerial responsibility for the Department of Christian Affairs from the Ministry of Religious Affairs to the Ministry of the Interior, he identifies intra-governmental and intra-Jewish politics as determining a greater influence on policy than any consideration of the minority themselves. 'It's a political issue, between rivals in the Israeli government itself rather than having something to do with anything else.'

However, other church representatives offered markedly different viewpoints. One suggested that there have been two main factors which have influenced the state's attitudes towards Palestinian Christians, and negatively at that: their Arab ethnicity and their Christian religion. However, both are moderated, in his view, by the continuing importance of Israel's foreign policy commitments and strategic relations.

> One view is they look at us as Arabs. It is true that they have an Israeli passport, but they still are Arabs. It means that they're different. So they want to make a Jewish state. The Arabs in a Jewish state seem to be foreigners. It is built on a Jewish state. This is one thing. Another thing is that they look at Christians in a different way also. Because Jews suffered from Christians during the ages, they consider that the persecution they endured after the death of Christ are motivated mainly by the fact that they are accused of killing Jesus. So, if they want to be very severe towards us they may consider us as traditional enemies. But now as they are supported by the USA, this feeling of . . . this anti-Christian feeling, doesn't appear clearly.

While the political bias against Palestinian Christians as Arabs remains clearly evident to him as an Arab, the 'hidden feelings' of anti-Christian bias are, on the whole, generally only experienced by church representatives and clergy. This bias is particularly evident for him in relation to the difficulty which Christian clergy have had in securing visas to come to Israel in order to administer to religious and personal affairs of their communities. This bias is understood to have become increasingly tangible in recent years. After the creation of the state, he recounts that it was relatively easy to acquire multiple-entry visas for Christian clergy in Israel. However, this situation has now changed with the cancellation of multiple-entry visas for all clergy except the very top leadership levels. In addition, an Arab bias has been introduced to the extension of visas. In the first instance, Arab clergy find it more difficult to acquire visas. Now they are granted only one-year visas, with the stipulation that if they should plan a trip outside of Israel within that year, their visa would be cancelled and re-entry refused if they don't apply in advance of their departure for a separate re-entry visa. The application for a re-entry visa is a lengthy and delayed procedure resulting in the fact that trips abroad are difficult to organise. These extra restrictions have made life very difficult for Arab clergy and the administration of religious services to Christian communities divided by borders and checkpoints.

In discussing the reasons behind the failure to implement the Fundamental Agreement (FA) between Israel and the Vatican, this respondent mentioned Israel's reluctance to continue giving the Christian churches privileges, particularly concerning tax exemption on church land holdings which they have traditionally enjoyed as part of the status quo arrangements. Once more, this change of attitude by the state towards the churches is observed as being a relatively recent development, originating only in the last ten years. In explaining possible reasons for this change of policy towards the church, he provides a number of possible interpretations.

> Maybe this displays the hesitation inside Israel itself to give privileges . . . as Israelis are not all agreed together on this. This is one thing. Then, the change of Ministers . . . There [are] a lot of changes in the Director General of the representations to these negotiations. This is [another] reason. But it is not enough to justify all this slowness in giving a final decision. Maybe they don't want to give us these privileges. Or the slowness is a kind of pressure: we can continue this way for years, you will not have what you want, so you have to accept a compromise. Maybe it's their way to [push] for a compromise. Maybe . . . So in this way they say, ok, we don't remain in the status quo, in the privileges given to us by the Turks and the French and the British, and they accept a compromise. In this case they will win, and we will lose something but we will not lose everything. And this compromise maybe they are looking for it, both of them, now. They've understood that . . .

It would, therefore, appear that the international power or influence which Christian churches traditionally had, particularly during the early years of the state, has declined. The Israeli state is seen to be increasingly independent from, and indifferent to, international and western Christian opinion. Thus, the balance of power in church–state relations is seen to be gradually shifting, and this confrontation with the most powerful church in Israel, the Latin (or Roman Catholic) Church, which also serves a leadership role on behalf of the other churches in Israel, signifies both a test-case of those relations and a potential watershed for future relations depending on the outcome or compromise reached in these negotiations.

Although church–state relations in Israel are observed by this respondent to be deteriorating, not all aspects of Israeli state policy are considered negative. On the positive side, this church representative mentioned the economic support given by the government to Catholic schools in Israel. The state, he observes, picks up 65 per cent of the budget of these schools which represents an important contribution in his eyes. Furthermore, he praises the general freedom of religion which is enjoyed in Israel, and the steps which the state has taken to allow full Christian worship whether it is in terms of holy days or religious processions.

While some respondents suggested that fear, opportunism or anti-Christian bias represent key factors motivating Israeli state policy towards Palestinian Christians, another leading church representative suggested that ignorance, resulting from their demographically small size, is the most relevant factor influencing both the state's and the general Israeli Jewish public's attitude towards Christians. 'In Israel, first of all, most of Israelis don't see Christians and don't know anything about Christians.' He then added:

> The attitude of the state, the first is ignorance. They don't care about Christians. We don't bring enough votes. But the church is important for foreign policy for if it speaks everyone listens . . . and generally speaking they don't like us so much. This is what I feel.

This suggests that while both pragmatism and foreign policy considerations have remained important, ignorance remains the primary trait of state attitudes. This ignorance is influenced by a number of factors. Firstly, changing demographics within Israeli society have allegedly resulted in fewer Jewish officials who are of European background who have direct experience, awareness of, or sensitivity to Christianity and Christian issues and are, thus, not sufficiently aware or open-minded to engage efficiently with the churches. Secondly, there has been a noticeable rise in the number of religious Jewish groups in powerful government positions that, he argues, care little about promoting or even discussing Christian matters. Finally, their demographic small size, together with these other forces, have rendered Palestinian Christians an increasingly negligible community in political terms. 'The state of Israel first of all does not think about the Christians, but when it thinks about the Christians, it thinks about the Christians mainly in Jerusalem.' This last factor demonstrates the close intersection between international Christian interest and the Jerusalem question. The fixation of international Christian interest upon Jerusalem has provided the authorities with more freedom and independence in the manner in which it engages with Christian communities living in other areas inside Israel proper.

As with other church representatives, this representative also integrated into his analysis an understanding of the negative role of differentiated internal Israeli Jewish politics. Generally speaking, he says, the churches and the Palestinian

Christians rarely experience state policy directly. The point of contact which they have for important issues of visas, land issues et cetera is usually not at the ministerial level, but at the level of local authorities. In describing the attitude of local authorities towards the church, he suggests that '[t]hey don't understand the Christian significance of the Holy Places, for instance . . . I don't think this is cynicism. Simply they don't understand the significance.' Elsewhere he commented that 'I don't think it's a deliberate policy. Sometimes maybe so, but generally speaking it's ignorance'.

By contrast, one local parish priest described state policy towards his village and its parishioners in strongly negative terms. One particular aspect of state policy which received his particular criticism concerned the issue of land. Describing the government designation of significant tracts of village-owned land as 'green' areas – on which the villagers have no further rights to build, farm or develop their land – he viewed this as symptomatic of state policy towards them. He also observed the continued negative impact which the construction of a neighbouring Jewish village (on land which had been expropriated from their village over twenty years ago) continues to have on the lives and livelihoods of the Christian villagers. His own family's personal history was also mentioned as testimony of the state's negative attitudes towards Palestinian Christians. Displaced from a destroyed Christian village, his family became internal refugees inside Israel before eventually settling down in Haifa.

One area in particular which revealed the state's discriminatory attitudes towards Palestinian Christians for this church representative was education. He viewed the state's policy on further education in Israel as deliberately, albeit indirectly, discriminating against the Palestinian minority, including the Palestinian Christian segment of it. Due to a minimum age restriction for enrolment in many university degree programmes – which is set at twenty-one years of age to coincide with the average age of Israelis who complete military service – a three-year vacuum for Israel's Christian and Muslim youth is created which, together with economic and family difficulties, pressurises many Palestinians to abandon education and enter the work-force as unskilled or semi-skilled workers, a situation from which they have great difficulty extricating themselves three years later. As such, they face various difficult choices; they must either 'put their lives on hold' until they are twenty-one, forego further education altogether, or continue their education abroad if they can afford it. If they choose the latter opportunity, the likelihood of returning to Israel diminishes starkly. Thus, state policy has, in his analysis, contributed directly to Christian emigration. Even in instances where Palestinian Christians persevere and re-enter the education system, emigration, he argues, continues to sap their numbers given the lack of suitable professional work opportunities which are available to Palestinians in Israel.

Government officials and politicians

In terms of the attitudes expressed by governmental and political figures, it is not surprising to find a wide variety of views. For one Palestinian respondent, no particular attempt by the state to create divisions or problems among the minority was identified. This was largely as a result of the absence of a Christian political party which could adequately reflect the political will of the majority of the Palestinian Christians and pass the electoral threshold in Israel, rendering them unattractive to the state as an independent pool of votes.

> Even if someone wanted to make a new party, a Christian party, I can't see that he will have a chance to do it because of the number of Christians on one side and because some of the Christians even don't want special parties and want to be part of the system, the Arab system, because they are not focusing on issues of the Christians but they are focusing on issues of the minority.

The subject of reserved seats on Jewish political party lists was also mentioned as evidence of the politically weak position of Palestinian Christians in Israel. In the elections to the Seventeenth Knesset in 2006, only one seat on the Labour Party list – seat number 19 – was reserved for an Arab candidate while approximately every fourth seat was reserved for a female candidate. Due to this unequal distribution of seats, it often makes more sense for Palestinian women who wish to put themselves forward as a candidate for election on behalf of mainstream Jewish political parties not to run for the seat reserved for Arabs, but rather for one of the relatively more numerous seats reserved for women. This was the case in the 2006 elections when Nadia Hilou ran for election on the Labour Party list and secured for herself the fifteenth of the 19 seats won by the Labour Party, which also happened to be the fourth of the five slots reserved for women on the list. The only Arab slot on the Labour Party list – the last slot, number 19 – was secured by a Muslim Labour candidate. Hilou lost her parliamentary seat in 2009 in large part as a result of the underrepresentation and low ranking of both Palestinian Arabs and women on the Labour Party list.

Notwithstanding the electoral obstacles which Palestinians must surmount to participate in mainstream Israeli politics, the view of this respondent on the role of state attitudes and policy towards Palestinian Christians remained, at best, ambiguous. While failing to observe any clear state policy towards Palestinian Christians in Israel, and acknowledging that the state had still to address some important residual gaps in society, the main focus of attention was given to what was referred to as the negative and contrary nature of Palestinian Arab opposition politics and the need for 'a vision of coexistence and a vision of equality and a vision of peace'.

> You know, I cannot say that the state has a special policy or a different policy towards Christians and Muslims. I can't say it. But, I want another policy of equality because I think that we haven't here a clear policy and a strategy of equality. (. . .) I think it's the same policy concerning the minorities in general. And I want, really, a very clear policy and strategy of closing the gaps that we can also measure. (. . .) Because if it's not, it's only words, it's only words and it's only giving promises and in general the Arab citizens are tired of these

words and tired of all the government and all the promises that they have said they will make better and promote and we will, we will, but we want facts.

Notwithstanding the perceived absence of any particular state attitudes or policies towards the minority, this respondent was comfortably able to reject the notion of Israel as a multicultural state. By contrast, another Palestinian respondent was able to describe state policy in more definitive terms. To begin with, the classification system used by the state in its presentation of official statistics is, for this respondent, a clear indication of state attitudes towards the Palestinian Arab minority.

> You know, the point here in Israel is that the government does not like to deal with so many minorities. They would like not to have so many minorities. So, if they put all of them in one basket, and that's what they do sometimes, they define all minorities in Israel as non-Jews. This is a huge basket in which you can put Arabs and Samaritans and Chechens, and then again you have the Christians and the Muslims and everybody. So, they're non-Jews and easily defined type of minorities. You scramble all of them in one category.

The non-Jewish category of Israeli census material illustrates the common marginalisation of, and discrimination against, Christians together with Muslims, Druze and other non-Jewish communities in Israel. Similarly, the reluctance of the state to use the internationally acceptable definition of the Palestinian minority as a national minority reveals the problematic nature of state attitudes towards the minority as a whole. The Palestinian Christians are, as a result, understood to be inextricably associated with the common political problematisation of the Palestinian Arab minority as a whole. Similarly, this respondent could not observe any meaningful extension of religious freedom, contradicting the assumption that freedom of worship is widely respected in Israel. The general lack of observance of, or respect for, Christian holy days, particularly with regard to the scheduling of national school examinations or parliamentary voting dates by the state, Knesset and the Ministry of Education demonstrates this point. This, however, is no different to Israeli state attitudes towards the Palestinian Arab minority as a whole.

> The attitude of the state towards the Christians is almost exactly the same as the attitude towards the Muslim community. All are Arabs, all are Palestinians, all are suspected citizens of the state. And the state discrimination that is implemented against Muslims is the same as implemented against the Christian community.

The discrimination which towns and municipalities that are predominantly Christian face in terms of budget allocations illustrates this shared experience of discrimination. Budget discrimination faced by Christian municipalities is comparable to the discrimination experienced by predominantly Muslim or Druze municipalities. However, it was suggested that certain elements within the Israeli authorities and central government, such as the security branches, do observe or follow differential approaches in their evaluation of potential security threats.

> So, in general, the attitude is exactly the same. I think that maybe the security branches and institutions here in Israel and especially regarding the theories on terror might not suspect, from a security point of view, the Christian community exactly as they do the Muslim community because of the religious background. But this is almost unseen. This is between the lines that I can read that. But in the development policies, status, citizenship, I can see that the government and the establishment has the same attitude towards all.

Despite this, the differentiation of the minority by the state is observed to be less evident in concrete policies than it is with regard to the more symbolic areas of language, media and political propaganda.

> Sometimes [the differentiation of the minority is done] only verbally. Just trying to revive, trying to give Christians the impression that they are preferred, that they do not belong to this Arab community. And in the definitions, Arab mainly means Muslims here. So sometimes they say Arab community, including Christians and Druzes. So, this is the wording used. 'Arabs including Christians and Druzes', and this is actually to give the impression that Christian and Druze communities are something else, not really Arab, and that is the reason why they should emphasise 'Arabs including', which means that if they accept the theory that Christians and Druze are Arabs but they emphasise that in order to give the impression that anyway there are some differences between the Muslim, Druze and Christian communities.

These selective terminologies are understood to be used deliberately by the state in order to sow divisions or exacerbate tensions within the minority and, it is argued, that they have found resonance only within small sectors of the Palestinian Christian community, usually for opportunistic reasons.

One application of this language of difference concerns the area of electoral politics within the minority. Describing the Labour Party initiative of launching a separate Christian political movement during the 1980s, this respondent commented upon the efforts made to generate feelings of Palestinian Christian difference during this period. Reference to one such attempt was briefly described in a previous chapter when the Labour Party supported a Christian list formed under the leadership of Hanna Haddad in 1981. However, this list failed to pass the electoral threshold at the time and was subsequently dissolved. Suggesting that the emergence of a separate Christian political movement in the 1980s was timed to coincide with the civil war in Lebanon, leading political figures are viewed as wishing exploit the deep religious tensions there in order to sow religious dissension between Muslims and Christians at home in Israel. These attempts are, however, all understood to have failed due to the lack of receptivity from Palestinian Christians themselves and the inability of such a movement, even if it had secured a wider swathe of the Christian popular vote, to pass the minimum electoral threshold necessary for a political party in Israel to sit in the Knesset.

Similarly, another Palestinian respondent considered the manner in which the state uses language to identify and categorise the minority as representing a solid indicator of its general political approach to Christians, Druze and Muslims in Israel. The state's preference of identifying the minority as a series of 'minorities' in spite of the common implementation of state policy is indicative of this general dichotomy between spoken and concrete policy.

> We will not accept, not now and not in the future, the governmental attitude and the governmental policy of dealing with us as "minorities". (. . .) Of course we do not accept that, and actually I believe that the behaviour of the government towards all the Palestinian minority in Israel is almost the same.

Considering Israel's foreign policy and the significance of Christianity within international diplomatic circles, particularly with respect to Europe, the Vatican, and the US, to have an important influence on the formulation of state policy towards Palestinian Christians in Israel, this respondent argued that the positive concessions which accompany such associations are largely limited to the level of appearances. While it often appears that a different policy results from external interest in local Christian issues, this respondent argues that a parallel, and more important, differentiation of Israeli state policy exists which often focuses on, and sometimes also caters to, the interests of the Muslim majority.

Ultimately, however, Israeli state policy is described as being the same, single-minded, opportunistic and exploitative policy regardless of occasional differences in application. Internal political competition between Israeli Jewish political parties is also attributed an important role in his analysis, particularly with regard to the electoral strategies and political gamesmanship which took place between Likud and Kadima during various national election campaigns in the 1990s, and the impact that this had on communal relations within the minority. The role of anti-Christian attitudes within government circles and within Israeli Zionist ideology, or the deliberate disassociation by elements within the government from issues or events which have important Christian cultural or religious significance, is also mentioned as having motivated the state's attitude and approach towards Palestinian Christians in Israel.

Regardless of their religious affiliation, the issue of intervention reveals the true nature Israeli state policy towards the Palestinian minority. The manner in which state intervention, or 'interference' as it is often referred to, occurs has changed according to shifting international opinion of Israel and Israel's increasing political awareness of how its policies may be received or interpreted internationally.

> Well, there is interference all the time. They will not stand looking from the side without trying to interfere, but I think that the regional and international atmosphere has changed and of course the political practices of the government have also changed . . . it's not the same. (. . .) Israel at the end [of the

Nazareth affair] paid also a very high price because of its policy, internationally and locally also. That was a short-term policy. They did not think about the long-term. They thought only about the very short-term policy. It was a plastic policy.

Another respondent was even more resolute and single-minded in his attitudes concerning state policy.

[F]rom my view, the policy of all the governments of Israel in taking decisions inside the Israeli institutions [is that] they have an agenda, or they deal with all the Palestinians like a problem. It doesn't matter to which religion they belong. They may use this division to serve their policy, not to serve any group of the Palestinians. The policy is one of dividing. They use it all of the time.

State policy is understood as being one that is primarily and consistently based on divide-and-rule strategies. As such, this respondent categorically rejected the notion that such a policy could benefit any segment of the Palestinian population. Instead, it is a policy which is seen to be implicitly structured against the interests of the minority as a whole and in favour of the interests of the Israeli Jewish majority only. What unites all Palestinians in view of this policy is their common identification and treatment by the state as a problem. As such, there is only one real division within Israeli society, and that is the division between Israel's Jewish and Arab populations which has created two separate realities across all fields, whether it is according to employment, income, socio-economic, or development figures.

They try to use it all of the time, in every field. It doesn't matter. They try to use it all of the time, in the media, in the terminology, [the] language they try to use. And they try all of the time.

The viewpoint of another minority representative who was interviewed for this study was markedly different. Arguing that the state does indeed take positive and affirmative steps towards all segments of the minority, including the Palestinian Christian segment of it, this respondent argued that the impact of state policy was limited by the tendency of certain elements within the minority to identify themselves with negative Palestinian Arab elements. Describing Palestinian Christians as having failed to fulfil their fair share of duties as citizens, particularly with regard to the performance of military service, they are understood to receive not only all but more than their fair share of rights and benefits from the state.

This respondent also described Palestinian Christians as being overrepresented in both government and civil service positions, and recommended that the figures provided by the Civil Service Commission's report be examined in order to confirm this. Consultation with the office of the Director of the Civil Service Commission, however, revealed that this claim was at best misleading. Of the total number of civil service positions filled by Palestinian Arabs in 2007, 60 per cent were taken by Muslims, 21 per cent by Christians and 11 per cent by Druze remain. Given that Muslims make up 84 per cent of the Palestinian Arab minority and Christians and Druze both account for a further 8 per cent each, it can be concluded, on the basis of strict statistics, that both Christians and Druze are overrepresented. In subsequent discussion with Henia Markovic, the Director of the Civil Service Commission, the reason for the inflated Christian representation in civil service positions became clear. While the figures for civil service employees exclude the military, security and police branches – areas in which the Druze distinguish themselves numerically – as well as public school teachers and the recently privatised postal, transport and communication companies, it includes not only government and ministerial workers but the entire personnel of Israel's general health and hospital staff, including nurses, doctors, maintenance and cleaning staff who have been classified as Ministry of Health employees. In total, employees of the Ministry of Health account for half of the total number of people categorised as civil service employees. As medicine and health care are generally recognised to be popular professions for Palestinian Christians, conclusions regarding the number of Palestinian Christians employed in the Israeli civil service can easily be skewed.

NGO representatives

While avoiding a focused analysis of the role and nature of state policy towards Palestinian Christians, one NGO representative addressed the factors underlying what was perceived to be the currently poor state of Jewish–Christian relations in Israel. Through wide-ranging public opinion surveys, this respondent revealed that the attitude of the Israeli Jewish public towards Christianity and Christians remains negative. This conclusion is supported by his former experience working within the Department for Christian Affairs during the 1970s and 1980s. Observing that it was, in fact, his experience working there which inspired in him the need to pursue non-governmental opportunities to focus on, and improve, Jewish–Christian understanding in Israel, he stated that the Jewish majority in Israel harbours deeply antipathetic views of Christians.

This antipathy and even antagonism is, he argued, primarily rooted in feelings and experiences of historical persecution at the hands of Christians in Europe and their resulting deep sense of continued victimhood. The creation of the state of Israel and the reversal of the traditional Christian–Jewish majority–minority relationship to one of Jewish political power and dominance over a Christian minority did not result in any significant change in Jewish attitudes. In fact, indigenous Christians in Israel are seen to suffer disproportionately more than other segments of the minority due to the maintenance of old Jewish attitudes and stereotypes which portray Christians as being an historical source of threat and danger.

> [W]e're working with a lot of Jewish baggage that comes from another place and another time, from the past centuries of persecution and so forth that obviously

feeds in to relations here. If I say that the local Christians are a double-minority, I have reason to believe that many Jews view them as a double-majority: once as part of the vast Arab world, because they emphasise that they are Arabs, once as part of the vast Arab world with which we have a decades-old conflict here, more specifically with the Palestinian people, with whom the conflict is more severe, and once again as part of the vast and huge Christian world with which the Jewish people have certain problems. (. . .) What is clear is that the Arab Christian gets it twice. Whichever card he puts forward, the Arab or the Christian, it doesn't serve him well . . . in the eyes of the Jew.

This historical bias is understood to have had an even more determining influence on Jewish–Christian relations and Jewish attitudes towards Christians than the wider Arab–Jewish political conflict. He argues that the majority of Israeli Jewish society is, in fact, difference-blind when it comes to attitudes towards the Palestinian minority. 'I'm never very certain how much Israeli Jews understand that this is a Christian Arab and not just an Arab. I think there's a tendency to treat all Arabs as one.' Moreover, Jewish religious antagonism to Christianity is understood to represent a growing factor in these relations.

The intersection between negative historical and religious attitudes is revealed in the results of a recent JCJCR survey into Jewish attitudes towards Christianity and Christians in Israel (JCJCR 2008). Discussing the significance of this survey he focused on a number of findings in particular. The survey was conducted across a representative sample of the Jewish population broken down according to age, gender, level of education, country of origin and degree of religiosity (the options being secular, traditional or orthodox). According to the results of this survey, it was found that 52 per cent of the overall sample group do not have any Christian friends or acquaintances. Furthermore, only half of the sample believed that the city of Jerusalem is central to the Christian faith. Even more surprisingly, 24 per cent, or nearly a quarter, of the secular sample, compared with 42 per cent, or just under a half, of the total Jewish sample, believed that Christianity was an idolatrous religion. By contrast, only 71 per cent of the total sample believed that the State of Israel is obliged to guarantee freedom of religion and conscience for its Christian citizens, while only 37 per cent believe that the New Testament should be taught in Israeli schools. Given the dialectical relationship between Israeli state policy and Israeli Jewish public opinion, these findings are enormously suggestive of the general attitudes towards Christians in Israel.

These negative attitudes are explained as being the combined result of inherited stereotypes, religious antipathy, ignorance and fear. While ignorance and stereotypical attitudes are understood to be typical attitudes of majorities throughout the world, the role which fear is described as playing is unique to the Israeli Jewish experience. The creation of the State of Israel is understood to have been an attempt at the restitution of Jewish 'normalcy' following the disastrous impact of the Holocaust on Jewish communal identity and confidence. However, a series of wars and the persistence of political deadlock with its Arab neighbours have kept the deep sense of fear and insecurity alive.

And I think this is a nation that is so afraid. With all our power . . . When you become afraid, you close yourself off, you start becoming defensive. Everybody is the enemy. You start demonising everybody around you. Where is the next blow coming from? That may sound really strange for a country that has the kind of military power that we do, but you blow these things up . . . [F]or all our economic and military powers I don't think people in this country are confident – they're afraid. I think many Israeli Jews are much more afraid than the Palestinians are. Palestinians stopped being afraid. They don't have anything to lose. That's my experience . . . All these things operate, and that also creates a deterioration in relating to people. So, it's not just a matter of growing ignorance, it's growing fear. And of course the two are probably very interrelated.

Therefore, the JCJCR's efforts to run educational seminars and workshops in conjunction with various ministries, particularly the Ministry of Education (and their school networks) and the IDF (in particular during the five-day seminar on Jerusalem which the IDF provides to new recruits to familiarise them with religious and communal diversity in the city), as well as attempts to engineer religious dialogues and 'cultural encounters' between Jews and Christians are understood to be necessary, but generally sufficient, measures to eradicate hostility and create a more harmonious relationship between Jews and Christians in society. These efforts are supported, firstly, by his belief that the nature of the relationship between the state and one of its smallest minorities represents, essentially, a 'good litmus test' in the determination of Israeli democracy. Secondly, Palestinian Christians share with Jews a history of minority suffering and persecution which could serve to integrate them further into the hearts and minds of Israel's Jewish population. And, finally, if Israeli Jews can learn to accept Palestinian Christians as a non-threatening and integral part of their society, the path may potentially be cleared for a gradual reconciliation with Israel's Muslim community and a resolution to the wider Israeli–Arab conflict.

The only instance in which this respondent directly referred to the state or state policy was with regard to the current administration of the Department of Christian Affairs. To his mind, this department is negatively affected by a lack of personnel who are familiar with and sensitive to Christian issues. During his time in office, he recounted that ministerial staff were predominantly first-generation Jewish immigrants from European or Arab countries. They possessed a much wider linguistic skill-set and circle of friends and acquaintances from other religions, cultures and countries than is currently the case. By way of an example, he mentioned his role in the Capucci Affair of 1974 involving the case of arms-smuggling from Lebanon into Israel by the then Greek Catholic Archbishop, Hilarion Capucci. The Advisor to the Minister of the Police was a Jewish man originally from Aleppo, Syria, who went to the same school as the Archbishop. This connection is understood to have facilitated a speedy resolution of the affair with, he argued, minimal negative impact upon the situation of Palestinian Christians in Israel. Similarly, the then Minister of Religious Affairs, who was originally from Berlin, was described as being 'a man of the world'. However, with the passage of time, and the evaporation of first-generation immigrant expertise, a gaping hole has emerged in Israeli Jewish awareness of Christianity and Christians.

> They're gone! And our education system has done nothing to prepare their replacements. People don't know how to relate to anybody else. I know I'm very extreme in my words, but it's true. These people were what I call cultured, or cosmopolitan, whether they got it from Arab Muslim countries or Western Christian countries . . . Our Israelis growing up in this society don't know anybody but themselves! And therefore it's only a downhill thing, and it's there in our strategic plan. Many people feel there's a tremendous deterioration.

This respondent was also sceptical of the government's appointment of a Palestinian Christian as the first non-Jewish Director of the Department for Christian Affairs within the Ministry of Interior. Considering the role of the job, the nature of the state and the amount of personal networking with other ministries and department that is required of this post-holder, he believes that the position should have been given to a Jew. As a Palestinian Arab Christian, his ability to influence a largely Jewish civil service is seen to be severely limited. As such, he sees this appointment as being 'more of a token thing' which is ultimately a sign of the 'downgrading of that office than [of] upgrading Caesar'. To which he adds that: '[i]t might look on the surface like you're being multicultural by putting Arabs into seemingly significant posts but it might also be saying we don't really give a damn about that area'.

As such, this respondent rejected a description of Israel as a multicultural state. To his mind, multiculturalism is the careful orchestration of competing cultures and religions, not the dominance of any particular one over others. He uses the Church of the Holy Sepulchre in Jerusalem to represent a model of 'true' multiculturalism. Despite the ongoing frictions and periodic tensions which have surfaced between various competing sects within it, the division of space and time which it employs as part of the status quo arrangements is, to his mind, what multiculturalism is really all about.

> [W]hen all is said and done they're all using the same building. They bump into one another. There are clashes . . . It's never always going to go totally smoothly, and in many cases it doesn't go smoothly at all . . . People don't love one another. People can exist together and separately in a good balance. The classroom for me is Jerusalem and the ultimate classroom for me the Church of the Holy Sepulchre.

In describing existing state policy, he has nothing to say other than that the state is 'so obsessed with the security thing'. In such an environment, true multiculturalism cannot exist as the 'obsession with security is anti-multiculturalism'.

However, other respondents from the NGO sector have provided a more specific and targeted analysis of the role and nature of Israeli state policy. For one, there was no question that a differential state policy towards the Palestinian minority as a whole exists. However, the notion that the state pursues an affirmative policy towards particular communities within the minority was categorically rejected. Describing the objective and impact of state policy, a respondent stated: 'It's the same. The same. There is no but. Absolutely the same.'

> The most important thing is the control part. The best way to control the Palestinian minority, anything that would serve in favour of the control, the ruling of the Palestinian minority, how to stop their development, to block their development, how to control them, maybe even to stop them even from reproducing, to limit their numbers inside the state because you see the Israeli policy explicitly sees the Palestinian minority as a demographic threat, and they repetitively say that. And what they will be willing to put up with is a limited number of Palestinians inside Israel and with a certain kind of behaviour. A little bit of marginal freedom of speech within a very clearly defined frame. You do not go over that. And with explicit loyalty to the state of Israel as the Jewish state. Whatever falls in favour of this policy they will not hesitate to do.

From this perspective, there is no difference in the levels of funding or political representation accorded to Palestinian Christians over and above other segments of the minority. In support of this, a law proposed a number of years ago in the Knesset by former Palestinian Christian MK, Azmi Bishara, to accord proportional representation to Palestinians in governmental institutions was mentioned. Although this law was passed, it has yet to be implemented, confirming the deeper structural discrimination that this respondent views as existing against Palestinians in Israel. 'And this law is not yet implemented because nobody cares to enforce it.'

Another Palestinian Israeli respondent argued that Israel can, at best, be described as a 'democracy of scale'. At the uppermost levels of this scale are Jewish Ashkenazi men who enjoy the full benefits and privileges of Israeli democracy. However, those at the lowest end of this scale, suffering the most from this incomplete form of democracy, are Muslim Arab women. Palestinian Christians are identified as lying somewhere closer to the bottom of this pyramid. This marginalisation is due to three main problems or obstacles. The first of these problems is the Arab ethnicity of Palestinian Christians, which places them within the same category of potential threat as all Arabs in Israel. The second problem concerns their Christian religion, particularly from the point of view of the increasingly powerful ultra-orthodox political elite in Israel. However, the third problem which pushes Palestinian Christians further down the order of importance in Israeli policy and governmental attitudes is the practical issue of their demographically small size. Given that Palestinian Christians make up less than 2 per cent of the total Israeli population and could not, as such, cross the minimum electoral threshold necessary to be represented in parliament, the state has not seriously sought to encourage Palestinian Christian difference through the extension of any preferential policies. Whilst not observing any significant affirmative action towards any segment of the Palestinian minority, this respondent suggested that if such a policy emerged it would first promote the Druze, because of their IDF service; second the Muslims, because of their numerical significance within the minority; and only lastly the Christians 'who get the crumbs of what's left'. In general, however, this respondent did not observe any 'clear-cut policy' towards Palestinian Christians. Christians are understood to have suffered similar discrimination and violations of rights as Palestinian Muslims, which has been compounded by the diminishing significance of the Vatican in recent years. In sum, Israeli state policy towards Palestinian Christians is identified as lying somewhere between 'stupidity' and 'conspiracy', while never consistently being one or the other. However, despite the inconsistency he observes in Israeli state policy, the outcome is consistently the same, and that is the fundamental weakening of the minority as a whole, including the Christian component of it.

Another Palestinian respondent similarly observed the existence of a common state policy towards the minority as a whole which is essentially based on the segregation of Arabs from Jews.

> They don't need us. They can live without us. But we, as a minority here, we need them. We need them. So, there is no difference between Muslim and Christian. It's the same. Maybe because the Christians are running schools or hospitals, they are well organised, more than the Muslims, there is the feeling that they have some autonomy. What you call cultural autonomy in some services. But these services are not the whole services that I need. I need the government. I need the state. But the state doesn't need us and doesn't want us to continue here. They want more land, less Arabs.

Despite this, little direct or concrete evidence can be found to support the claim that any particular policy, whether differential or discriminatory, exists towards the Palestinian minority in Israel. A clear disjuncture, however, remains between the declarative level of Israel policy which is couched in between the democratic language and legal provisions of the state and the real or practical level of policy consequences. Furthermore, in terms of the apparent cultural autonomy given to the churches, this respondent observed that such autonomy is, in fact, a convenient façade for the state which provides it with the opportunity to shirk its responsibility towards the minority in terms of a fair and equitable distribution of state services and resources.

Similar to the previous analysis, the demographic insignificance of Palestinian Christians in Israel is considered to motivate the absence of any real differential policy towards that community. As such, Christians are not considered to have any significant 'power of pressure'. Recalling a meeting which he attended in the mid-1990s in which a former Greek Catholic Bishop (Maximos Salloum) and Israeli Prime Minister (Shimon Peres) were in attendance, the following was observed:

He [Peres] said very well, and very clearly, that those people who are electing the Labour Party will take all the opportunities to be equal. He said that very well. So, I repeat that there is no policy. The whole policy is the same policy as it was forty, fifty or sixty years [ago] towards the Arabs – only to run their lives from day to day. There is no planning for the future for the Arabs. They are working, until now, in their way of colonial thinking, of how to separate the Arabs from the Jewish settlements, from the Jewish cities, or villages. So, you are there, and we are here.

As such, Muslims are understood to receive relatively more opportunities from the state than Christians do. By way of an example, it was mentioned that until approximately twenty years ago, the majority of teachers in Arab schools were Christian, as were most of the Arab inspectors in the Ministry of Education. Nowadays, only two out of a total of 45 Arab inspectors are Christian, despite the fact that there are 35 thousand school children attending church schools. This is indicative of the shift in the government's priorities and their attitudes towards the minority. Christians are, therefore, understood as being deliberately sidelined by the state in areas which have been traditionally dominated by, and provided for, by Christians. 'Because the way of thinking in the Ministry of Education is to give the opportunities more to Muslims than to Christians.'

Another Palestinian respondent could not identify the existence of any particular state policy towards Palestinian Christians.

I think that the state of Israel nowadays doesn't have any special policies towards Christians. I mean policies are allocations. Policy is money. Where do you invest, where do you not. There are no special decisions for the government towards the Palestinian Christians. For example, they don't give them more allocations, they don't invest in their schools, they don't treat them in a special way. So, there is no special policy towards the Christians.

This respondent also identified a number of contradictions between the practical and the rhetorical levels of Israeli policy. The Palestinian Christians are understood to represent a useful symbol and rhetorical device for the state, whether through media channels or political statements, in its attempt to both promote itself as a democratic state and to suggest by comparison that Muslim disadvantage within society is self-engineered. The state is, therefore, understood as exploiting and capitalising from opportunities which Christians have, by and large, created for themselves.

[T]he Christians are always a good excuse for the government to blame the Muslim Palestinians, because the most educated part of the whole Israeli population is the Christian women. The most educated. More than Jewish women. It's not because they are more clever, it's just that they continue more with education. There are many reasons for it, but that's a good excuse for the government to say that we're not discriminating against the Arabs because, look, here we have Christian women who are very well educated, and here you have Muslim women who are not. So, it's the Muslim mentality that is responsible for many of the gaps between Palestinian citizens of Israel and Jewish citizens of Israel. So, the Christians here are a good excuse for the government that they are doing ok, it's just the Muslim mentality that is not.

Accentuating differences within the minority is seen as occurring frequently particularly in situations of government neglect. 'Everywhere that the government is not doing its job and there are huge gaps between Palestinians and Jews inside Israel, it's very convenient for the government to make differences.' But by and large Israeli policy-makers are seen to be not particularly conscious or aware of Palestinian Christians when they develop or formulate their policies towards the minority. This is primarily due to the demographic insignificance of Palestinian Christians, and the identification of Palestinian Christians as Arabs by the state. Moreover, as Palestinian Christians are, by and large, mostly landless and urban-based, their political significance and level of threat are significantly reduced from the perspective of the state.

The state attempted to create divisions between Palestinian Christians and Muslims in the past. The registration of a citizen's religious affiliation on national identification cards, which was a mandatory requirement until it was challenged by orthodox Jewish groups questioning the Jewish identity of immigrants from the former Soviet bloc countries, is mentioned by this respondent as one such method. 'The government tried to show that being Christian is not being Arab.' Comparing this venture with the state's successful attempt to separate the Druze from their Arab identity and heritage, it was observed that 'Israel tried to do this thing with the Christians. They tried to divide the Arabs here among Christians and Muslims.' Results are understood to have been mixed, based on the complicated and layered nature of Christian identity; the weak position of Christians in Israeli society; and the regional distribution of the various Christian communities. Some Palestinian Christians from the northern villages of Jish, Mailiya or Fassouta, for example, which are villages located close to the Lebanese border, are understood to be 'trapped in a very problematic situation' between the demands of their Palestinian and Maronite identities. Similarly, the traumatic experiences of villagers originally from the destroyed village of Bir'am are understood to have placed different pressures on Palestinian Christian identity. Estimating that between a quarter and a third of all Palestinian Christians in Israel have chosen to emphasise their religious identity over and above their national identity, this respondent further suggested that there has been at least some measure of success for the state's divide-and-rule attempts. The lure of military and civil service is described as further emphasising these divisions. However, the lack of a central or a single hierarchical political leadership for Christians and the more individual nature of Palestinian Christian society, have limited the impact of any single trend. Ultimately, no particular benefit to those Palestinian Christians who have chosen to emphasise their Christian over their Arab or national identity is observed. In fact, emphasising religious identity has resulted in more rather than less discrimination.

By putting myself only as a Christian, I am losing a lot of my rights, because statistically I am in a better place than the average Arab in Israel. By that, I don't demand a lot more from the government. And this attitude is very convenient for the government: you're Christians, you're ok, so I don't have to give you anything. Look at the numbers, your situation is fine. I mean, the government doesn't give prizes if the Palestinian Christians are very well educated. No, it's not the way it is. The government says, oh, you Christians are ok, so you don't need anything from us, you're doing fine. And this is what the Christians don't exactly understand. They think, ok, we're happy about the compliments we get from the government, and that's it. This is not a smart thing to do. It's better not to get happy and say treat us as Arabs, as part of the whole Arab Palestinian community in Israel, and give us more allocations. Because the good place that the Christians are in some of the villages is because of their own hard work, it's because they know that they have no other choice, and being a minority inside a minority inside a minority anywhere in the world demands for you to work harder and harder to achieve what's easier for the Jews.

Another Palestinian respondent similarly identified Palestinian Christians in Israel as suffering from the same discriminatory policies as the rest of the Palestinian minority. However, contrary to the previous analysis, small differences in government allocations to Palestinian Christians do exist, particularly in the area of education.

In general, I would say that their status, their situation is very similar to other parts of the Palestinians in the sense that they are part of the Palestinian minority in Israel so they are treated in the same discrimination, or with the same policies that Muslim Palestinians are facing. With one major difference, in the sense that Israel is spending money, and policy and resources to try to develop a kind of separate culture, or separate identity for this minority so that it would be more close to the Jewish majority or the establishment of the state and to try to separate them from the other Palestinians in different ways, not just through trying to develop different or separate identity from the majority of the Palestinian people but also through investing in the education system in some of the schools, in some of the villages and even in some of the universities in trying to develop them.

The issue of church education reappears as a divisive issue in the testimony of the various respondents who have discussed it. To some, the state neglects its financial responsibilities to church schools which provide an essential service to Palestinian Arab education. To others, such as this respondent, the partial subsidies which the state extends to these schools represents a differential policy towards Palestinian Christians, even when such subsidies do not significantly alter the status of Palestinian Christians in Israeli society. What unites this and the previous analyses is the importance given to practical and rhetorical differences in policy. This contradiction reveals the 'hidden agenda' underlying state policy.

> I think there is a hidden agenda in the sense that you will not see something written that speaks about the Palestinian Christians differently than Muslim Palestinians. In the written and public policy you see one policy, while in the practice and with the investment of the government you see that. Not investment in the positive sense, but in the investment of time and resources, you will see this.

This investment of time and resources is observed to be particularly true of the state's efforts to recruit Palestinian Christians into the army and civil service. This pursuit of differentiation of the minority is understood to be achieved primarily through the channels of the media and the education system.

> I think what they are trying to do is two things: one is in the public media, its attitude that if you are Christian, you are different, and the way that things are dealt with in the media. But more important, I think, is their investment in the education system. I think when you have church-based schools the state is interested more in all the issues of military service, like encouraging children to do national service as a replacement to military service, trying to focus on the religious identity of the group as separate to the national identity. But this is mainly through the education system.

Such differential media coverage of the Palestinian minority is viewed as being rooted in rhetoric, slogans and insinuations which are rarely supported by empirical fact or concrete policy. Differential media coverage is particularly prominent in the run-up to various national and local elections, helping to fuel internal tensions within the minority to the anticipated advantage of Jewish national parties. Moreover, such an approach is understood to resonate with a growing 'culture of racism' in Israeli society which is based on the rejection of all non-Jews, who are considered *goyim*, as foreigners in their own home. Ultimately, Israeli policy towards the Palestinian minority in Israel, being fuelled by an exclusivist understanding of nationalism, is understood to be based on 'short-term strategies of apartheid' which have boomeranged on the state to the detriment of Israeli Jewish national interests.

> If you look at the policy of Israel towards the Palestinians inside Israel, I think that they are totally doing the opposite of their intention and interests. I mean, if their interest is that the Palestinians will stop becoming Palestinians and will become part of Israel and by this stopping any kind of demographic threat because they become an integral part of the region. But what they are doing on the ground is keeping this community outside any kind of consensus, which is the opposite [of their interest].

According to this perspective, the state's divide-and-rule attempts within the minority, whether among the Druze, Bedouin or Christians, are destined to fail in the long term. Evidence of this, it is argued, can already be found within the ranks of an increasingly oppositionist Druze youth.

Another Palestinian NGO representative saw absolutely no differences in Israeli policy towards the minority. Specialising in land and planning issues, this respondent could not identify any differences in the problems facing a Muslim village such as Wadi Ara and Christian villages such as Mailiya or Fassouta. Observing that while the government clearly wishes to create differences between the different segments of the minority, this aim has not ultimately been translated into different policies, particularly in the two key strategic areas of government policy relating to demographic and land issues.

In this analysis, the importance of these strategic concerns within Zionist ideology supersedes other state interests and ambitions. This is demonstrated, in particular, by government plans to merge a number of local authorities, both Arab and Jewish, in order to reduce municipal expenses. There are a limited number of Arab villages in which there are a significant number of Palestinian Christians. These villages reflect historically unique patterns of Christian residence. However, this did not stop the government from proposing mergers between municipalities with a significant Christian population and other Muslim or Jewish villages. It was recalled that in 2003, for example, the government proposed a merger between the municipality of Mailiya, one of only two Christian-only villages in Israel, and another non-Christian municipality. Despite the fact that the proposal was later dropped, the proposal itself suggests a disregard for the importance of Christian communal patterns of living. Similarly, an objection filed with the state by Adalah in 2001 on behalf of 26 local Arab authorities from the north of Israel demonstrates this point. The objection related to a Northern District Master Plan which placed a number of serious restrictions on future Arab development. A number of the local authorities who signed this petition were Christian, confirming the similar discrimination which Christian and Muslim local municipalities face. Finally, the government-proposed development scheme for border villages in the aftermath of the 2006 war in Lebanon illustrates the singular and uniform nature of the state discriminatory policy towards the minority. The scheme in question was designed to compensate villages and businesses damaged or otherwise negatively affected by the war. However, the initial plan excluded a number of Arab villages, including Mailiya, Fassouta and Jish. It was only after Adalah petitioned the Supreme Court on behalf of those villages that they were subsequently included in the plan.

The rhetorical dimension of Israeli policy towards the Palestinian Christians is also mentioned, particularly insofar as it brings important diplomatic rewards for Israel. 'It's also in their interest to show the international community that the Christians are somehow protected . . . On the ground it's not like that but, internationally, I think it serves their interests.' Similarly, the media is observed to play an important role in substantiating false claims of Palestinian Christian difference, 'especially at times of crisis where [they] try to manipulate and censor what kind of information people will get'. The role of the Israeli media in advancing and supporting differences within the minority is described as a form of 'marketing' which ultimately pays dividends to the state, but only to the state. This is supported by the claim that, particularly during times of crisis, but also in the run-up to local and national elections, the Israeli media rallies around and becomes supportive of the government and its aims.

The final respondent from the NGO sector also identified the existence of common discriminatory attitudes towards all segments of the Palestinian minority. As with the previous respondents, this respondent argued that the confusion surrounding the question of whether or not there is a differential policy lies in understanding the difference between policy and the impacts of policy. Therefore, the 'implications of discrimination' across the Palestinian minority are different, given the existence of a number of important pre-existing communal differences. However, even these communal differences have been influenced, to some degree, by the evolution of state policy, thus further complicating the matter. The *Nakba* (which refers to the 'disaster' of 1948), for instance, introduced seismic shifts in both the leadership structures and the demographic composition and distribution of the remaining Palestinian population. Thus, the implications of discrimination against the Palestinian Christians were different to those experienced by other communities, despite the fact that they originated in the same policy.

From this point of view, the experiences of Palestinian Christians in 1948 have continued to inform the nature of Israeli state policy towards them. The deportation of Palestinian Christians from the villages of Kfar Bir'am, Iqrit and Eilaboun, and the subsequent return of these villagers following international intervention is mentioned as an example of this. The state and, in particular, its security and intelligence services, are portrayed as 'using and abusing' the experience of these Palestinian Christians, particularly the Maronites, and their repeated demands to return to their villages in order to extract useful information and intelligence contacts from within the Maronite community in neighbouring Lebanon. It is suggested that the return of the internally displaced hinged upon their cooperation with the Israeli security services, which used them to develop relations with the Kata'ib (Phalangists) in Lebanon. Throughout decades, hopes of return were kept alive by the state in order to motivate their continued cooperation. However, with the Israeli withdrawal from Lebanon in 1999–2000, the need for this 'political link' ended, 'and this is why also the Israelis are not willing to talk about it [return to their villages] anymore and they stopped talking about it, because they don't need them anymore'.

However, it was not only Christian villages which were targeted by this policy. The Muslim village of Kafr Kara in the Triangle is cited as having been similarly abused and exploited by the secret service in a similar manner. What united all of these individuals and groups, in this analysis, was the common sense of vulnerability which resulted from the loss of Palestinians' homes and villages, and their cooptation by the secret service into the system of control which ultimately deepened discrimination against them.

Other different 'implications of discrimination' resulting from 1948 which are mentioned include the preservation of Christian communal properties and institutions. Contrary to the Muslim experience, it is argued that there was an explicit and deliberate policy not to confiscate properties or dissolve institutions belonging to the church. However this policy is understood to have been an exception to the rule that, indirectly, also proves the rule. Foreign policy constraints together with explicit demands placed on the state of Israel by the international community in return for recognition of its nascent statehood are recognised as having submerged an otherwise common policy based on the control of the Palestinian Arab minority as a whole. However, the maintenance of Christian institutions has, in this analysis, contributed to widening gaps and tensions within the minority. This, in turn, has strengthened the ability of the state to control it.

Particular discriminatory attitudes against Palestinian Christians are also mentioned. In order to counter the political leadership role of Arab nationalism and the Communist Party during the first number of decades of the state – movements which were synonymous with the Palestinian Christian intellectual elites – the government is understood to have nurtured a parallel political elite within the Muslim community, particularly during the 1970s and 1980s. The emergence of the Islamic Movement in Israel is identified as having been initially nurtured and encouraged by the state in the hope that it would offset the political influence and popularity of unitary Arab movements. Similarly, the political leadership role of the Nazareth municipality, which is headed by a Christian mayor, is understood to have resulted in government efforts to promote the municipality of the next largest Arab city in Israel, Umm al Fahem, which is entirely Muslim in make-up. A policy of government intervention and interference, therefore, together with other forces of change, eventually resulted in diluting the political influence of Palestinian Christians in Israel, a situation which has, ironically, come to be decried by establishment circles as a loss today. Therefore, it is possible to observe from this analysis that the state's interest in Palestinian Christians is dependent upon, and subservient to, wider strategic interests and perceptions of minority threat that make no distinction according to considerations of religious differences.

Conclusion

The findings presented in this chapter confirm the importance of each factor outlined in the previous chapter's analysis of Israeli state attitudes towards Palestinian Christians in Israel. Several themes, in particular, were popular among the respondents. To begin with, the notion that the Arab ethnicity and oppositional political behaviour of Palestinian Christians creates or increases the negative association of this community within the wider 'Arab problem' was commonly encountered. Equally popular was the argument that the numerical and electoral insignificance of Palestinian Christians in Israel increases the irrelevance and negligibility of this community to a political establishment that is preoccupied by more pressing concerns surrounding Muslim demographic and electoral strength. These findings also suggest that the numerical insignificance of Palestinian Christians in Israel has contributed to high levels of ignorance about, and indifference towards, them in society, rendering both the Israeli authorities and the general public increasingly blind to them.

While their 'Western' attitudes and non-Muslim identity are frequently referred to as reducing the level of threat that is otherwise associated with the Palestinian

Arab minority and as of having the potential to bridge the gaps between Jews and Arabs in general, the opinions encountered indicate that these two factors have not significantly affected or altered the concrete application of state policy. Instead, state policy is portrayed as being largely consistent with policies that are extended towards the Palestinian Arab minority as a whole and only different in such instances where foreign policy considerations relating to the international significance of Christianity have demanded an alternative or more concessionary approach. As such, it is generally understood that it is not affirmative or preferential state attitudes towards Palestinian Christians which generate differential policies where these are found to exist, but rather independent and external factors which have little to do with the daily lives of local Palestinian Christians. Even here, however, the diminishing power of the international community and, in particular, of the Christian churches to influence the Israeli authorities has been identified as resulting in a policy towards Palestinian Christians which is increasingly uniform and indistinguishable from state policy towards the Palestinian Arab minority as a whole.

This trend has been accelerated by growing Jewish religious antipathy towards Palestinian Christians and Christianity as a whole which ensures their isolation at the periphery of both society and state interests. The role of increasingly overt Jewish anti-Christian sentiments receives markedly more attention in the respondent feedback than it does in the literature, suggesting that this factor has potentially more influence on state attitudes than was hitherto anticipated or expected.

The findings also indicate the relevance of two issues or topics in particular which were repeatedly referred to by the respondents to demonstrate, or testify to, claims concerning the nature of Israeli state attitudes towards Palestinian Christians in Israel. The first relates to a conflict which emerged in Nazareth and which dominated intra-communal relations there throughout much of the 1990s and the particular role of the state in that conflict. The second concerns growing Druze–Christian tensions in a number of Arab mixed villages in Israel and the response of the relevant Israeli authorities to these events. While each of these topics, together with the perspectives provided by the respondents, will be addressed separately in the next two chapters in more detail, their selection is firmly anchored and motivated by the broader perspectives outlined in this chapter.

6   Conflict in Nazareth

With a population of over 70,000 people, Nazareth is not only the largest Arab city in Israel, but is home to approximately 24,000 Palestinian Christians who make up one third of the city and one fifth of all Palestinian Christians in Israel (Sabeel 2006: 47 and Forman 2006: 337). Variously described as the unofficial Arab capital of Israel, this city which also remains an important destination for Christian pilgrims around the world is widely recognised to be an influential political trend-setter for the Palestinian Arab minority in Israel (Landau 1969: 6, 206; Frisch 2001: 163 and Israeli 2002: 38).

It is within this context that this chapter seeks to explore the response of the Israeli authorities, its government ministries and various political parties to a particular conflict which emerged in the city in the mid-1990s and which went on to dominate intra-communal relations within the city for several years thereafter. Referred to as either the Nazareth 2000 affair or the Shihab ad-Din conflict, the dispute arose between the city's DFPE-led municipality and the local Islamic movement over the development of a small piece of land at the centre of the city.

In order to understand how this conflict can inform this study's investigation of state attitudes towards Palestinian Christians, this chapter offers a brief overview of the history and political role of the Nazareth municipality. This will be followed by a chronology of events surrounding the conflict and a description of the various players and factors involved in it. The final section of this chapter will integrate this study's interview-based findings with the available literature and provide an analysis based on the insights developed in the opening chapters.

The Nazareth municipality

Nazareth has one of the oldest and longest-functioning municipalities in Israel today, dating back to the Ottoman reforms of 1877. Despite this, the first Israeli municipal elections to be held in Nazareth took place only in 1954, six years after the creation of the State of Israel in 1948 (Forman 2006: 337). The delay in re-instituting the powers of the Nazareth municipality is often explained away with reference to the prevailing security concerns which the new state faced at the time which necessitated the extension of military rule involving tight control and super-vision over the Palestinian Arab minority. However, more nuanced explanations, such as that provided by Geremy Forman, have pointed to the significance of the particular demographic (read security) threat posed by Nazareth as an Arab city in the midst of a predominantly Arab Galilee, and the state's practical fears of the Communist Party (CP, Maki) which had by then established a strong base of support in the city and which was emerging as the main source of opposition to the hegemonic status of David Ben-Gurion's Mapai party.

The authorities' fears of Nazareth's political potential were confirmed in 1954 when the CP won the municipal elections in Nazareth. Despite winning the majority of seats in these local elections, Maki representatives were pushed out of the leadership level of the municipality by a government-backed sectarian coalition which was more accepting of, and submissive to, government demands (Forman 2006: 342–7). As a result, the city was, until the mid-1970s, led by a series of Mapai-aligned mayors who were considered to be deeply unrepresentative, inefficient and corrupt in their administration of the municipality (Smooha 1989: 113; Dumper 2006: 274). The predominance of Mapai-affiliated lists within the Palestinian Arab sector is documented in the literature as a typical feature of the period of military rule and the neo-patrimonial politics of the early state. The first mayor of Nazareth, a Greek Orthodox Christian by the name of Amin-Salim Jarjara, ran on the Mapai-affiliated list known as the Democratic List of Nazareth and served as mayor of Nazareth from 1954 to 1959 until he was replaced by Seif id-Din el-Zu'bi, a Muslim who ran on the same list until 1974 (Knesset 2010).

As a result of growing levels of local dissatisfaction with the municipality as well as increasing discontent with government policy in general, a number of May Day protests, spearheaded by the CP were initiated in Nazareth in May 1958, later spreading to other villages in the area (Emmett 1997: 538). Although these protests were quickly squashed by the authorities, resulting in the injury of 17 and the arrest of 350 others, they provided an important indication of the growing confidence of Palestinian Arabs in Israel, particularly through the political channels provided by the CP (Hadawi 1959: 37–8). Signalling the weakening hold of Labour-affiliated 'satellite' lists in Nazareth, the Democratic Front (which was primarily composed of members of the Arabic faction of the CP (Rakah) but also included members of the Association of Nazareth Academicians, the association of Nazareth students known as Sons of Nazareth and the Nazareth Chamber of Commerce), took control of the Nazareth municipality in December 1975 in a landslide victory (Kaufman 1997: 100; Rabinowitz 2001a: 104). Tawfiq Zayyad, a Palestinian Muslim who was well known for his 'poetry of protest against Israeli treatment of the Arab minority in Israel' and had been a senior member of the CP for some time became mayor of Nazareth and remained in that post until his death in 1994 (Institute for Palestine Studies 1976: 178).

The 1975 municipal elections represented a watershed for the Palestinian Arab minority in Israel as this was the first time in which 'an Arab candidate, affiliated with a nationalist-oriented party such as Rakah, [had] been successful in winning the mayoralty of any major Arab town such as Nazareth' (Rekhess 2007: 10). The important leadership role of Palestinian Christians in Rakah (later known as the Democratic Front for Peace and Equality (DFPE), or Hadash) has been described in previous chapters. This is consolidated by the leadership role of Palestinian Christians within the Nazareth municipality itself. Not only did Nazareth become the first Arab locality to be led by an Arab Communist-led political coalition, but Rakah/DFPE/Hadash itself remains the only local party to have participated and won seats in all 12 Israeli municipal elections between 1954 and 2008 (Emmett 1997: 540). When Zayyad was re-elected mayor in 1979, Christian-born Ramiz Jaraisy, who was then only 27, became his deputy-mayor until he himself became mayor of Nazareth following Zayyad's death in 1994 (Israeli 2008: 252–4). Since then, Jaraisy has been consistently re-elected as mayor of Nazareth by the majority of the city's residents.

As 'the only non-Zionist Israeli party officially permitted to function in Israel since its establishment', the survival of Rakah/DFPE depended in no small way upon its formal character as a Jewish-Arab party (Jiryis 1979: 35). Notwithstanding this, the results of the election were not received well by the authorities who saw it as indicative of an emerging threat 'from within'. In fact, Rakah's platform was frequently described by the authorities as representing a 'radical' and 'extremist' threat to the state. That this 'threat' was centred on Nazareth should not be minimised. According to one report 'the Israeli press was unanimous in describing the [1975] election returns as an expression of anti-Zionist sentiment among the Arab citizens of Israel' (Institute for Palestine Studies 1976: 178). This same report includes comments made at that time by Moshe Dayan (who was to become Foreign Minister in 1977) to Haaretz that the results should be no surprise to those who understood the 'true aspirations' of the people of Nazareth.

> We must remember something that is absolutely fundamental. The Arabs of Nazareth did not become Israelis of their own free will. (. . .) We forced Israeli [citizenship] on them. The only other option open to them was to leave the country. They neither sought nor asked for the State of Israel to be established. (. . .) For some years, at least, some of them have voted and acted not in accordance with their true aspirations, but rather in accordance with their daily needs. They were afraid of an angry reaction of some kind if they expressed views against the government of Israel and therefore acted through the framework of established parties, party agents or other interests. None of these things can be relied on, and I am not sorry they have vanished or will soon vanish completely. I have never thought that relations could be established with the Arabs of Israel, or even with the Arabs of the occupied territories, through a party agent – whoever he may be – who tells them how to vote.
>
> (Institute for Palestine Studies 1976: 178)

From the point of view of the authorities, therefore, Rakah and, by consequence, Nazareth for the platform which it provided it with, represented the main, and most serious, source of internal political threat to the Israeli political establishment and to the state's national priorities at the time. One account of the run-up to the municipal elections of 1975, in fact, claims that 'the Israeli government felt so threatened by the prospect of this "radical" [Tawfiq Zayyad] becoming Mayor that it had warned the residents of Nazareth that, should they elect Zayyad, they would lose all government assistance to their community' (Zogby 1994). Notwithstanding these threats, Zayyad was elected. However, the government delivered upon its threat by drastically cutting the already meagre municipal and development budgets which the city had been receiving up until that point (Institute for Palestine Studies 1978: 134–5).

This is also evidenced by the contents of the Koenig Report which were leaked to the public in 1976 and which contained several references to the so-called threat posed by Rakah and the Nazareth municipality. In particular, it warned of 'the nationalist manifestations in the voting in the Nazareth municipal elections on 9 December 1975' and 'the devious and unexpected call-up of the inhabitants of Nazareth to help the municipality pay off pressing debts' accumulated as a result of the government's retaliatory budget cuts. In addition to a system of 'rewards and punishments', the Report recommended providing an alternative political 'valve for communities still sitting on the fence', whether through new Mapai-affiliated parties or through the promotion of alternative political movements and parties among the minority (MERIP 1976). It was within this context of 'radical' Arab communist activity that a significant proportion of the government's energies were invested in promoting the fledgling Islamic movement.

Despite this, the 1975 local elections mark the beginning of a new period of Palestinian Arab minority politics characterised by the growing power of Rakah/DFPE/Hadash which was centred on Nazareth and, particularly, on its local municipality. In effect, these elections transformed Nazareth into the 'de facto capital of Israel's one million Palestinian citizens' and the place from which 'the basic political consensus of this community' would henceforth be forged (Usher 2000: 2–3). As the driving force behind the first Land Day (Yaum al-Ard) of 30 March 1976, the Nazareth municipality organised a series of strikes in order to protest government plans to expropriate Arab land in the Galilee for Jewish development and settlement purposes, which resulted in the death of six Palestinian Israeli citizens and which marked 'a watershed in the relations between Jews and Arabs' in Israel (Landau 1993: 21).

As a result, the Nazareth-based Rakah party represented a real threat to the Israeli establishment not only because of its novelty in offering 'state-wide national leadership' on a universal and non-sectarian basis to the disenfranchised Palestinian Arab citizens of Israel, but because of its active opposition to government policy within the minority sector (Smooha 1982: 77–8). One report suggests that in 1981 the then Prime Minister, Menachem Begin, who was also the Minister of Defence, barred a conference of Arab representatives scheduled to take place in Nazareth, confirming the negative reputation which the city had in the eyes of the authorities (Ghanem 1998: 437).

With the emergence of the Islamic movement in Israel in the late 1970s, it became clear that a substantive thematic shift was occurring not only at the level of local minority politics, but on the national level as well. A number of national, regional and international developments contributed to the loss of Rakah/DFPE/Hadash's political monopoly and to the growth of political Islam. In the first instance, mainstream Israeli Jewish politics witnessed a sharp swing to the right with the 'reunification' of Jerusalem in 1967 and, more particularly, with the Likud victory of 1977, which, when coupled with the increasingly powerful role of ultra-orthodox Jewish religious movements in government, resulted in an accentuation of the significance of religious identity across Israeli society as a whole (Rouhana 1997). Secondly, the recognition by the Palestinian Liberation Organisation (PLO) of Israel in 1988 (and Israel's reciprocal recognition of it in 1993), and its acceptance of the 1947 UN Partition Plan, led to the marginalisation of the wider political leadership role of Rakah/DFPE/Hadash, and an increasing sense of disillusionment, isolation and abandonment by the Palestinian Arab minority in Israel who felt cut adrift and forgotten by the PLO and the Israeli-Palestinian peace process. Thirdly, the decline and ultimate break-up of the Soviet Union itself seriously undermined the credibility of the CP and its ability to provide effective leadership. And, finally, the 1980s witnessed widening socio-economic gaps between Jews and Arabs in society, resulting in increasing competition and tension between both sides, and within Palestinian Arab society itself. The combination of all of these factors contributed to the emergence of the Islamic movement not only as an attractive alternative to Rakah/DFPE/Hadash, but, for a number of years, as its primary opposition (Kaufman 1997: 40–1; Tsimhoni 2002: 131–4).

The Islamic movement, which was established in Israel in the late 1970s by Abdullah Nimr Darwish of Kfar Qassem, emerged primarily as a grassroots organisation providing social welfare support for Muslims in the area known as the Triangle in Israel (Emmett 1997: 546). However, its roots date back to 1967 with the regional growth of Islamic movements on the one hand, and the relaxation of military rule over Israel's Palestinian citizens on the other (Peled 2001b: 379). Its popularity continued to grow into the 1980s, particularly as a result of the support it received from the Israeli government itself which sought to undermine the power of Rakah by promoting alternative political avenues within the minority (Peled 2001a: 132–3). When the Islamic movement campaigned for the first time in municipal elections in 1984, it won seats on several local councils and, by 1989, had secured mayoral positions in five Arab municipalities which had previously been held by Rakah. This it achieved under religiously themed campaign slogans such as 'Islam is the answer' (Peled 2001b: 383). Therefore, Hadash/DFPE suffered not only 'the defection of part of its Muslim supporters' in 1989 but also experienced the beginning of a more general decline in its electoral significance in local politics (Emmett 1997: 541). This trend had also begun to affect the Rakah/DFPE/Hadash stronghold of Nazareth. While still managing to secure the majority of the vote (50.8 per cent) in the 1989 elections, Rakah/DFPE/Hadash nonetheless suffered a significant decline in its percentage share of the vote from 1983 when it commanded a clear majority (65.1 per cent) of the local vote (Emmett 1997: 551–2). And while the Islamic List did not win control over the municipality in Nazareth in 1989, it nonetheless secured an impressive 30 per cent of the vote (and, thus, six out of the 19 available seats in the municipality). While failing to secure the Nazareth mayoralty, the new Islamic List won control of six other local municipalities in 1993, testifying to the wide distribution of its political influence and growing popularity in Israel (Peled 2001b: 384; Israeli 2008: 255). Of these, the most significant were Taybeh and Umm el-Fahim, the latter of which would, in many respects, come to replace Nazareth as a centre of gravity for significant sections of Palestinian Arab (Muslim) minority.

The 1989 elections were, therefore, pivotal for two main reasons. Firstly, they resulted in the loss of the CP's political standing in Israel and the growth of political contest within the Palestinian Arab minority. Secondly, they introduced a more pronounced sectarian character to minority politics, with the Islamic movement commandeering large swathes of the Muslim vote and the CP becoming increasingly associated with its Christian electorate (even though it was not, in and of itself, a sectarian party). As one observer put it, '[re]ligion re-entered the political arena of Nazareth in full force in the 1989 elections' (Emmett 1997: 546) with the result that, by the year 2000, Muslim parties came to command approximately 25 per cent of the total Arab vote in Israel, making them a political force to be reckoned with (Usher 2000: 3).

The growth of political Islam in Nazareth is also rooted in the experiences of the city's internal refugees. When, after 1948, large numbers of predominantly Muslim internally displaced refugees came to settle in the city, they established separate quarters on the periphery of the old city (Emmett 1995: 153–60, 176–97). The spatial segregation of these communities from the 'core' areas of old Nazareth introduced socio-economic and infrastructural disparities and imbalances between old and new residents. With the passage of time and the persistence of gaps, the Communist-led municipality of Nazareth came to be targeted by accusations of neglect and, given the religious affiliation of the mayor (post-1994), of religious bias and favouritism. That traditional, or pre-1948, Muslim neighbourhoods of Nazareth remained on the same level of development (or, rather, underdevelopment) as Christian ones did little to mitigate this potentially incendiary situation (Emmett 1997: 546; Tsimhoni 2002: 140). Instead, the strong Christian atmosphere of the city with its dominating Basilica and plethora of churches and shrines, together with the prevalence of European-administered church schools and institutions, served to reinforce the notion of Christian advantage, chauvinism and exclusivity (Emmett 1997: 547).

With the split of the Islamic movement in 1996, the power of this party to effectively challenge Hadash/DFPE was momentarily checked (Kaufman 1997: 119). Issuing from this split, however, the more politically moderate southern branch of the Islamic movement, based around the figure of Abdallah Nimr Darwish, came to provide important ideological support to the newly formed United Arab List (UAL) which would soon overtake Rakah/DFPE/Hadash as the single largest Arab party in Israel (Usher 2000: 4). Although it does not campaign on an explicitly religious or sectarian political platform, all of the MKs who have represented the UAL since 1996, or Ra'am-Ta'al (when UAL merged with the Arab Movement for Renewal) since 2006, have been Muslim which has important consequences for voting patterns (and electoral strategies) in subsequent Israeli national and municipal elections.

In the Nazareth municipal elections of 1993, only 23 per cent of Nazarenes voted for any of the three Muslim parties, with a parallel upward shift in electoral returns for Hadash/DFPE to 56 per cent of the overall vote (Emmett 1997: 552). By the time of the 1996 municipal elections, Hadash/DPFE had won back even more electoral support. However, this figure fell to 44 per cent by the time of the 1999 municipal elections, demonstrating that Muslim parties had come to represent 'CPI-Front's most formidable rival in the 1990s' even in Nazareth (Kaufman 1997: 4, 117). Having said this, the electoral returns for DFPE/Hadash in Nazareth were more than twice the national average for that party in 1999. This suggests that while its regional popularity was waning, Nazareth continued to be 'a traditional DFPE stronghold' in Israel (Frisch 2001: 163). It also, however, suggests that political trends in Nazareth were no longer entirely representative of general political trends occurring within the minority and across the country as a whole. Despite the erosion of the singular significance and centrality of Nazareth and the increased distribution of Palestinian Arab political weight across other Arab urban centres in Israel, political competition for control over its municipality demonstrates the continued importance of this city to the aspirations of various political parties and movements within the Palestinian Arab minority in Israel.

The Nazareth 2000 affair

In the mid-1990s tensions developed in Nazareth between members of the Islamic movement and the Communist-led municipality over the fate of a 6,000 square foot plot of land in the city centre adjacent to the Basilica of the Annunciation and the tomb of Shihab ad-Din (nephew of the legendary Salah ad-Din) who died in Nazareth of wounds he received during the Battle of Hittin in 1187 against the Crusaders (Rabinowitz 2001a: 96).

The plot of land, which had previously been the site of a state primary school, had been levelled in 1996 by the municipality in order to create space for a plaza in front of the Basilica in time for the city's 2000 millennium celebrations (Cohen-Hattab and Shoval 2007: 706). The initiative, referred to as the 'Nazareth 2000' project, was originally launched by the municipality in 1991 under the leadership of its former (Muslim) Mayor, Tawfiq Zayyad, to coincide with the millennium and the anticipated mass influx of tourists who were expected to come to celebrate 2000 years of Christianity in Nazareth and the visit of Pope John Paul II to the Holy Land in March (Jabareen 2006: 16–17). The project 'aimed to use the millennium as a springboard for urban renewal in Nazareth' and, as such, was specifically designed to promote the largely tourist-based economy of the city, develop infrastructure, renovate the old *suq* (market), build museums and other public buildings, as well as to remodel the heavily congested city centre (Rabinowitz 2001a: 96).

Despite efforts made by the municipality to capitalise on the singular opportunity afforded by the millennium to develop the city for all its inhabitants within the confines of Nazareth's only niche market (and dependent economy) – tourism – the initiative was vigorously opposed by members of the Islamic movement who protested that it marginalised the city's majority Muslim population and heritage in what was, they argued, an exclusivist Christian project. This antagonistic view was exacerbated by the insensitive relegation of the Shihab ad-Din shrine to a small, closed-off area behind utility buildings in the architect's original master plan for the area (Rabinowitz 2001a: 97).

Instead of the proposed open plaza, Muslim protestors demanded that a new mosque be built on the site, the dimensions of which would have overshadowed the Basilica as the dominant landmark of the city (Tsimhoni 2002: 135; Israeli 2008: 260). Fearing the rapid progress taking place at the site and the potential damage to the delicate dome of the shrine, Muslim protestors led by Salman Abu Ahmad, a local council member who represented the newly formed Muslim Action Committee (which incorporated the local Islamic movement and the Waqf Committee of Nazareth), declared the contested area to be Muslim *waqf* (Jabareen 2006: 17). Abu Ahmad and his followers moved in and took over the site on 21 December 1997, set up prayer tents and erected a 10-metre fence south of the shrine, thus interrupting any further construction on the site (Rabinowitz 2001a: 97–100).

In the meantime, the municipal elections of November 1998 took place in which the DFPE, led by the incumbent mayor, Ramiz Jaraisy, won only nine out of the total 19 seats available. With only 135 votes separating them, the United Nazareth List, a Muslim list headed by the UAL, won the remaining 10 seats thus becoming the majority coalition power in the municipality (Israeli 2002: 158). Notwithstanding this, Jaraisy himself was successfully re-elected as mayor after winning 52 per cent of the popular vote in the direct elections which were held separately for the mayoralty (Frisch 2001: 157). As runner-up in the direct elections for the office of the mayor, however, Abu Ahmad, as leader of the majority coalition, became deputy mayor of Nazareth (Israeli 2002: 104–5).

It soon became evident that the mayor and his municipality were pitted against each other in their respective struggles for control over the municipality which resulted in a complete political and administrative deadlock of the city. Demonstrating the high level of tensions between both sides, the first council meeting following the elections descended into a fist-fight (Rabinowitz 2001a: 105). Jaraisy himself hired a number of bodyguards suggesting that he himself felt a direct level of personal threat against him (Israeli 2002: 109).

This political conflict between the mayor's office and the Islamic List did not remain within the confines of the municipality for long. It spread to the street, when on 3 April 1999, one day before Easter, violence broke out (Rabinowitz 2001a: 105; Tsimhoni 2002: 136). In an attempt to explain the outbreak of violence, it has been suggested that a group of young Christians passing by the compound of the shrine initiated the trouble by making insulting remarks about the Prophet Muhammad with the result that, during the night, angry Muslim rioters set fire to a number of cars on the main street and broke several shop windows (Rabinowitz 2001a: 105). Another account, citing local media sources, claims that following a fight between drunken Christian youths and Muslim protestors, the violence became targeted against innocent Christian passers-by.

Christian women driving their cars were dragged off and badly beaten; Muslims who were considered to be collaborating with the Christians were attacked and their property vandalised.

(Tsimhoni 2002: 136–7)

Whatever its origins, there was a clear fear that this violent outburst would escalate into 'large-scale bloody clashes' between Muslims and Christians in the city (Rabinowitz 2001a: 105). As Head of the Committee of Arab Heads of Local Councils in Israel, Mohammed Zeidane called an emergency meeting between local leaders to take place the following day in order to resolve this 'ticking time bomb'. His actions succeeded in averting a general strike which was organised to take place by the Muslim Waqf Committee (Rabinowitz 2001a: 105–6).

Within the context of these developing tensions the role of the authorities became the focus of much attention. However, descriptions of the nature of that role have not always been consistent or uniform. Some have, for instance, argued that the Israeli central government 'sided with the municipality' (Rabinowitz 2001a: 103), but even accounts such as these describe the state's actions as highly inconsistent reflecting the changing priorities of different governments and political parties. To begin with, the municipality's Nazareth 2000 Master Plan, which was first drafted in 1993, was originally coordinated alongside the Labour government of Yitzhak Rabin (Tsimhoni 2002: 135), who is accorded a positive and affirmative role in his desire to narrow the developmental and economic gaps between Arab and Jewish cities in Israel (Jabareen 2006: 16; Cohen-Hattab and Shoval 2007: 702–5).

In 1996, however, a new government under the leadership of Likud's Benjamin Netanyahu took power which openly endorsed and supported the Muslim protestors' demand to build a mosque, which fundamentally undermined the efforts made by the previous Rabin government. In particular, the occupation of the construction site by Muslim protestors in late 1997 involved the office of the Prime Minister himself through his personal envoy, Danny Greenberg (Tsimhoni 2002: 136). Greenberg, who had been presented in the media as 'the Prime Minister's Advisor on Arab Affairs' was, in fact, the Likud Party's independent consultant on Arab Affairs. He was seen in the city as early as December 1997 (before the riots began) and met frequently with the various heads of the Islamic movement as well as with their lawyer, Dan Shafir, coordinating meetings between them and various governmental representatives. Mayor of Nazareth, Jaraisy, wrote directly to Netanyahu to complain about 'Greenberg's suspicious activities' and his 'meddling' in the issue to little avail (Israeli 2002: 89–90).

The Likud policy even contradicted the wishes of the Israel Lands Authority (ILA) which had jurisdictional authority over the plot of land and which, in early 1998, appealed to the court to have the protestors removed (Rabinowitz 2001a: 103; Tsimhoni 2002: 135). However, despite the power and influence of the ILA, these appeals were deliberately delayed and neglected. Instead, the first inter-ministerial commission of inquiry was appointed in April 1999 which was headed by the then Minister of Tourism, Moshe Katsav and the Minister of Tourism, Eli Suissa. Testifying to a broader policy of neglect, the commission failed to present any immediate formal recommendations on how to proceed with the plot of land, thus extending the conflict in the city further (Tsimhoni 2002: 138).

In terms of the government's role during the violent outburst of April 1999, a deliberate 'hands-off' policy by the police has been observed:

> A large police force was mobilised, but abstained for hours from stopping the attacks . . . due to received orders [by Northern District police commander, Alik Ron] from 'higher levels' not to interfere.
>
> (Tsimhoni 2002: 137)

Similarly, a blank cheque policy with regard to the arrest and prosecution of known perpetrators of the violence was noted.

> Rather than punishing the rioters, representatives of the Likud and several religious parties that were members of the government coalition visited the Islamic movement protest tent and publicly expressed their support for the building of the mosque in front of the basilica.
>
> (Tsimhoni 2002: 137)

On 9 April 1999 the then Minister of Tourism, Moshe Katsav, publicly endorsed the protestors, announcing his 'personal support' for the construction of the mosque on Israeli television and, nine days later, the government announced the allocation of 504 square metres of the disputed square for construction of a mosque, with the remaining area to be developed in line with the original master plans (Tsimhoni 2002: 137–8). This offer, however, was rejected by local Islamic leaders who presumably hoped that their stand-off would bring even greater concessions from the government. This was, in part, confirmed when, in addition to his open support of the Muslim protestors' cause and their demand to build a mosque on the site, Netanyahu 'caused the freezing of nearly all government projects and finance connected with the Nazareth 2000 project' (Tsimhoni 2002: 135).

Notwithstanding the publicly stated commitment of Netanyahu's government to the cause of the Muslim protestors, other developments contradicted their apparent allegiance. For example, the pledge made by former Foreign Minister, Ariel Sharon, to the Pope on his visit to the Vatican on 26 April 1999 that the Israeli government would not allow the construction of a mosque in front of the Basilica, cast a reasonable measure of doubt over the real intentions of the government and suspicion over their tactics (Tsimhoni 2002: 140).

It has been widely acknowledged that Netanyahu's position was heavily motivated by pragmatic electoral politics in the run-up to the parliamentary and direct prime ministerial elections of 1999 in which the 'Arab vote', which was essentially viewed as a Muslim vote, was prioritised and aggressively courted. For instance, Greenberg, who worked personally for Netanyahu's re-election as his special envoy 'was appointed by the Prime Minister to meddle in the Nazareth controversy informally, as a contractor of votes in the Arab sector' (Israeli 2002: 89, 93). However, these attempts to win the popularity of marginal Islamic elements within the Muslim minority alienated the more moderate majority of the Muslim electorate, demonstrating that their policy not only miscalculated the response of Palestinian Muslims but underestimated the strength of their Palestinian national identity. These factors ultimately contributed to the collapse of the Arab support for Netanyahu and his fall from power following the May 1999 general elections.

Demonstrating their dissatisfaction with Netanyahu, the vast majority of the Arab electorate supported Labour candidate Ehud Barak as a vote for change in the direct prime ministerial contest of 17 May 1999 (Frisch 2001: 153). One analysis describes the factors which brought Barak to power as follows:

> The mood among the people in Nazareth was that if the right-wing Likud won the Islamic movement would get the upper hand, and if the Labor bloc won the Christians and the moderate Muslims in Nazareth would strengthen their position.
>
> (Tsimhoni 2002: 138)

Others, however, acknowledge the equally important role of Israeli electoral politics in the Labour Party campaign, suggesting that Barak's victory was, in no small part, due to promises he made to the Islamists regarding the construction of a mosque and the promotion of 'Arab-Muslim' enclaves in Israel (Israeli 2002: 98–9 and 2008: 262–3). This view is supported by the fact that when Barak took over the reins of power in 1999 no noticeable change in either his wider policy towards the Palestinian Arab minority or in his local policy on the Nazareth issue itself occurred. In fact, the former government's position on the Nazareth issue became, to a large extent, solidified under Barak's term in office. A second ministerial commission of inquiry, this time under the authority of Shlomo Ben-Ami, who served as Minister of Internal Security and was also responsible for the Israeli Police, was set up on 14 April to deal with 'this sensitive issue'. However, this committee 'was mainly concerned with the possible reactions of the Islamic movement to their decisions' rather than with issues of legality or local Arab consensus (Tsimhoni 2002: 138). In fact, Barak's government decided to allocate an even greater proportion of the site (700 square metres) towards construction of a new mosque. This decision, which was taken on 5 October 1999, came just one day before the Nazareth District Court released a report refuting the Islamic movement's claim that the entirety of the site represented Muslim *waqf*. Tracing historical land deeds and ownership documents for the site, the court found that only 135 square metres of land surrounding the shrine itself was Muslim *waqf*. The remaining area was traditionally, since the time of the Ottoman period, state-land (Peled 2001b: 395; Tsimhoni 2002: 139).

Barak introduced one important condition to his offer to the Islamic movement which was that 'in return for a governmental guarantee that a mosque would be built, the Muslim activists were to evacuate the area no later than 8 November' (Rabinowitz 2001a: 106). On 2 November 1999, the government-appointed office of the architect responsible for the construction of the mosque issued its proposed blue-prints for the mosque. This was immediately followed by a wide-scale and unified strike by the Christian churches in Israel as well as condemnation by the Vatican and several Arab leaders both of the Israeli authorities and of the Muslim protestors themselves. Notwithstanding these protests, government representatives officiated at the cornerstone-laying ceremony for the new mosque on 23 November 1999 (Rabinowitz 2001a: 106–7; Tsimhoni 2002: 139). Losing patience with the slow progress of building, the Islamic movement reneged on its deal with the government and, defying regional and international protests, paved large sections of the disputed area, installing a loud-speaker system for prayers (Peled 2001b: 395). It became increasingly apparent that the Islamic movement was, through its actions, attempting to create a 'fact on the ground'.

The millennium came and went in Nazareth without the anticipated hype or celebration which had been planned seven years earlier. On 25 March 2000, the Catholic holy day commemorating the annunciation of the Virgin Mary in Nazareth, Pope John Paul II arrived in Natzeret Illit by Israeli Air Force helicopter from Jerusalem. He was escorted down into the old city in order to preside over a short mass for the occasion (Rabinowitz 2001a: 94–6). Notwithstanding the anticlimax of the millennial celebrations in Nazareth, international pressure against the construction of the mosque was growing ever stronger and more impatient. The Vatican was growing ever more restless (it had, in fact, threatened to cancel the Pope's visit), while Arab leaders became ever more vocal and critical. Even international leaders such as George W. Bush and Vladimir Putin made direct intercessions with Israel on behalf of the municipality (Peled 2001b: 395; Tsimhoni 2002: 140–1).

Ariel Sharon of the Likud party took office becoming not only the eleventh Prime Minister of Israel but the third Israeli Prime Minister to officiate over the protracted conflict in Nazareth. As with each of his predecessors, Sharon appointed his own ministerial commission of inquiry to investigate the matter anew, this time led by his Minister of Construction and Housing, Natan Sharansky. This inquiry which was appointed in 2001 reached the conclusion one year later that the construction of a mosque on that spot would be deleterious both to intra-communal relations in the city and to the state's diplomatic relations abroad. On 1 July 2003, the foundations of the new mosque were destroyed and the tents removed with little to no resistance from the local community (Cohen-Hattab and Shoval 2007: 710). Four months later, in November 2003, when the next municipal elections came around, Jaraisy won an outright majority of the popular vote and his party was similarly successful in winning the necessary majority to lead the municipality.

Only in 2004, eight years after the demolition of the school, did construction of the new city square begin. However, given the long delays and the protracted nature of the conflict, hopes of securing the development of the city on the basis of the unique, one-off funding package earmarked for the millennium were permanently dashed. Moreover, the city's tourist trade, which had virtually come to a halt during the eight years of conflict, political deadlock and governmental procrastination has still not recovered from the major economic setback it experienced during this period and, arguably, is worse off in economic terms today than it was before the initiative was first launched (Arab HRA 2000).

Media coverage of the Nazareth 2000 crisis has also played a pivotal part in the conflict, stressing different areas of responsibility. Mainstream media generally provided a 'Huntingtonian' analysis of events centring on a presumed clash of civilisations between Christians and Muslims. However, attention was also brought to bear on state policy itself as well as on internal electoral competition and rivalry between the DFPE-dominated municipality and the aspiring Islamic movement (Usher 2000: 2). However, in a 2004 survey conducted by Jabareen among a sample of 250 local residents of Nazareth, the public perception and assessment of blame followed a more distinctive pattern. The respondents were asked to grade eac of the five different 'players' in the crisis according to their perceived role (whether it was strong, moderate or non-existent) in contributing to, or aggravating, the crisis. The five different players in the conflict were listed as follows: the municipality, the Islamic movement, the Israeli government, the Islamic Waqf Committee and the planners. According to the survey's findings, the vast majority of the respondents (88.8 per cent) considered the Israeli government to have played a strong role in bringing about, or contributing to, the crisis. A strong role was also assigned by 65.6 per cent of those surveyed to the Islamic Movement, 50.2 per cent to the Islamic *Waqf* Committee and 47.7 per cent to the Planners. By contrast, only 37.2 per cent of all respondents considered the Municipality of Nazareth to have played a strong role in the crisis (Jabareen 2006: 18).

Analysing state attitudes

In this section, the particular viewfs of the respondents interviewed for this study will be incorporated with the available evidence from the literature. Three individuals directly involved in the crisis were interviewed by this author. The first was Ramiz Jaraisy, a Palestinian Christian by birth and active member of Rakah/DFPE/Hadash who has accumulated over three decades of experience within Nazareth municipality since his initial election to the City Council in 1978. Serving as Deputy-Mayor of Nazareth until the death of Tawfiq Zayyad in 1994, Jaraisy has since held the position of Mayor of Nazareth for 15 years through three successive elections (in 1998, 2003, 2008) and will continue to hold this position until the next Israeli municipal elections take place in 2013. The second individual who was directly connected with the Nazareth conflict and who was interviewed for this study was Raphael Israeli, an Israeli Jewish academic from the Hebrew University of Jerusalem who specialises on topics relating to Islamic fundamentalism. Called as an expert witness to the 1999 government-appointed inter-ministerial Committee of Inquiry on Nazareth, Israeli was not only responsible for writing that Committee's report, but he later developed his findings into a book dedicated to the subject, *Green Crescent over Nazareth* (2002). The third respondent who was directly involved in the conflict was Mohammed Zeidane, a Palestinian Muslim by birth who is currently Director of the Arab Association for Human Rights. During the 1990s, he served as Head of the Committee of Arab Mayors and the National Follow-Up Committee for the Heads of Arab Local Authorities in Israel, and played a key part during the conflict which unravelled in the city. In particular, he called for and chaired the emergency meeting of local Arab leaders which took place following the outbreak of violence in 1999. In addition to these three figures, the views of other respondents who were not directly involved in the events but were, nonetheless, contemporary witnesses to them are also addressed here.

In line with the findings produced by Jabareen's survey of public opinion in Nazareth on the sources and origins of the conflict, the Mayor of Nazareth also found the Israeli political establishment to be the main party responsible for the events which unfolded in the city. Not only did he argue that the authorities developed the dispute, but they were also instrumental in raising it in the first place. In particular, he identified the role of 'common goals' between certain local interest groups (namely, the Islamic movement) and the national interests of the state. Nonetheless, he rejected the notion that the conflict can be characterised as an essentially religious clash between Muslims and Christians in Nazareth. For him, the goals of, and decisions made by, the Islamic movement in Nazareth were purely political, as they were for the state itself. The Islamic movement is understood to be not just a religious movement but an aspiring political party which seeks to capitalise on Muslim demographic strength in its competition with the DFPE/Hadash for control over the municipality.

Citing the destructive role of Netanyahu's envoy Danny Greenberg, the significance of the state's support to the Islamic movement is also understood by Jaraisy to have been motivated as much by pragmatic electoral concerns as it was by strategic national interests in the run-up to the hotly contested prime ministerial elections of 1999 in which the Arab vote played a determining role. This factor underlines the view encountered in previous chapters that the numeric weakness and electoral insignificance of Palestinian Christians represents a central determinant of state attitudes towards them. It also suggests that the religious difference of Palestinian Christians is submerged or overruled by the crucial factor of political activity and orientation in the formulation of state attitudes towards them.

For Jaraisy, the fundamental reason why this dispute, which could have been easily contained or averted had the state been so inclined, became so protracted and long-winded was the cynical attitude of the state itself towards Palestinian Arab intra-communal relations. The constant intervention and meddling of various political envoys such as Greenberg and the three highly ineffective ministerial committees which were set up to deal with the issue by successive Israeli governments, but which ultimately prolonged and worsened the conflict, testifies to the disposability and inconsequentiality of Palestinian Christian needs and interests to the state. Ultimately, Nazareth as a whole is understood to have fallen victim to cynical Israeli political gamesmanship. Neither side in the conflict (whether the DFPE-led municipality with its Christian mayor or the local Islamists) benefited. No mosque was ever built and the Nazareth 2000 initiative was, for all intents and purposes, shelved. Instead the political integrity and unity of Nazareth was called into question and seriously undermined by the dispute, with the only possible benefactor being the state.

In fact, Jaraisy suggested that the government never really had any intention of proceeding with either the mosque or the Nazareth 2000 project in the first place.

In terms of the mosque initiative, for instance, he mentioned that the government had solicited three architectural companies from around the world to propose different designs for a new mosque on the contested site. This selection process alone cost the government three million shekels, which would suggest a real commitment by the state to this project. However, once the plans were ready and about to be put into effect on the ground, the Islamic movement suddenly and illogically lost patience, choosing to proceed with construction themselves. For Jaraisy, this was no coincidence, but rather the result of a careful governmental orchestration. As such, the government is understood to have quietly encouraged the protestors to take over the site, 'to turn the situation to violence', and to dig a make-shift foundation for a new mosque, so that, as a result of their legal violations, construction of the mosque 'which was at a very advanced stage of planning' could be stopped. This highly irrational move by the Islamic movement is understood to have been motivated by the state's desire to outwardly appear as a defender of Muslim rights while, covertly, making every effort to undermine and limit any real advancement of Muslim interests in the city.

This discomfort with Muslim communal gains, however, also extended to the Palestinian Christians. For Jaraisy, the state, particularly under the government of Netanyahu, was deeply uncomfortable with the Nazareth 2000 project on several grounds. In the first instance, there was a clear discomfort with the central status of the Christian-associated and DFPE-led Nazareth municipality within Palestinian Arab society and Palestinian oppositional political activity. As such, the state is understood to have feared the increased potential that the Nazareth 2000 project would have given to the already problematic political leadership of the municipality.

> The municipality of Nazareth created a new model for the Arab local authorities. On one side, holding the basic and principal positions concerning the struggle against the policy of the government based on discrimination, for equal rights, national rights and civilian rights, for the rights of the local authorities, the issues of confiscation, of lands, Nazareth was in the front of that struggle inside the Committee for Arab Local Authorities and the Follow-Up Committee. The role of Nazareth and the Nazareth municipality [had] a very important role . . . We were in the front as a leader. So, creating that model from one side, the city was developing deeply and [proposing] very important positive changes everywhere in the city, infrastructure projects, buildings, preparing the old part of the city, a lot of investment internationally, nationally, all that, and at the same time with the positions of defending rights.

Accordingly, Netanyahu's government is described as having 'wanted to break this model' and, in order to achieve this, they sought 'to use this dispute and to create this problem and to develop it' in the hope that the power of the Nazareth municipality to lead the city, let alone the wider national minority, would be effectively 'neutralised'.

However, the desire to undermine Nazareth as the centre of political gravity for Palestinian Arabs in Israel was not the only factor which affected state attitudes towards the dispute. Jaraisy considers Jewish religious antipathy towards Christianity to be an important additional factor affecting both the state's decision-making process and its strategies of intervention.

> I think that when the Likud Party came to power, I'm sure of it, they decided that the state of Israel should not be part of these preparations for celebrations towards 2000 because of ideology, because these celebrations don't have any roots in Jewish history in the area, but Christian history in the area.

In particular, Jaraisy points to the decision made by Benjamin Netanyahu together with his new Deputy Prime Minister, Moshe Katsav (who was then also Minister for Tourism and his Advisor on Arab Affairs, and who would become President of Israel in 2000) to change the name of the 'Nazareth 2000' project to 'Nazareth in 2000'. While this may appear to an outside observer to be only a minor change in the project's marketing slogan, this change of name provides Jaraisy with ample evidence of the anti-Christian religious bias of the state. Fearful that 'Nazareth 2000' reinforces not only the association of an Israeli city with Christianity but implicitly recognises the historically continuous presence of local Christians in Israel, thereby challenging the exclusive nature of Jewish claims to the land, the more sanitised and historically disconnected 'Nazareth in 2000' label was adopted.

Given the distancing tactics of the Likud government in relation to the millennium project, the Nazareth municipality decided to proceed with their preparations alone. The municipality advertised internationally for proposals to organise the millennial celebrations in Nazareth and received three bids. They chose the proposal made by the London-based Clinton Group who were prepared to pay the municipality three million dollars in advance of the celebrations to fund the necessary infrastructural improvements to the city, including the construction of an amphitheatre. However, just as they were about to sign the contract, the Easter riots of 1999 broke out. As the new year celebrations were due to be broadcast all around the world in just eight months' time, including guest appearances by a number of high-profile stars (including U2), the Clinton group decided that, despite having already invested 100,000 dollars of their own money in the project, the risk to any further investment by potential intra-communal conflict in the city was too great and they pulled out. Given the ambivalence and antagonism of the Netanyahu government to a project which would underscore the Christian atmosphere of the city, the authorities are said to have been secretly pleased.

However, a third factor which according to Jaraisy influenced the state's attitudes towards the Nazareth dispute was the peace process. Towards the late 1990s, momentum was building in political talks between Ehud Barak and Yasser Arafat as part of the Oslo peace process. In particular, international attention was focused on final status arrangements with regard to Jerusalem. As the European governments were generally supportive of the Palestinian demand to have East Jerusalem as the capital of a future Palestinian state and for the PA to have control over the Holy Sites within the Old City, the emerging intra-communal conflict in Nazareth became a useful political playing card for the Israeli government. According to Jaraisy, Israeli representatives approached EU and Vatican officials arguing that if the PA had control over Jerusalem and its Holy Sites the same level of instability and intra-communal hostility as was apparently happening in Nazareth would plague Jerusalem as well. As a result, stoking up the conflict in Nazareth and portraying the conflict in exaggerated terms signifying a clash of civilisations between radical Muslims and a united Christian-Jewish 'West' paid important political dividends to the state.

However, despite gloomy prognostications made in the media about the future of intra-communal relations in Nazareth, Jaraisy remained upbeat. Stating that relations in the city have returned to normal, he argued that the conflict represented nothing more than an artificially inflated 'blip' on an otherwise calm horizon. Testifying to what he described to be the true sign of Muslim–Christian relations in Nazareth he argues that, in a city which is 70 per cent Muslim, he, as a Christian-born candidate, has been twice re-elected since the dispute first occurred. As such, the vast majority of the people of Nazareth remain united in their support of a DFPE-led municipality with a nominal Christian figure at its head, and are not as influenced by ideological rhetoric as some analyses might suggest. He also suggests that it is very unlikely that the state would ever again take such a direct interventionist role in intra-communal relations within the Palestinian Arab minority. While interference is to be expected ('Well, there is interference all the time. They will not stand looking from the side without trying to interfere . . .'), the significant and costly internal and international backlash which the state received for its role in Nazareth has had a deep impact both on its diplomatic relations and on how the state moves forward with respect to its Palestinian Arab minority.

For Muslim NGO Director, Mohammad Zeidane, the Israeli government also received the greatest measure of blame for the Nazareth affair. For him, it was 'the manipulation of small things in the election campaign' of the main Zionist parties that is understood to have influenced the state's particular line of intervention. Such government intervention is identified as occurring on several different levels. In the first instance, media coverage by both the Israeli and international press is understood to have manipulated the conflict and to have distorted the true significance of the affair.

> I mean Israel can demolish a whole village in the Negev and nobody will hear about it. It won't even be mentioned in the Israeli media let alone the international media. I mean, 25 houses were demolished in the Negev and nobody mentioned it even in the Israeli media, while a small event around a religious thing in Nazareth suddenly becomes a New York Times and BBC item.

However, even with international press coverage, the state is considered to have played an important part in directing and even encouraging these newsfeeds. Given the timing of these press releases which he observes to have generally coincided with electoral campaigns, he suggests that not only particular political parties but the state itself exploited the fall-out of this sensationalist and Huntingtonian coverage of the conflict upon Muslim–Christian intra-communal relations in Israel to its own advantage.

Zeidane also stressed the poor socio-economic situation of certain neighbourhoods in Nazareth which have exacerbated tensions between communities in Nazareth and provided the state with another angle of opportunity. The disenfranchised neighbourhoods in question emerged from the post-1948 settlement patterns of predominantly Muslim internal refugees in the periphery of the old city mentioned earlier which Jersaisi likened to modern-day refugee camps. The emerging gaps between these neighbourhoods and the more traditional Muslim and Christian core areas of the city are not, however, attributed to discrimination by the municipality but to the natural development of the area in line with continued budgetary discrimination from the central government. Ironically, it was these socio-economic gaps which contributed to the growing popularity and strength of the Islamic movement in Nazareth which, in turn, fed off and exploited the clear social and economic gaps for its own quasi-religious political purposes. Similarly, he accused the state of manipulating the conflict by persistently portraying it as an essentially religious problem, overlooking the deeper political and socio-economic problems which it was ultimately responsible for.

Unlike analyses which portray the conflict in Nazareth as a 'watershed' marking the deterioration of Christian–Muslim relations in Israel, Zeidane believed the opposite to be true. A growing public awareness of the 'real' root causes of the conflict has, to his mind, led to a growing internal criticism of the intentions of both the state and the Islamic movement among the majority of the Muslim population in Nazareth. It did not usher in a collapse of the 'communal balance' in Nazareth, as some have prophesied, but rather it represented an isolated and unfortunate incident which – notwithstanding sensationalist media coverage and opportunistic state policy – has been overcome.

Testifying to this and to the importance of other underlying factors obfuscated by the media, he discussed the response of local Nazarenes to a Jewish terrorist attack at the Basilica of the Annunciation which took place in 2006 (Arab HRA 2006). On Friday 3 March 2006, a special Lenten mass was being held in the upper floor of the Basilica at which several hundred local Christians, together with a handful of foreign pilgrims, were present. A Jewish man from Jerusalem together with his Christian wife and 20 year-old daughter entered the church posing as tourists. Pushing a baby stroller filled with firecrackers, kerosene, gas canisters, inflammable material, as well as metal shards and marbles, the home-made bomb which they carried failed to detonate properly with the result that no one was killed or seriously injured.

Panic quickly spilled over from the smoke-filled church onto the surrounding streets and soon large crowds of locals, shocked by this brazen attack on such a venerated holy site and a central landmark of the city, gathered around the front gates of the church in a gesture of solidarity and protection. This rapid response was, Zeidane suggests, spurred on by the still fresh memories of a Jewish terrorist attack which had occurred six months previously in Shfar'amr which resulted in the death of four Palestinians (two Muslims and two Christians), and the still open wounds of the events of October 2000 in which 13 Palestinian Israeli citizens were killed by Israeli security forces (Arab HRA 2005a and 2006). The inability or reluctance of the authorities to apply basic criminal procedure in a swift and just manner led many to fear that those responsible for the 2006 incident in Nazareth would also escape justice. Demonstrating the biased and overzealous nature of the state's security apparatus, riot police were dispatched in large numbers to Nazareth to contain the demonstration which ensued and to protect the attackers from what was described in the Israeli media as the fast-multiplying 'Arab mob'. The police then entered the church where the attackers were being held and, disguising them in police uniforms, escorted them to a local hospital whereupon they were released from police custody. The police then used teargas and stun grenades to disperse the unarmed crowd.

The following day hundreds of locals marched through Nazareth protesting the police response and the inability or unwillingness of the authorities to prosecute the law in an impartial manner. At the front of this march were communal and political leaders from across the religious spectrum, underscoring the new sense of solidarity between Christians and Muslims. Ironically, it was the Basilica of the Annunciation which only a decade earlier proved to be so divisive which now inspired renewed intra-communal solidarity. Over the course of the following days, the police began to arrest individuals who they claimed were responsible for brutality against the police. By contrast, no criminal procedure against the attackers was observed. In fact, the local Hebrew press downplayed the attack altogether, dismissing those responsible as mentally unstable or 'crazy'. Simultaneously, the then President Moshe Katsav accused local Muslims, who made up the majority of protestors, of interfering in affairs which had nothing to do with them, while it is said that acting Prime Minister Ehud Olmert tried to undermine the sense of renewed intra-communal solidarity with claims of persistent Muslim intolerance towards Christians (Roffe-Ofir 2006; Cook 2006b; Bannoura 2008).

Zeidane was present in the crowd subsequent to the attack on the Basilica. He recalls that 95 per cent of the crowd who gathered outside the church gates were Muslim, confirming his view that there is a unity of feeling amongst the people of Nazareth that supersedes sectarian differences. In fact, the Basilica of Annunciation came to represent an important symbol of Palestinian Arab unity against what was perceived to be a Jewish racist attack and an indifferent government. And while religious differences will continue to provide new and easy opportunities to create problems amongst the minority or to promote particular local political agendas, particularly around election time, he believes that the Shihab ad-Din issue is now very much a thing of the past.

The third central figure in the Nazareth 2000 affair who was interviewed for this study was Raphael Israeli. A Professor of Islamic, Middle Eastern and Chinese History at the Hebrew University of Jerusalem, Israeli immigrated to Israel from Morocco when he was 14 years old. He has written several books on 'radical Islam' and the 'Islamisation' of the Palestinian Arab minority in Israel as well as on the alleged dangers surrounding the presence of Muslim minorities throughout Europe and the US (Israeli 2002; Israeli 2003 and Israeli 2008). He has been called as an expert witness by the state on three separate, and highly publicised, trials and commissions of inquiry in Israel: the first inter-ministerial commission of inquiry into the Nazareth dispute in 1999; the Or Commission of Inquiry in 2000; and the trial of Sheikh Raed Salah, mayor of Umm el-Fahem and spiritual leader of the northern wing of the Islamist movement in Israel. It was his role in the inter-ministerial commission of inquiry into the Nazareth dispute of 1999 which is of interest here.

The Commission of Inquiry which Israeli gave evidence to was appointed on 14 April 1999 by the former Minister of the Interior Eli Suisa who was a member of the ultra-orthodox Mizrahi Shas Party. The Committee itself was quite small and was composed of four core members: a Bedouin (Amram Kalaji) who was a former Director General of the Ministry of the Interior and had risen through the ranks to become Commissioner for the Northern District; a former intelligence officer in the IDF who was also a former Director General of the Ministry of Police (Gad Aviner); a former General and IDF spokesman (Ephraim Lapid); and Israeli himself who was appointed to this panel made up primarily of defence and security officials 'in order to lend to it an aura of objectivity, respectability and thorough research which would be free from biases and political scheming' (Israeli 2002: 115–16).

The Committee was charged with three tasks: to examine the tensions between the different groups in the city; to find a resolution to the conflict without having to resort to governmental measures; and to investigate how the normal functioning of the city council could be restored (Israeli 2002: 116). However, the conclusions reached by the Committee, which were submitted as a report three months later and which basically endorsed governmental support and further concessions to the Islamic movement, contradicted the views of Israeli himself. As the only academic on a committee consisting primarily of politicians and officials, he claims to have been given the task of researching the historical context of the conflict, particularly with regard to the claim that the disputed plot of land was Muslim *waqf.* However, when he submitted this report together with his conclusions, the committee chose to replace his final recommendations with their own while keeping the main body of the report intact. He was most indignant and refused to sign the new report which became known as the Majority Report. In his own conclusions, which he submitted as the committee's Minority Report, he recommended against the construction of a mosque which would only 'yield' to the demands of a radical Islamic movement and which would, in turn, be understood as a provocation by the local Christian population.

He subsequently converted this Minority Report into a book, *Green Crescent Over Nazareth: The Displacement of Christians by Muslims,* in which he detailed in greater length and detail his dissatisfaction with the Committee's conclusions.

> Taking into account the political machinations behind the scenes (. . .), the slow pace in the proceedings of the Commission, and the parallel measures

and decisions that were adopted by the Government as the Commission was being set up, it is now evident that the latter was no more than a fig leaf to cover the already adopted resolution to give in to the Islamists with a façade of respectability, proper government and good manners. At no time, indeed, did the Minister who appointed the Commission think about dissolving the city council, or denying the Islamists their actual illegal possession of the plaza, or move to ensure that the plaza would be ready at the deadline for the 2000 celebrations. His alliance with the Islamists described above in fact may have dictated his negative approach to the whole idea of the millennium, and he did not seem to be in any rush to advance that cause. The fact that the Commission was not pressed at any time, neither before the national elections of 1999 nor subsequent to them, to expedite the report of its findings, also tends to corroborate this view. Moreover, the repeated individual attempts made by various members of the Commission, apparently under its Chairman's prodding or assent, but never reported beforehand at the Commission's meetings and only reluctantly confirmed after the fact, is evidence enough that what was happening behind the scenes was more important than outward appearances. The assumption must have been that any attempt at mediation behind the scenes, which pleased the Chairman who acted on orders from his Minister, would be at any rate rubber stamped by the Commission.

(Israeli 2002: 116–17)

Notwithstanding the alliance between the government and the Islamic movement, which he disapproved of in the strongest terms possible, he was no fan of the local municipality either and of the 'radicalising' nationalist position he considered it to espouse. Given the paralysis of the municipality, the state would, to his mind, have been entirely within its rights to have dissolved it and appoint central control over it instead. Unlike Jaraisy, who identified a measure of Jewish anti-Christian religious feeling in determining state policy, Israeli blames the state's proximity to the Islamic movement, arising from electoral opportunism, as well as the (mis-guided) political choices made by Christians themselves, as indirectly sidelining local Christians and their particular issues within the priorities of the state. In all, he identifies state policy as a 'mixed bag'. He was adamant that the state was concerned with providing a peaceful resolution to the conflict, which he sees as an essentially religious conflict between Muslims and Christians but that, due to electoral politics on the one hand and the hostile attitude of the minority towards it on the other, the state is caught in a 'no-win' situation resulting in their ultimate 'hands-off' approach to the conflict.

Because whenever, like in Nazareth, when Israel interferes or tries to estab-lish some order between the two camps, because they were attacking each other and so on, and the Israeli Home Office needs the municipality to func-tion, they need to bring services to 60,000 people and so on. So, both Chris-tians and Muslims accused Israel. It's Israel that's causing the rift, causing the rift between the two, and so on, and therefore the Israeli police say whatever we do will be damned and, therefore, let them settle their problems, unless it gets into open conflict or criminal acts and so on and the authorities have no choice but to intervene. But usually they prefer not to intervene as far as possible.

This view of stand-off government policy is confirmed by other respondents. One Israeli Jewish academic described it in the following terms:

When problems come up such as the great feud over the mosque in Nazareth, the government is ambivalent. On the one hand, they would like to appease Muslims. They don't want to fight Islam. On the other hand, they would like to protect the Christians who are the weaker party and the party in the right apparently in that particular case. And they just try to navigate through the crashing waves with no great degree of success.

According to this view, no particular or affirmative state policy towards Palestinian Christians is identified and while the government is described as wanting to protect this community it is understood to be preoccupied with the more numerous Muslim segment of the Palestinian Arab minority primarily for electoral purposes. Notwithstanding this, it is suggested that Palestinian Christians are already well equipped, in socio-economic terms, to withstand government discrimination towards the Palestinian Arab minority but this factor, ironically, serves only to compound, not reduce, the indifferent attitude of the state.

By contrast, the Greek Catholic Bishop Elias Chacour considered state attitudes towards the conflict in Nazareth to have been essentially an extension of the state's more traditional divide and rule policy. Having no objection to the construction of mosques anywhere else in Nazareth, he considered the decision to build a mosque directly adjacent to the Basilica to be a deliberately provocative gesture which would never have gotten off the ground, particularly given the widespread condemnation of it by important Arab and Muslim leaders, were it not for the intercession and support provided to the Islamic movement by the Israeli authorities.

The only one who wanted the mosque, apparently, was a Jewish minister with the Jewish authorities with a few Muslims. And the aim was not the mosque. Israel is not missionarising [sic] for Mohammed. The aim was to divide the Christians from Muslims in Nazareth. And they succeeded greatly in doing that. (. . .) But it left a trauma, a wound in the heart of both the Muslims and the Christians.

Similar to the views expressed by Zeidane, the attitude of the authorities to the Jewish terrorist attack of March 2006 is singled out by him for criticism.

And God arranged that some weeks later that famous Jewish family brought these fireworks and exploded them in the church and everybody thought the church would be destroyed, [which] brought thousands and thousands of

Muslims with their top leaders to join into the church, more than the Christians did. Why? Because they wanted to protect the church of Mary, the Mother of Jesus, *Maryam, bint 'Aman.* We found ourselves there hugging each other and forgetting all the misunderstanding. That evening, Mr. Olmert called me on the telephone. I was just two weeks Bishop. He said, Bishop Chacour, we are sorry that what happened in Nazareth happened. You know that it does not represent the Jews. It must he handicapped persons, surely, and we are not with them. We reject all that. But also we want to encourage you to see clearly, these Muslims who came and gathered around the Church, they don't like you. They come flattering you to win your votes for the election. Please, don't fall in the trap. I said, Mr. Olmert, we have been dreaming to see the Muslims come with us in the church, around the church, to show solidarity. Not to show flattery, but solidarity. And I want you to be sure that your place as a Jew is very well respected. If you come, instead of me hugging you, we would be hugging you, me and the Muslim sheikh.

Another Palestinian respondent, this time from the academic segment, considered the state to be interested, for its own purposes, in creating or promoting divisions between different segments of the Palestinian minority. However, in his analysis of the factors which can be said to determine the state's response to intra-communal conflict in Nazareth as well as in other localities, the role of internal electoral politics and Israeli foreign policy considerations are also attributed equal weight to Israeli state attitudes and interests. Ultimately, the final resolution to the Nazareth 2000 dispute was one which reflected the wishes of the international community, not necessarily the wishes of the Israeli establishment. Within this, the preferences of local Christians as well as of the majority of Muslims in Nazareth are considered to be quite irrelevant to the overall decision-making process of the government.

This is reiterated to some extent by one Palestinian NGO Director. While recognising the conflict in Nazareth to be one between three main players – the Israeli government, the Nazareth municipality and the Islamic movement – this respondent stressed the hierarchical relationship which exists between each of these three different and unequal parties to the conflict and which reflects the broader picture of socioeconomic inequality and discrimination in Israel.

You know, in Nazareth the fight was not over the Shihab ad-Din. It was over the institutions: schools, local councils, etc. Shihab ad-Din, this half *dunam* [one *dunam* = a quarter of an acre], was abused because Upper Nazareth was taking everything around them, so suddenly what do you have? You have a stupid fight over the margin. The struggle on the margin is very tough, and the elites, the leadership of any community has to be aware of the fact that marginalised communities can be very tough in fighting over the margin instead of fighting and getting people to fight over the centre. Instead of fighting for our rights from the government and to distribute the resources of the state in a fair way, we have elites in our community that are concentrated in fighting each other on the margin of the margin. So, you find it in every Arab village and city . . . Suddenly you have Christians against Muslims, [saying] that we want a Christian mayor. Why is a Christian mayor better than a Muslim mayor? I don't know. I'm not sure that a Christian mayor is better. (. . .) So the fact that he's a Christian mayor and he is educated didn't help Nazareth. It didn't help Nazareth to improve the situation of the city because the Arab community took the decision that they want to develop Nazareth, so the state doesn't want to develop Nazareth. So they encourage and develop and feed Umm al-Fahim, and you have parallel local forces in Umm al-Fahim, Islamic movement, that want to develop Umm al-Fahim.

For this respondent, therefore, the mosque dispute is symptomatic of the widespread underdevelopment and marginalisation both of Nazareth and the Palestinian Arab minority as a whole. Within this, the Islamic movement as well as elitist elements within the Christian community, which both sought to capitalise from the divisive framework of government-promoted sectarian identities, are both guilty of losing sight of the bigger problem of state discrimination. In fact, this respondent suggested that, on a purely pragmatic level, a Christian-led municipality may have, given the nature of the state and the religious appeal of the Nazareth 2000 initiative, worked more to the socio-economic disadvantage of Nazareth as a whole than a Muslim-led municipality.

Conclusion

The Nazareth 2000 affair, and the role of four successive governments (under Rabin, Netanyahu, Barak and Sharon) in responding to it, allows a number of observations to be made on the nature of Israeli state attitudes towards Palestinian Christians in Israel. While external foreign policy considerations may have moderated, or even determined, the final outcome of the conflict, it can nevertheless be concluded that, internally at least, the state did not pursue any particular, affirmative or multicultural policy towards local Palestinian Christians in Israel. This assessment is due to the significance of several other factors in the determination of state attitudes towards Palestinian Christians.

The electoral significance of the demographically stronger Muslim population and the desire of successive Israeli governments to appeal to or, at the very least, not to alienate that electoral base, resulted in a higher level of political indifference shown by the state towards Palestinian Christians and their local interests than that shown towards Palestinian Muslims. However, it must be noted that the conflict in Nazareth, and particularly the role of Israeli electoral politics in contributing to and developing that conflict, coincided with the short-lived period of separate direct elections for the position of Prime Minister which was abandoned after 2001, thus diminishing the relevance of the Arab vote to mainstream Israeli Jewish parties.

Another factor which motivated state attitudes towards the conflict in Nazareth was Jewish religious antipathy towards Christianity as manifested in opposition to the symbolic nature of the Nazareth 2000 celebrations. While this factor has been observed by the respondents to have grown in line with the increase in the number of ultra-orthodox and other Jewish religious parties in Israel, its role during the conflict in Nazareth was particularly strong during the government of Netanyahu. This factor, when combined with Israeli electoral politics, indicates a particular form of discrimination against Palestinian Christians in Israel which, in turn, increases the level of isolation and neglect experienced by them.

Finally, the historically active role of Christians in Palestinian Arab national politics both in Nazareth and on the broader national level also contributed to the marginalisation of this community from the central priorities of the state during this conflict. The important political leadership role of the DFPE-led Nazareth municipality has been a continuous source of annoyance and even of threat to the Israeli authorities. That this municipality is led by a Christian-born mayor did nothing to dispel this negative association or to moderate the government's support of and alliance with the local Islamic movement. In fact, it can be convincingly argued that the opposite is true, particularly given the political salience of the Christian community's external network of powerful contacts and of growing anti-Christian religious antipathy within government circles.

To conclude, Israeli state attitudes towards the dispute in Nazareth and, by extension, towards both the Palestinian Arab minority as a whole and Palestinian Christians in particular can be described as being highly opportunistic and indifferent. It consisted of different approaches which were, in turn, highly interventionist (on behalf of the local Islamic movement) and 'hands off' (with regards to local Palestinian Christians). At no point were the aims and wishes of local Palestinian Christians, or even the majority of Palestinian Muslims, taken into account by the state, and while the Islamic movement was initially singled out for support by the government, this support was ultimately a poisoned chalice which left both communities (Muslim and Christian) disadvantaged and marginalised.

7   Military service and village conflict

This chapter investigates another aspect of intra-communal conflict involving Palestinian Christians in Israel which was frequently identified by the 36 respondents who were interviewed for this study as typifying or demonstrating current state attitudes towards them. Unlike the conflict in Nazareth which took place between the local municipality and the Islamic movement, and has often been described as a Muslim–Christian conflict, the conflicts which are under discussion in this chapter have taken place in Arab mixed villages in the north of Israel (but in one instance in an Arab mixed city) between Druze and Christians. As such, this chapter broadens its analysis in order to measure the impact of intra-communal conflict between two non-Muslim segments of the minority upon state attitudes. In addition to the typical factors associated with inter-communal conflict in the previous chapter – most notably the political engagement and electoral strategies of various segments of the minority and the state itself in line with demographic, religious and socio-economic differences – one new factor which this chapter will consider is the role of military service both as a cause of, and response to, Druze–Christian inter-communal conflict in Israel.

In order to assess the particular relevance of military service to state attitudes and inter-communal conflict, this chapter provides a brief introduction of the goals and ethos of the Israeli Defence Forces (IDF) together with a discussion of the consequences of the legal exemption of Muslims and Christians (but not of the Druze) from compulsory military service in Israel. This approach, which outlines a number of important structural limitations to state attitudes towards the Palestinian Arab minority, is followed by an overview of Palestinian Arab voluntary service within the IDF both in terms of numbers and factors which can be said to influence or encourage their enlistment. On this basis, this chapter will then address a number of Druze–Christian conflicts – the majority of which have occurred over the past decade – and address the significance which military service has played in each case. In particular, differential state attitudes towards its Druze and Palestinian Christian populations as symbolised by each community's respective inclusion and exclusion within the framework of compulsory military service are discussed. Also discussed is the state's observed differential response to the conflicts and the significance of this response to this study's analysis of state attitudes towards Palestinian Christians in general.

Palestinians in the IDF

More than any other institution in Israel, the IDF (or Tzahal as it is known for short in Hebrew) plays a central role both in Israeli state- and nation-building efforts. It remains the main symbol of national unity as well as a badge of honour, identity and belonging for the vast majority of those who serve in it. Described as Israel's melting-pot, the army has critically functioned as an important and indispensable socialisation device, particularly with regard to the integration and assimilation of Jewish immigrants (*olim*) into society. In addition to its nation-building role, military service has also been referred to as 'the great equaliser' of Israeli society, as it is understood to represent an equal platform through which social differences and cleavages can be overcome through the performance of military service alone (Gal 1986; Cohen 1995; Peled A. 1998 and Lomsky-Feder and Ben-Ari 1999).

In their investigation of *The Military and Militarism in Israeli Society*, Edna Lomsky-Feder and Eyal Ben-Ari have observed the centrality and dominance of all 'things military' in the social and political fabric of Israeli society. They have, however, also pointed to the problematic status of Arabs in Israel as having been compounded rather than alleviated by the ethnic and political salience of military service. In as much as the Israeli army is a central location in the social construction of Jewish national identity, it has also been directly involved in the social construction of the Arab as its permanent 'other' (Lomsky-Feder and Ben-Ari 1999: 1). In other words, the 'othering' of Palestinian Arabs is not only found within Zionist discourse, but is also a central and persistent feature of military service and military discourse.

By creating new avenues of social mobility and integration for its Jewish majority population, military service has simultaneously become the 'great divider' of Israeli society along national lines. The inclusive framework of military service which was established not only for the protection and the security of the state, but also for the production of a new, homogenised Jewish nation-state, has become an exclusive and differentiating framework underlining the non-compatibility of Palestinian Arabs within it. In discussing Ben-Gurion's 'nation-building vision of the new military', Alon Peled identifies the Palestinian Arab citizens of the new Jewish state as remaining 'outside the boundaries of this military melting pot' (Peled, A. 1998: 130). As a result, military service which engenders a sense of pride and belonging amongst the majority of Israeli Jews has, for the Palestinian Arab minority, become a badge of difference, suspicion and exclusion. This point is developed by Rhoda Kanaaneh who investigated the role and motivations of Palestinian Arabs who serve in the IDF. Acknowledging the twin melting pot and nation-building roles of military service, Kanaaneh observes that these roles are exclusively to the benefit of, and in the service of, the Jewish community and to the direct detriment of the Palestinian minority which retains 'the embodiment of Arabs as a source of insecurity' in the Israeli Jewish mindset (Kanaaneh 2009: 7).

It is within this context that Palestinian Arabs have, with the exception of the Druze, been legally exempted from military service since 1954. This decision was taken by the Ministry of Defence, which was then under the sole jurisdiction of one of Israel's founding fathers and former Prime Ministers, David Ben-Gurion (Ghanem 1998: 433). While some suggest that this exemption was requested by the local Palestinian Arab leadership as a temporary measure 'until the problem of Arab refugees was settled', it is generally accepted that the state's decision was at the very least based upon the mutual suspicion of the authorities, on the one hand, who saw in Arab military service 'the Trojan horse dilemma', and of the local Arab leadership, on the other hand, whose 'overwhelming suspicion and distrust of the state's real intentions' undermined any initiatives to recruit Palestinian Arab citizens into military service (Peled, A. 1998: 131–6).

One account which has explained the exemption of Palestinian Muslims and Christians from mandatory conscription as an unfortunate but necessary require-ment brought about by the so-called 'security risk' posed by Palestinian Arab citi-zens, on the one hand, and by the state's desire to 'spare' Palestinian citizens the difficult dilemma of being forced to choose between their Palestinian and Israeli identities, on the other, is that provided by Reuven Gal, former chief psychologist of the IDF and later Director of the Authority for National Civic Service in Israel (Gal 1986: 32). Similarly, S.N. Eisenstadt has observed that military exemption of Palestinian Muslims and Christians was an 'institutional innovation' which was created by the state in order to 'avoid a situation of conflicting loyalties, as well as not to endanger the security of the Israeli Army' (Eisenstadt 1967b: 395–6).

This view is somewhat challenged by Peled who suggests that the state was not solely interested in encouraging the compulsory conscription of the Druze com-munity. Mentioning the ultimately futile attempts of various government officials to 'test the waters' with local church leaders in the mid-1950s, he recognises a broader attempt by the authorities to encourage the leaders of smaller communi-ties within the Palestinian Arab minority (but never those of the larger Muslim community) to consider the possibility of mandatory conscription for Palestinian Christians in Israel.

> There were also rumours that in 1955 Israel approached [the Greek Catholic] Archbishop Hakim in Beirut, requesting his support for the conscription of young Christian Arabs, and that Archbishop Hakim consulted the pope and declined the offer.
>
> (Peled, A. 1998: 137)

These attempts to foster the communal conscription of Palestinian Christians in Israel were short-lived and ultimately abandoned not only because of the lack of receptivity from within the Christian community but, more importantly, because of the state's inability to control or overcome the complicated and fragmented nature of Palestinian Christian religious communal leadership in Israel.

The inability of the state to co-opt Christian communal leaders has resulted in the tendency of pro-establishment analyses to explain the exemption of Palestinian Muslims and Christians from military service on the same basis of a potential security threat. This does not, however, adequately explain the phenomenon of

Palestinian voluntary conscription into the IDF and the reaction of the authorities to those Muslims and Christians who have sought to be included within it. This phenomenon is particularly remarkable given that, until the late 1980s at least, the voluntary enlistment of Palestinian Muslims and Christians was severely restricted by the state due to its persistent distrust of the Palestinian Arab minority and its desire to maintain the Jewish national character of military service. A number of obstacles were placed in the path of any aspiring Arab recruit.

> Formally, Muslim and Christian Arab citizens had the option of volunteering for military service. But the conditions for the acceptance of such volunteers were difficult to satisfy. To gain approval, Arab volunteers had to command the Hebrew language, complete at least ten years of schooling, have paternal approval, and be twenty-two years of age or less. They were also required to serve in field units because the IDF had enough conscripts and regulars staffing its headquarters. (. . .) Finally, Arab volunteers needed strong Jewish recommendations to support their applications. Needless to say, none of these requirements were ever applied to Jewish conscripts.
>
> (Peled, A. 1998: 138)

A number of these restrictions still apply. For example, it is still a requirement that voluntary Palestinian recruits must provide two formal recommendations in order to serve in the IDF. These recommendations, however, must come either from individuals already connected with the military establishment or from communal leaders with whom the authorities have close relations, thus illustrating the continued importance of state control and patronage and the impact that this policy has on creating or re-creating patrimonial relations within Palestinian Arab society (Kanaaneh 2009: 45–6). Furthermore, all potential Palestinian volunteers are subjected to rigorous 'security' checks which often involve assessments of the political suitability of both the individual recruit and his wider family. Kanaaneh describes the experience of one Palestinian Christian volunteer in this regard.

> One Christian man I interviewed was asked to identify himself and his family members in photographs of legal and peaceful political demonstrations before being turned down by the military as 'incompatible'. The very definition of compatibility with the military carries ethnic significance.
>
> (Kanaaneh 2009: 64)

Given these obstacles, the number of Muslim or Christian recruits during the first forty years of the state 'was close to nil' with estimates suggesting that as little as only four or five Muslims and Christians were successfully registered for service each year from 1978 to 1983 (Peled, A. 1998: 139). Ascertaining the number of Palestinians currently serving in the IDF today is more difficult. While the Israeli military authorities do not disclose the exact number or religious breakdown of Palestinian Arab volunteers, partial figures do exist.

Illustrating the close relationship between print media and the political establishment in Israel, selective figures concerning minority presence in the army have been sporadically leaked to the Israeli press over the years, shedding some light on the matter. One article published by Haaretz in 2004, for example, stated that the combined number of Muslim and Christian recruits to the IDF did not exceed 150 individuals in any given year (Harel 2004). The International Institute for Strategic Studies (IISS) estimated that the total number of Israeli conscripts in 2009 was 109,500. It can, thus, be deduced that the 150 Palestinian conscripts remain a statistically negligible proportion (less than 0.2 per cent) of the total number of Israeli conscripts (IISS 2009: 249–51). Another Haaretz article from 2005 stated that '[i]n 2002 and 2003, the Christians were 0.1 percent of all the conscripts', suggesting that, if this data can be relied upon and continues to be true, approximately half of all Muslim and Christian recruits in Israel, amounting to no more than 85 individuals, were Palestinian Christian (Stern 2005). As Palestinian Christians represent less than 10 per cent of the minority, it has therefore been possible to argue that Palestinian Christians are statistically overrepresented in the IDF, a fact which belies the small size of Palestinian and Christian recruits in absolute numbers.

The improbable and contradictory phenomenon of Palestinian voluntary military service in the IDF is usually explained with reference to structural considerations of the nature of the state and the negative impact of their formal exclusion from mandatory military service upon their general status and opportunities in society. In identifying the necessity of their exemption from within a national-security perspective, for example, Eisenstadt identifies the obvious practical drawbacks of this policy upon the Palestinian Arab minority.

> While this might have been seen as a release from an onerous duty, it was also an exclusion from a sphere which epitomised the essence of Israeli citizenship and identity and it therefore emphasised the ambivalent relations between the Arabs and the state. Wider repercussions of this involved the availability of occupational opportunities, as suspicion and a reluctance to employ Arab labour developed in legitimate security areas as well as those not directly affected. As this widespread attitude was not fully articulated, it was also not easy to overcome.
>
> (Eisenstadt 1967b: 395–6)

In another study investigating the role of the Druze in the Israeli military, Hillel Frisch has observed this same connection between military service and the extension of the full rights and benefits of citizenship which he argues has been clearly understood and accepted not only by the state but by the majority of the Israeli (Jewish) public as well.

> Paradoxically, the Jewish Israeli majority accept to a far greater extent the exemption of Muslim and Christian Arabs from the army [than ultra-orthodox Jews]. First, security considerations justify it. Second, the Arab sector

receives small per capita allocations from the public purse. The bulk of Israeli society justifies this biased allocation by the fact that the Arabs do not bear the military burden. Arabs feel that burden is not theirs to begin with and demand allocations on an equal basis due to common citizenship.

(Frisch 1993: 59–60)

While both of these analyses acknowledge the clear correlation between state discrimination against Palestinian Arabs and the non-performance of military service, a more detailed elaboration of the practical implications of this attitude is missing. Ian Lustick overcomes this in his analysis of the structural impact of Israel's military-defined 'social-evaluative system' upon the Palestinian Arab minority which equates both social worth and equal rights with military service.

The fact that the army is not an integrated Jewish-Arab institution is of enormous significance for Arab citizens. The position of veteran status is a prerequisite to a wide variety of jobs and public assistance programs. The personal associations, as well as the rank and service records, a soldier establishes in the course of regular service and reserve duty are among the most important elements in the determination of a future career in Israeli society – the officer corps being, perhaps, the primary conduit for administrative and managerial personnel in all branches of Israeli industry, commerce and government.

(Lustick 1980: 94)

On an individual level, military service can affect not only a person's ability to advance in society but their basic employability in a range of sectors. Careers which are understood to relate in any way to Israel's defence, national priorities or security industries such as engineering and even computer science are subject to the same military preconditions (Kanaaneh 2009: 40, 43). The decision to dismiss 150 Palestinian Arab employees of the Israeli state-owned railway company (Israeli Railways) on the grounds that they did not perform military service and could, therefore, not be trusted with the 'security'-related duties of their jobs, represents a more recent case of this form of discrimination (Cook 2009a).

On a collective level, military service has also been used by the state to determine the distribution of various subsidies and welfare allocations. One area in particular in which the criterion of military service has been used to discriminate against Palestinian Arabs is education. In 1987, for example, the government attempted to condition the award of tuition subsidies upon the performance of military service, directly targeting the educational aims and aspirations of Palestinian Arab youth. However, following public outcry from both Palestinian Arabs and their Jewish supporters, this initiative was soon thereafter dropped (Rouhana 1997: 263 n. 16). Similarly, the Ministry of Education has set the minimum enrolment age for many university degree programmes at 20 or 21 on the grounds that this is the age when conscripts typically finish their military service (Kanaaneh 2009: 41). However, given that this policy has not been applied universally to all university subjects, but to those which are the most competitively sought after, such as medicine, pharmacy, social work, physiotherapy and speech therapy, many young Palestinians are either obliged to sacrifice further education or, if they can, pursue their studies abroad (Cook 2009b). Palestinian Israeli NGO Adalah has also filed several complaints against Haifa University both for making enrolment into certain courses contingent upon military service and for using this same criterion to discriminate against Arab students in the allocation of student dorms (Adalah 2006 and 2008).

Military service has also been used as a precondition in the award of numerous social welfare and other material benefits. In order to avail of these benefits, applicants are expected to produce certificates of release from the Israeli army.

> The status of "released" qualifies the individual and his family for a wide range of financial assistance in the areas of education, professional training, housing, and starting a business, as well as exemption from or reduction in municipal property taxes, credit points on income tax calculations, free driving courses and so on.
>
> (Kanaaneh 2009: 39)

Critically, 'released' soldiers are given the unique opportunity to lease land from the state at preferential rates, representing an obvious incentive to land-deprived Palestinian Arabs with no other way of securing a plot upon which to build a home for themselves and their families (Kanaaneh 2009: 36, 41–2). The contingency of this and other subsidies upon the performance of military service reflects not only the suspicious and rejectionist mentality of the state but their fear of the so-called 'demographic threat' posed by Palestinian Arabs to the future Jewish majority status of the state.

> According to regulations that don't explicitly use the term Jewish or Arab, Jewish families with children were awarded larger financial allowances per child than Arab families. Formulating an explicit policy of supporting a higher Jewish birth rate would have contradicted values of equality inherent in the state's second guidelines of democracy; however, the tension between these two principles came to be obscured (though not resolved) by using military service as the qualifying factor for receiving the higher subsidy. Since few Arabs serve in the army, this criterion functionally channelled the larger funds to Jews without explicitly stating so. But with increased awareness that the criterion was manipulated to include as many Jews as possible regardless of their actual military service – yeshiva students, for example – and as few Arabs as possible, and with the increasing pressure from the Arab community and their Jewish supporters on this issue, the Knesset revoked differential subsidies as of 1997.
>
> (Rouhana 1997: 83)

Despite the formal revocation of differential subsidies based on military service, the Knesset passed new legislation in 2002 legally condoning reductions in economic subsidies payable to families not covered by the criterion of 'entitling service' which refers to financial entitlements based on the performance of military service by a family member. As such, 'the law is a thinly disguised means to deny Arab families the benefits available to virtually all Jewish families' (Rouhana and Sultany 2003: 12).

It is within this context that the obvious economic incentives of military service to individual members of the Palestinian Arab minority become apparent. Volunteering is rarely understood to be motivated by ideological commitments. Instead, the phenomenon is generally understood to reflect a pragmatic strategy of self-advancement by a small number of deprived individuals who have recognised the structural limitations imposed upon them by the state and who seek to bypass the worst aspects of state discrimination through the performance of military service. In response to growing criticism of the discrimination faced by Palestinian Arabs in this regard, the state has launched a national civic service initiative whereby a non-military alternative to national service has been provided. However, this scheme has been identified by a number of groups within the Palestinian minority as the government's cynical attempt to neutralise the legitimate and democratic demand that Israel relinquish its discriminatory policies towards the Palestinian Arab minority. In the Committee set up by the Minister of Defence in 2004 the government's intentions with the national service scheme were outlined.

> The committee argued that Arab citizens would thereby gain similar benefits to those received by individuals who serve in the military. Thus, the committee explicitly linked Arab citizens' entitlement to equal rights with an obligation to perform national service. The committee also made a connection between national and military service.
>
> (Adalah 2007b)

This deliberate coupling of military service with civic service is, for some, indicative of the continued conditionality of Arab equality in Israel upon the prerequisite that Palestinian Arab citizens perform some form of national service (Baladna 2008). By providing an alternative avenue for military service, civic service reduces the financial pressure on Palestinian Arabs to perform military service. However, given the relative socio-economic advantage of Palestinian Christians and their higher concentration in the areas of education and professional careers, economic need does not adequately explain the voluntary enlistment of Palestinian Christians. As such, other factors motivating their enlistment must be considered.

One factor which explains Palestinian Christian voluntary conscription is connected to the historical experience of the Druze in the IDF. All Palestinian Arab recruits to the Israeli army were originally concentrated by the state within the military's 'Minorities Unit' which was first created during the Israeli War of Independence. Receiving official status as a regular military unit only in 1954, the history of the Minorities Unit has been dominated by the Druze and is, in fact, closely connected with the evolution of Druze political identity in Israel. Kanaaneh has, for instance, indicated that it is no coincidence that the Unit received formal recognition just two years before the Druze themselves became liable for mandatory military conscription in 1956. In fact, she suggests that their formal conscription not only predated but was contingent upon their subsequent recognition as a separate religious minority in 1957 (Kanaaneh 2009: 11).

In any case, the concentration of Druze soldiers within the Minorities Unit predates the 1956 decision to make military service for Druze compulsory in Israel. However, given the much smaller number of other Arab recruits over time, this legal provision has maintained the Druze character not only of this unit but of Arab military service with the result that in 2008 alone it was estimated that approximately 850 of all 1,000 Arab recruits in Israel were Druze (Ronen 2009). The Minorities Unit remained an essentially segregated battalion within the IDF until 1972 when minority volunteers were first given the opportunity of serving in other mainstream military units, but on a limited basis only (Peled, A. 1998: 161). Even with the disappearance of the Minorities Unit, the majority of Arab soldiers today still serve in separate units associated with different segments of the minority, such as: the Druze unit known as the Sword Battalion; the Bedouin Desert Reconnaissance Battalion; and the Bedouin Trackers Unit (Kanaaneh 2009: 52).

The traditional segregation of Arab recruits within the IDF not only marginalised the role of Arab recruits but of the units in which they served. Although allowed to participate in its War of Independence, the Minorities Unit was 'denied participation in the battles of the 1956 and 1967 wars' due to the persistence of security fears and suspicions of disloyalty by the establishment (Peled, A. 1998: 158–9). This suggests that despite the performance of military service and the fulfilment of this ultimate 'test of loyalty', minority recruits remained marginalised and suspected by the state. Despite growing incorporation of the Minorities Unit within mainstream military operations, the military duties of Palestinian Arab recruits remain today largely confined to more perilous and unpopular border-guard and patrol duties, as typified by the Druze Reconnaissance Unit and the Bedouin Trackers' Unit.

This marginalisation of minority recruits, and the inability of their military service to create the anticipated improvement of their socio-economic status in society, has contributed to growing feelings of frustration and resentment within certain segments of the minority. Criticising the empty rhetoric of the state which conditions equal rights upon military service, one report discusses the continued deprivation of Druze and Bedouin communities in Israel.

> Under Israeli law, the whole population must complete military service. The Minister of Defence does have limited power to excuse certain members of society from serving – namely Orthodox Jews and the majority of the Palestinian community. However, in the case of the Palestinians, this is used to justify their unequal status in society. In truth, there are now more and more Jewish Israelis who are dodging enlistment, and yet, like the Orthodox Jews, they still receive all of their rights. The Israeli Defence Forces' statistics of 2007 show that 25% of draft-age men obligated to complete military service do not enlist (Haaretz), and the number of women thought to be eluding service is thought to be even higher. On the contrary, many Druze Israelis have

the same military obligations as secular Jews, and there is a long-standing policy of persuading those from impoverished Bedouin communities to enrol for military service. Despite serving in the IDF as they are supposed to, it is widely accepted that both of these groups remain two of the poorest and most neglected areas of Israeli society, and live without their individual and collective rights. The dire conditions within the 37 unrecognised Bedouin villages warrant special emphasis, as despite paying taxes to the government and completing military service, 80,000 people in these Bedouin communities are without running water and electricity.

(Baladna 2008: 1)

The lack of positive returns for military service is particularly evident within the Druze community not only because of their exemplary military service record but also because of the 'ethnicisation' of both their identity and their military duty by the state. Over 40 per cent of the total Druze male labour force is today dependent upon the army for jobs (Firro 2001: 42). That the military has become a 'niche' market for Druze is a consequence of both their mandatory conscription and the parallel destruction of the Druze agricultural economy by the state (Hajjar 2000: 304). By 1962, the Druze had already lost more than two thirds of their lands, and by the late 1990s, less than 1 per cent of this traditionally rural community was able to support itself through agriculture (Firro 2001: 48).

Poverty, the lack of further education and the hierarchical nature of the Druze communal leadership structure further restricted the occupational avenues open to the Druze and increased their dependency upon the military. The official rhetoric of state favouritism made little material difference to the Druze. The impact which it did have, however, was that it increased both the sense of Druze entitlement based on their military service and their resentment of other segments of the minority which were exempt from military service.

These policies of separating and distinguishing Druze from other Arabs have been resoundingly effective overall. Although Druze and Arabs are discriminated against in comparable ways as non-Jews in a Jewish state, because the state *rhetorically* favours the Druze, they have been presented with a strategic incentive to maintain and even to use the sectarian divisions by lobbying for equality with Jews. This is the ideal they have been led to believe that they deserve because of their service to the state, rather than aligning themselves with Arabs to work for universal equality for all citizens. The importance of military service to reinforcing the separation cannot be overstated: Druze are 'different' from Arabs (more 'Israeli') because they serve; discriminatory policies like land confiscation and insufficient investment in Druze villages are unjust because they serve, and so on.

(Hajjar 2000: 307)

These feelings of frustration, however, are not of recent origin. Peled suggests that despite being 'natural allies' of the Jewish state and having an impeccable service record within the IDF, Druze units have not received 'the same level of professional military support' from their higher command that other Jewish units have, often suffering far higher casualty rates as a result. Similarly, military service did not protect the Druze from government programmes of land seizures and expropriations. Referring to 'greedy state institutions interested in confiscating the assets of their communities' in the 1950s, Peled refers to attempts made by individual Jewish officers at the time to compensate affected Druze soldiers by providing their villages with 'food supplies, weapons licenses, and travel passes' (Peled, A. 1998: 146).

This form of side-payment, particularly through the provision of additional weapons' licences to the villages of serving Druze soldiers during the 1950s, is also mentioned by Kanaaneh. However, for her, this was not a compensatory gesture but rather a deliberate scheme by the government to provide incentives to Druze to support the idea of mandatory military service which was at the time being actively pursued by the authorities (Kanaaneh 2009: 11 137 n. 11). As it is illogical that the state would provide weapons' licences to the Druze in order to help them defend themselves against government expropriations of their land, the question arises why weapons' licences represented such an attractive incentive to the Druze.

Kanaaneh believes that the explanation lies in the tradition of military authorities to interfere with and stoke tensions between different segments of the Palestinian Arab minority, both inside the military and in society as a whole. In particular, she observes the segregation of Arab recruits along communal lines and the different military functions given to separate communities – particularly the segregation of Druze and Bedouin recruits in separate border patrol and tracking duties – as part of the state's wider divide-and-rule policy (Kanaaneh 2009: 52–4). The manipulation of intra-communal tensions by the military establishment is, however, not restricted to the separate designation of military duties alone. Kanaaneh also observes the state's deliberate attempts to exploit communal divisions within the minority as a whole for the sake of military recruitment purposes. One area of concern which she mentions is the manipulation of inter-clan rivalries by the IDF. However, a more explosive area is the manipulation and exploitation of sectarian differences and religious tensions within the minority, within which 'conflicts between Christians and Muslims are used as opportunities to recruit Christians into the military' (Kanaaneh 2009: 14).

> Beyond the ethnic labelling of units, recruitment centres, and benefits, authorities take advantage of disputes in Arab communities at a more ad-hoc level, encouraging parties to the conflict to enlist in the military in order to gain access to weapons and state protection. After the Shihab ad-Din conflict in Nazareth between Muslims and Christians, especially the violence that erupted in 1999, many Christians were encouraged to enlist with the argument that the state is the only entity able to protect them from their Muslim neighbours.
>
> (Kanaaneh 2009: 57–8)

While avoiding any discussion of the role of Druze–Christian tensions on recruitment efforts, the situation in Nazareth illustrates that intra-communal conflict is not only of interest to the political establishment in terms of the electoral significance the Arab vote, but is also of interest to the military establishment in terms of its wider recruitment potential. One central component of the state's recruitment drive within the minority is, according to Kanaaneh, their exploitation of the conservative and patriarchal nature of Palestinian Arab identity, particularly with regard to concepts of family honour and masculinity. As 'Palestinian masculinity centres on the ability to provide for and protect home and family', this strategy of equating military service both with concepts of masculinity is understood to have found resonance with segments of disenfranchised and conservative male youth (Kanaaneh 2009: 80). It is also understood to have affected the manner in which the state 'markets' military service within the Palestinian Arab sector, particularly in its use of local Arab officers to entice new recruits.

> Palestinian soldiers are accused of 'seducing' other young men into soldiering, under direction from Israeli authorities, by showing them their guns. Soldiers are supposedly instructed to intervene in local conflicts – family feuds, wage disputes, and religious tensions – by suggesting to young men involved in the conflicts that getting a gun (by joining the military) will resolve such problems with ease.
>
> (Kanaaneh 2009: 81)

As such, gaining access to a gun is, in many instances, understood to be a pivotal factor motivating Palestinian Arabs to volunteer for military service. While the lure of having a gun may, as Kanaaneh suggests, be linked with either a skewed sense of male pride or the need to overcome feelings of social disenfranchisement, it may also be motivated by rational feelings of personal or communal insecurity and vulnerability and the individual's desire to defend and protect his family, property or community in instances of intra-communal conflict.

> When one party to a conflict has soldiers among its members and thus access to weapons, this puts pressure on the opposing party to have members volunteer for the military so that it too can acquire guns.
> (Kanaaneh 2009: 58)

While the role of intra-communal conflict on voluntary conscription is often overlooked, it represents a critical dimension of this study's analysis of what motivates Palestinian Christians to volunteer for military service.

Four village conflicts

This section looks at four Druze–Christian conflicts which have taken place in mixed Arab villages in Israel which have either a Palestinian Christian majority (Kfar Yasif and Rameh) or a significant Palestinian Christian minority (Mughar and Abu Snan). Significantly, these four mixed Arab localities represent the only villages and towns in Israel where significant numbers of Palestinian Christians live together with Druze. Equally significant is that all of the conflicts under discussion here have taken place in relatively recent times. With the exception of the first conflict which took place in 1981, all have taken place between in a short two-year period between 2003 and 2005, suggesting a real contemporary relevance to these conflicts.

On 11 April 1981, Kfar Yasif witnessed the first major conflict between Druze and Christians in Israel (Shihade 2005: 32). Kfar Yasif is a mixed Arab village close to the city of Akko with a population of 8,700 people. The largest community in the village is Christian (55 per cent), but the village also has a large Muslim minority (40 per cent) and a smaller Druze community (5 per cent). On 11 April, a football match was taking place in the village between the local team and that of the smaller nearby Druze village of Julis. As this was an important soccer match, the local team managers requested a police force be present as a precautionary measure (Shihade 2005: 33). As predicted, fights broke out during the match between supporters of both sides and a young man from Julis was stabbed and killed (Mansour 2004: 274). Reconciliation talks were arranged between leaders from both communities, but following the unwillingness of the local council to release the name of the man suspected of the stabbing, a large crowd of several hundred armed men from Julis descended on Kfar Yasif. Fearing that a failed reconciliation would lead to even more violence, the reconciliation committee together with the head of Kfar Yasif local council contacted the regional Israeli police headquarters requesting immediate back-up. Their request was denied (Shihade 2005: 34) and, in the violence which ensued – described by Mansour as a 'pogrom' – the role of the police was singled out for criticism.

Two days later [after the stabbing], as a group of Arab leaders were negotiating a traditional peace agreement (*sulha*), a large police force was deployed in the field separating the two villages – Julis and Kafr Yaseef. Suddenly a crowd of heavily armed Druze from Julis arrived seeking revenge against the Christian village. A police force of 60 armed officers did virtually nothing to prevent the ensuing pogrom. Houses, cars, stores and workshops were torched. Three people were shot dead, others were injured. Only one police officer behaved with honour for he blocked the entrance to the high school and told the mob's ringleaders they would enter the school over his dead body.

> This slowed the massacre, but the other officers refused to act claiming they had insufficient arms to do anything and were waiting for reinforcements – which did not show up for two long hours of terror and looting. I interviewed General Hayem Avinoa'am, the north district police commander a few days later, who assured me the police knew the perpetrators and they would be brought to justice. Some 20 years have passed, yet not one of those criminals who acted in front of 60 armed police witnesses have been convicted in court.

(Mansour 2004: 274–5)

It is clear from this account that the vast majority of the Israeli police officers present shared responsibility for an attack which lasted only two hours and which killed three people, destroyed 85 homes, 17 stores, 31 cars and damaged the local church (Shihade 2005: 34). An important number of off-duty Druze military personnel also took part in the violence.

> A number of the attackers were wearing either Israeli army or border police uniforms. Arms and equipment (such as vehicles, automatic machine guns, and bombs) from the Israeli military and different security unity were used in the attack. This added to the fear of the people in Kfar Yassif who realised that the state seemed to be behind this serious attack.
>
> (Shihade 2005: 34)

Other military and police personnel who did not take a direct part in the attack nonetheless assisted the Druze attackers by blocking the entrances of both villages to outsiders while at the same time keeping the road linking Julis with Kfar Yasif open for the duration of the attack (Shihade 2005: 34–5). One of this study's respondents personally witnessed the attack and described the role of the police as follows:

> I was a witness to that. From that neighbouring Druze village of Julis a lot of people came in destroying houses and homes and eventually killing a guy who was also my friend, and I could see the police just standing and doing nothing.

However, in discussing the role of the authorities, this respondent distinguished between that of the Druze-dominated police and the Jewish authorities.

> I don't know, but it's not that they [the authorities] don't want to intervene in order to let all of this damage happen, like they like seeing the damage. It's not that. Maybe they didn't want to intervene because they don't want to take sides in this dispute. It's like a kind of a hands-off kind of a policy more than, ok, let's let them burn and kill each other, we're happy with it. That's not what I think is at issue. What is more at issue [is] that such a conflict is not perceived as a national threat in the establishment's mind. It's not like a guerrilla from Hezbollah coming from Lebanon and doing something in some northern village where you would find the whole Israeli army mobilised in one hour. When these conflicts happen, they are not perceived as a national threat or as something that threatens something, so the establishment does not really know how to handle it.

While the state is not blamed for the outbreak of violence, its indifference towards the plight of the targeted Palestinian Christian community is understood to have indirectly given a green light to the attackers to continue without fear of restraint. To worsen the situation, the authorities showed no inclination towards pursuing criminal prosecutions against those responsible or towards providing financial support to repair the damages which had been inflicted upon Christian homes and properties in the village. While an international church organisation paid for some of the damages, it was the uninvolved Muslim *waqf* which picked up the bill for the majority of the damages.

> The World Council of Churches partly compensated the damage in Kafr Yaseef, but the cost of the rituals for the traditional 'peace' was paid from the Muslims' Waqf revenue – collected to help needy Muslims, repair Muslim mosques, subsidise the maintenance of Muslim cemeteries or met similar community needs. In Israel these funds are run by Jewish officials, so the ministry of religious affairs and the prime minister's advisor on Arab affairs decided to finance peace celebration between Druze and Christian from these Muslim funds – a typical demonstration of how the Israeli 'civil servants' treat the minorities.
>
> (Mansour 2004: 275)

For another respondent who was interviewed for this study, the attack in Kfar Yasif was a clear case of anti-Christian violence which, through the actions of its security services, was indirectly condoned by the state. The attackers, after all, used Israeli army weapons in their attack against the Christian villagers, which was neither investigated nor corrected by the authorities subsequent to the attack. Citing several reasons why the Christian villagers of Kfar Yasif did not seek revenge for the attack or pursue the matter through the courts, Shihade suggests that a combination of pragmatic awareness and fear represented the main reasons.

> The village of Kafr Yassif did not seek revenge for the damage and fatalities caused by the assailants from Julis, but sought a truce with the attacking village. People I interviewed from Kafr Yassif viewed the event as a plan by the Israeli government to stir up communal fighting and divide the Palestinian Arab community along religious lines. In addition to this political analysis for not resorting to revenge, the local Palestinian Arabs understood that Arab tradition was opposed to violence because it upsets the normal, peaceful, daily life of the community. They realised that revenge leads to a cycle of violence. People from Kafr Yassif that I interviewed also said that the residents of their village did not respond in a like manner because they were afraid to do so, knowing that Julis was an armed village and the government seemed to be backing them.
>
> (Shihade 2005: 35)

The next instance of Druze–Christian confrontation occurred in Rameh, a mixed Arab village of just under 8,000 people the majority of whom (53 per cent) are Christian but which also has smaller Druze and Muslim communities (30 and 17 per cent respectively). Against the backdrop of government plans to merge the Christian-majority municipality of Rameh with two neighbouring Druze villages (Sajur and Ein al-Assad), tensions between Christian and Druze youths in the village spilled over on 22 February 2003 when an anti-tank missile was fired through the wall of the local Greek Catholic church (Ettinger 2003). While several nuns were inside the church when the missile hit, no one was seriously injured, and although the identity of the perpetrators was never uncovered, it is widely accepted that, given the sophistication of the weaponry used in the attack and the religious nature of the building targeted, individuals from the Druze community were responsible.

A similar attack against Christians involving a bomb took place two years later in Abu Snan on 18 February 2005. Abu Snan is a mixed village close to Akko where at 19 per cent of the population Christians represent the smallest of the three communities there, while Muslims and Druze account for 55 and 22 per cent of the village population respectively. While the roots of Druze-Christian tensions in the village are understood to be connected with electoral competition over the municipality, it is the military superiority of the Druze and the asymmetry of arms which allowed these tensions to spill over into open conflict.

> Similarly, in the longstanding and violent electoral conflict in Abu Snan, where military weaponry has been used, the police have been at best ineffectual. Local policemen are both party to the conflict and involved in the investigations – the authorities have not removed them from investigating the case although they are accused of some of the crimes. This impunity and that of soldiers and policemen in other incidents give Palestinians the sense that the state wants Arabs – soldiers included – to fight with each other.
>
> (Kanaaneh 2009: 59)

Despite the seriousness of the attack, next to no media coverage within the Israeli English-language broadsheets exists of the attack in Abu Snan. This suggests a broad level of indifference to the plight of Israel's Palestinian Christian population. Moreover, in instances where Druze assailants have used military weapons against civilians, the media have not commented upon the relationship between violent outbursts and the possession of IDF-supplied weapons and, by extension, on the responsibility of the Israeli authorities to ensure that military weapons are not used to harm or harass any segment of the population.

Testifying to both the nature of media coverage and the common occurrence of attacks involving military weapons by Druze, the *Jerusalem Post* reported two incidents which occurred on the same day on 6 February 1995. In one case, an IDF fragmentation grenade was thrown at a house in Rameh while the owner and his family were asleep inside. The house was badly damaged but nobody was hurt. In another incident that day, it was reported that a bomb exploded under a car parked outside a house in Abu Snan. Once again, nobody was hurt, but the car and surrounding houses were damaged. In both cases, the article downplayed the attacks and stressed that they were 'criminally motivated' incidents and nothing more. In neither case did the journalist attempt to identify the victims (or the attackers), nor did he or she find anything noteworthy in the fact that IDF weapons had been used to attack civilians in their homes (Rudge 1995).

The casual nature and common recurrence of Druze attacks against Christians as well as the general absence of media coverage was personally evidenced by the author on a visit to the mixed Arab town of Rameh. In an informal meeting with the local Greek Orthodox priest and the Druze headmaster of the local (state) school, I asked how relations between the different communities have been in the village since the bomb attack (of 2003). I was expecting that the answer would reflect the positive stress which both individuals placed on inter-communal relations within the village, but they paused and then the priest, in confusion at my question, asked 'which one?' Apparently, just one week prior to my visit to the village (in August 2008) there had been another incident in which a grenade had been thrown at a Christian house in the village. This innocent response to my question revealed not only how common such incidents have become in the village, but how unchecked they are by the authorities. A similar pattern of non-intervention by the police, non-identification of the attacker/s and non-prosecution through the courts was observed in this case, which increases the sense of vulnerability experienced by Christians as well as the impunity and disregard of the attackers who both consider themselves to be and are generally treated as though they are above the law.

Of all the violent attacks perpetrated by Druze against Christians, the one which overtook Mughar for three days between 10 and 12 February 2005 has become the most well known, with the then Minister for Internal Security, Gideon Ezra, going so far as to describe it as 'the worst sectarian riots I have ever seen in the Israeli Arab community' (Urquhart 2005). A small mixed Arab village with a population of just under 20,000 people, Christians and Muslims both separately represent 20 per cent of the village, while the Druze comprise the remaining 60 per cent of the village. Mughar is also the only locality in Israel with a significant Christian population to have a Druze majority.

Following rumours that Christian youths in the village had digitally manipulated and uploaded pornographic pictures of local Druze girls onto the internet, a group of several hundred Druze men descended upon the Christian quarter of the village on the night of Thursday 10 February and went on what was variously described in the newspapers at the time as a 'rampage' and a 'pogrom' (Sedan 2005; Mitzna 2005). Twelve people were injured, two by bullets; the local Greek Catholic church was damaged and dozens of Christian-owned businesses, homes and cars were broken into, vandalised or set alight; and over two thousand Christian villagers fled the village in fright (Kanaaneh 2009: 58).

Despite the fact that the rumour which sparked the riots turned out to be a hoax spread by a local Druze boy, analyses of the attack suggest that the incident in Mughar represented 'nothing new' in Druze–Christian relations, which have become dominated by feelings of Druze jealousy and resentment at the allegedly more privileged socio-economic position of Palestinian Christians in Israel. The non-performance of military service by the more educated and economically secure Palestinian Christian population compared with the lack of opportunities and the economic instability facing returning Druze soldiers who have forgone further education in order to serve the state which has nonetheless chosen to neglect them represents an essential aspect of these recurring conflicts. For one Druze respondent, the conflict in Mughar was first and foremost the result of the disparate contributions made, and benefits received, by each community.

> They [the Druze] asked to be under all of the duties that Israel asks from its citizens. They serve in the compulsory service in the army and they are part of the Israeli community. Even though they have made all of their duties, they did not get all of their rights. The Christians, they don't join the duties of the Israeli population but they got a lot of their rights.

According to this respondent, the Druze are not oblivious to what he describes as the opportunistic behaviour of Palestinian Christians who play both sides of the political field (the Palestinians and the Israelis) in order to secure for themselves the best position possible in society. Given this view it would, however, be anticipated that Druze jealousy would also extend to Muslims who are similarly exempt from military service. While this sentiment may very well exist, it is unlikely to be acted upon. As one Palestinian Christian respondent explained, the Palestinian Christians are an easy target for the Druze precisely because they are the smallest and most politically weak community within the Palestinian Arab minority. 'You see, they can't attack the Muslims. They know they can't do it. They are too strong for them.' But according to the Druze respondent, this factor alone does not satisfactorily explain Druze attitudes towards Palestinian Christians which, he argues, are also partially rooted in local politics and Christian electoral strategies.

> We know the background of the elections for the local council. The Christians supported the chair [mayor] of the municipality. Because of the support of the Christians they won the head of the municipality. And when [the Druze] saw that Christians do not serve in the army, they finish high-school, go to university, return back with all . . . the professional jobs – doctors, advocates, teachers – the [Druze] said, listen, we are going to the army, we are going to serve three years for nothing, only to be part of this country. The Christians within these three years will finish university, come and take the good jobs, have all the places of trade because they have the time and ability to be more educated . . . And [because] they are the minority, and the [Druze] majority feel that . . . they are not the same as us, they didn't serve in the army, they didn't pay nothing for the Israeli community, and they got all of their rights . . . This situation makes those that are less educated to be jealous of them. And when you see that he has the good life, he has a car, he has a house, he is educated, he is beautiful. That means, I work very hard, I finish the army, the trade is not in my hands in my village, and I am jealous of him. Those who are more or less educated, people come and ask them, look what's going on there, and this brings the people to be very tough in their thoughts.

For another Palestinian Christian respondent, a measure of responsibility is attributed to Christians themselves for their role in adding to Druze–Christian tensions in Mughar. For instance, the exclusive and aloof attitudes of the church, which owns the local school and which insists upon maintaining sole jurisdictional power over all administrative decisions relating to education, teaching and employment within the school, disregards the demographic reality of the village and the rights of other communities to have an equal stake in the running of the school. Furthermore, it was the inability of certain segments of the Christian community to reconcile themselves to their minority status within the village and to accept the natural rights of the Druze majority to have more of an input into their own education that primarily motivated many Christian families to leave the village and educate their children in neighbouring villages subsequent to the riots.

While this account may seem a little harsh, it does, at the very least, provide a broader contextual understanding of Druze–Christian tensions in Israel. Notwithstanding this, most accounts accept that it is military service itself which has had the greatest influence on the nature of Druze–Christian relations in Israel today. This point of view is summed up by another Palestinian Christian respondent:

> But, they do have this problem, this mental problem. They want to prove to the Israelis that they are good citizens, that they are very faithful to the army, to Israel, more than the Jews themselves even. For example, in the uprising in the First Intifada from 1987 to 91, it was the Druze soldiers who committed the most awful crimes against Palestinians. Jews as well, but a lot of them were by Druze. Because they are a very, very conservative community that is not educated, but they have the power and for the first time they are discriminated against. They have weapons, and they all work in the Border Police, and they are the first line against the Palestinians, and this is where all their shortcomings come to the surface. They have someone they can abuse as they have been abused. It's a very understandable thing in psychology. The victim can be the most horrible victimiser sometimes. They have weapons . . .

The issue, therefore, returns to one of weapons. Beyond the issue of Druze resentment and jealousy, the riots in Mughar were exceptional not solely for the role played by Druze officers and the use of military weapons – which is evident throughout the Druze–Christian conflicts encountered earlier – but because of their organised and premeditated nature.

> One witness said: 'The attacks on cars and people are nothing new. But this time they were very well organised. They had petrol and tubes to pour it through doors and they had tools to break into the houses. The Druze have no fear. They are in the police and army.'
>
> (Urquhart 2005)

However, what stands out in accounts of the riots in Mughar is that they went unchecked by the authorities for so long. The violence commenced on Thursday night but it was only on Saturday afternoon that the Israeli police finally responded, sending in 350 officers and using tear-gas to disperse the crowd which had by then reached 1,500 people (Rudge 2005a). For failing to intervene earlier and for allowing the Druze mob to go about destroying Christian properties, the Israeli police have been singled out for particular criticism.

> Although Christians are angry at their treatment at the hands of the Druze, most of their anger is reserved for the Israeli police, who they say could have halted the violence. Witnesses said they saw police in cars watch as the mob stoned and burned buildings.
>
> (Urquhart 2005)

For one Palestinian Christian respondent, the behaviour of the police in Mughar was indicative of deeper attitudes of state indifference and religious antipathy against Christians.

> They [the police] stood back all the time in Mughar. For three days they were battling in the city. And they put [the police] there, and they didn't move, they didn't say a word, they didn't try to prevent. And there are rumours – they're not rumours, they're facts – that some of the police, who were Druze, took part in what happened. OK, what happened, happened. What about . . . I don't know, I could show you pictures. How many houses were burned? How many shops were looted? I mean, why doesn't somebody go and investigate and order some arrests? Nothing! In Kfar Yasif they attacked the village, they burned 68 houses, many cars . . . and the police didn't interfere at all. They stayed out. They prevented people from coming in and trying to help . . . [I]n Rameh, they fired a rocket on a school. It's going on all the time. I mean, they start something and the police are happy about it, let's say . . .

This is confirmed by another account which suggests that the attitude of Israeli police was not one based on political apathy alone.

> [O]ff-duty Druze policemen, along with soldiers and ex-soldiers, were suspected of participating but were not punished. The Druze police on duty were reportedly 'apathetic' during the worst peaks of the violence, which they watched but failed to stop. They reportedly ignored residents' pleas for help, and instead stood around 'watching and eating baklava'. Yet in the end there was no official sanction for their behaviour.
>
> (Kanaaneh 2009: 58)

While the inability of the Israeli police to deal swiftly and fairly in ending the conflict increases the sense of vulnerability experienced by Palestinian Christian citizens of Israel, it was the indifference of the political establishment to pursue justice on their behalf which has compounded it. Despite claims by the authorities to the contrary, their inability or disinclination to follow standard criminal procedure against the culprits has undermined their status as a protector in the eyes of many Christians.

> The local police commissioner, Dan Ronen, told the Knesset committee on interior affairs that it was not the job of the police to become involved in inter-communal violence. 'Police have no say in the matter. Don't expect the police to solve all communal internal conflicts. This is the responsibility of the heads of the community,' he said.
>
> (Urquhart 2005)

Despite the rather flippant manner in which the northern Police Commissioner distanced himself and the Israeli police from the affair, the lack of police intervention in Druze–Christian conflicts has nonetheless been viewed as either symptomatic or representative of state attitudes towards Palestinian Christians in Israel. For one Israeli Jewish respondent, the police response followed a more general 'hands off' policy of the state in dealing with sensitive intra-communal issues within the Palestinian Arab minority. Given that the state is generally suspected and mistrusted by the minority, non-intervention is presented as being the most preferable and least exacerbating position that it can take.

> So, both accused Israel [of interfering]. It's Israel that's causing the rift, causing the rift between the two, and so on, and therefore the Israeli police say whatever we do will be damned and therefore let them settle their problems, unless it gets into open conflict or criminal acts and so on and the authorities have no choice but to intervene. But usually they prefer not to intervene as far as possible.

Clearly, however, 'open conflict' and 'criminal acts' in Mughar did not speed up the police response. Another respondent suggests that the lack of police intervention in Druze–Christian conflict is not necessarily motivated by ideological concerns alone. For this respondent, a downturn in the police's financial resources and manpower has limited their ability to act swiftly and efficiently in instances of intra-communal conflict. In addition, he believes that regional police forces lack the necessary authority from above to deal with these cases. To support this, he recalled one occasion where he had been advised by a Jewish policeman that the central government was reluctant to get involved in unnecessary high-profile cases due to the high volume of political corruption charges it was facing and its desire to avoid becoming embroiled in any situation which would invite further bad publicity.

Regardless of what factors underpin this policy of non-intervention by the police in intra-communal conflict, their non-intervention is universally acknowledged. What is less acknowledged is the impact which it has had upon the local Palestinian Christian population. Their confidence in the ability or desire of the authorities to protect them when required has been significantly undermined. This has been aggravated by the rejection by the authorities of numerous calls from within the Palestinian Christian community to open a formal public inquiry to investigate the conflict in Mughar. More damning still was the decision taken several months later by the government to close criminal cases against four Druze police officers who were identified as taking part in the attacks (Khoury 2005b and 2005c). To this is added the lengthy struggle the local Christian community subsequently had with the authorities in their attempt to secure financial compensation for damages done to their properties and livelihoods. Given the extensive damages done to property in Mughar, it was estimated that the cost of repairs would require tens of millions of shekels. A Haifa-based Jewish law firm represented over 100 individual Christian claimants from the village seeking financial restitution from the government. Initially, the government refused to accept that it was in any way obligated to cover these costs. However, the claimants' legal representation argued the opposite.

> These people were abandoned to their fate. If the police, who were aware of the tensions in the village, had acted immediately and taken the appropriate measures, the violence would have been prevented. (. . .) The state failed to protect them and, as such, has to take responsibility.
>
> (Rudge 2005c)

Eventually, the government agreed to pay out NIS 10 million (approximately US$2 million) to compensate for damages and to allow reconstruction of the village to begin, but the pay-out was delayed for several months, causing even further economic suffering to the already frozen local economy of the village (Khoury 2005d; U.S. Department of State 2006).

All of these factors explain why military service has become an attractive option for certain quarters within the Palestinian Christian population. Military service provides weapons which in turn equips individuals and families with the means through which to defend themselves in instances of intra-communal conflict. Interestingly, the military authorities have shown that they are well aware of this. As one respondent noted, the authorities send military representatives, both Arab and Jewish, to visit village schools in these small mixed villages in order to advertise and market military service among the local youth. According to Nadem Nashef, an important part of their recruitment strategy has been to emphasise the patriarchal nature of Palestinian Christian identity.

> And also they play on macho stuff, like, if you go to the army you're a man because you have a gun. In some villages, the motive is also because of tensions. For example, in one of the villages a part are Druze, and most of them go to the army so they have guns in their houses. Sometimes there are fights, so the Druze have guns and you don't ask questions. So they come and tell you to go to the army and you'll have a gun and you'll be more of a man. They play on different levels. It's not only sectarian thing. It's also about macho stuff.

Other respondents have pointed to the tendency of Palestinian Christians to volunteer for military service based on feelings of fear and vulnerability and an awareness that they must look to themselves, and not to the state, for protection.

> We want to go and serve in the military and basically in the police only to take a weapon to feel safe. This is the only answer of why Christians in these specific areas they are ready to go and serve in the army or the police or the civil service.

This factor is also understood to influence the manner in which military service is 'pitched' or marketed to Palestinian Christians by recruiters. Moreover, the practical or economic incentives of military service which are typically cited as motivating Palestinian Arab recruitment are considered to have had less impact, or influence, on the decision-making process of Palestinian Christian who are deemed relatively more economically advantaged and secure than their Muslim and Druze neighbours. This desire to acquire a weapon for the sole purpose of self-defence is widely understood to be an important factor motivating Palestinian Christians to volunteer for military service.

> Among the villages themselves . . . and it happened in the past, it's happening now, it happened before, especially in the '80s . . . Druze and Bedouins who go to the army have their weapons, and in every communal village [or] family struggle, they use these weapons against Christians when the struggle is with the Christians. So, the Christians in the'80s found themselves without any protection at all. Many of them, a big number, from the villages in the north, go to the army just to get a weapon. So, it's not connected to their political point of view. They just want to go to have a weapon and keep it in case. It especially happens in Mughar, in Kfur Yasif, in Abu Snan, in the villages where around you, you have Druze villages.

Another respondent, suggested that the two main areas through which the government achieves its goal of encouraging Palestinian Christians to volunteer to national service are the media and the education system.

> I think what they are trying to do is two things: one is in the public media, its attitude that if you are Christian, you are different, and the way that things are dealt with in the media. But more importantly, I think is their investment in the education system. I think when you have church-based schools, the state is interested more in all the issues of military service, like encouraging children to do national service as a replacement to military service, trying to focus on the religious identity of the group as separate to the national identity. But this is mainly through the education system. (. . .)
>
> And [in the schools] you will see more programmes concerning identity, more programmes, more lectures putting the children in direct contact with political propaganda basically which is making them closer to the state, in the

sense that you are Christians and not Muslims . . . Through funding, through lectures, through visits, through tours, like taking children to meet with Jewish children, like coexistence programmes, taking children on Independence Day to meet with army people, bringing army and military people to lecture about the army to the schools. It's the same programme, more or less, that was used against the Druze. (. . .)

And also the way it's presented in the media. You'll see from time to time in the media, like in the Arab media, somebody writes about the fact that you have more and more Christians participating in the police service, or in the armed service. And sometimes it's not factual, just propaganda to send a message also to the Muslim community that the Christians are integrating. Like to try to separate the two communities from each other.

The tendency of military recruiters to target mixed villages, particularly for Christian volunteers, is confirmed within the literature (Peled, A. 1998: 166). Although their recruitment is understood to be motivated by existential concerns brought about, in no small way, by the indifference and neglect of the Israeli authorities, Christian recruits are welcomed by the military authorities who use them as a political symbol for the possibility for Arab integration into Israeli society; the more amenable nature of Palestinian Christians and the fragmented nature of Palestinian Arab identity.

One city conflict

While the previous incidents of Druze–Christian conflict which have been discussed in this chapter were essentially village-based conflicts, one further conflict will be discussed in this chapter which was a city-based conflict. The conflict which took place in Shfar'amr in 2009 was the first conflict to take place in Israel in a major Arab city between Druze and Christians. With a population of almost 35,000 people, Shfar'amr is the only Arab city in Israel in which Palestinian Christians (28 per cent) and Druze (15 per cent) live side by side.

As one of only a handful of Arab cities in Israel, the city of Shfar'amr represents both a demographic and political cause for concern for the authorities. This was demonstrated in 2005 when an off-duty Jewish soldier from the OPTs by the name of Eden Natan Zada climbed aboard a bus travelling from Haifa to Shfar'amr wearing an IDF uniform and opened fire on its Arab passengers with an M-16 rifle, killing four (two Muslim and two Christian) and injuring a further 10 passengers. When onlookers surrounded the bus in anger and attacked and subsequently killed Zada – described by the Israeli media as a 'lynching' by an Arab 'mob' – the authorities responded by aggressively pursuing several local Palestinians from Shfar'amr through the courts for attempted murder (Izenberg 2009).

Five years later, on 6 June 2009, the state finally indicted 12 Palestinians from Shfar'amr on charges of attempted murder and aggravated assault against the Israeli police officer who had attempted to protect Zada. In response, the city declared its intention to hold a one-day general strike three days later on 9 June to protest against the state's 'double standards' (Khoury 2009a). It is within the context that one week later, quite out of the blue, violence broke out between Druze and Christians on 16 June 2009.

The violence was triggered by a rumour that local Christian youths had digitally manipulated and uploaded video clip to YouTube which showed the image of deceased Druze spiritual leader, Amin Tarif, alongside a pig (Raved 2009). Unlike the case in Mughar, which was also triggered by a similar rumour involving a manipulated online image, this rumour turned out to be true (Nasr 2009), and, in the violence which ensued, nine local teenagers were stabbed (none fatally) and several houses and shops, mainly in the Christian part of town, were damaged or torched (Khoury 2009c).

Representing a significant departure from the pattern set by previous conflicts involving Christians and Druze, the police, Border Police and anti-riot squads were quickly deployed to Shfar'amr and, significantly, did not demonstrate any bias whatsoever in favour of the Druze (Khoury 2009b). Roadblocks were established, and in their attempt to disperse the crowds, the police themselves came under attack from rocks thrown by both Druze and Christians. Four policemen were injured by stones and, in one instance, by live ammunition (Khoury 2009b; Lappin 2009). However, as with previous violent incidents, the issue of where these weapons could have originated from was dealt with in local press in the same evasive manner as before.

> 'It's clear they have many guns, but we don't know from where. Some could be legally owned. Last night, they were turned against us,' Galilee Spokesman Eran Shaked told *The Jerusalem Post* on Wednesday.
>
> (Lappin 2009)

The incident was critically and publicly scrutinised by the media and was, for some time, the subject of both disbelief and suspicion. Given that the conflict had emerged as the city was experiencing an unprecedented level of political unity resulting from the indictment of 12 city residents, questions of whether external forces had deliberately sought to engineer the conflict or instigate violence were raised.

> 'Some hooligans on both sides caused this whole commotion. I'm convinced that people from outside caused the conflagration in town. Only last week the people here were united in their response to the [state's] decision to indict 12 townspeople for being involved in killing the terrorist Natan Zada,' [a local Druze Hadash activist] said.
>
> (Khoury 2009b)

One week later, an unidentified local youth who was suspected of uploading the video was arrested by police, thus allaying to a large extent these suspicions (Khoury 2009c). Notwithstanding this, the extent to which the Druze–Christian riots in Shfar'amr may be understood to represent a continuation of, or a break with, previous conflicts in mixed Arab villages in Israel remains unclear. While certain factors, such as the asymmetry of arms, echoes previous incidents, others are inconsistent with them, such as the quick and even-handed response of the police which did not take the side of the Druze rioters, and the subsequent cross-sectarian violent confrontation between the authorities on the one hand and the local residents on the other. While this may be indicative of changing attitudes to intra-communal conflict in Israel, it is just as likely, if not more so, that, compared with the small and politically irrelevant villages, the political significance of Shfar'amr as an Arab city dictated a firm and swift response from the authorities which, in turn, elicited a different response from the local population. Only future cases of Druze–Christian conflict in Israel, if they are found to persist, will indicate whether the conflict in Shfar'amr was an exception or part of an emerging trend of intra-communal conflict and state–minority relations in Israel.

Conclusion

This chapter investigates four instances of intra-communal violence in Israel involving Palestinian Christians and Druze and finds that the mandatory conscription of Druze in the IDF has not only accentuated Druze–Christian tensions, but has directly enabled violent confrontations between both groups. This it has done in two main ways. On the one hand, military service equips the Druze with military arms which are unavailable to other segments of the non-serving minority, thus determining that Druze–Christian conflicts remain largely one-sided and asymmetrical in nature. On the other hand, the concentration of Druze in the police and military forces has compromised the ability of these important state institutions to intervene in a fair and timely manner, thus prolonging the duration of attacks and maximising the amount of damage inflicted on Christian lives and properties.

What does this say about the nature of Israeli state attitudes towards Palestinian Christians in Israel? Given the reluctance of the authorities to ensure that weapons provided by them which are supplied in order to maintain internal order and protect and defend the state and its citizens from external threats are not abused and exploited by certain Druze individuals and groups wishing to act out their frustrations or act upon their petty grievances against Christians; given their track-record of protecting Druze individuals and officers involved in violent attacks against Christians from standard criminal procedure or even reprimand; given their rejection of various calls for inquiries into the substandard role of the police in these conflicts; and given their reluctance to provide adequate or timely financial compensation to those Christian individuals and families whose properties and livelihoods have been destroyed by individuals using military weapons, it is possible to argue that the state is, at best, guilty of neglecting and, at worst, guilty of targeting the interests and needs of Palestinian Christians in Israel. In this, the state's indifference is facilitated by the indifference of international players whose attention is focused almost exclusively on the key religious and geopolitical cities of Nazareth and Jerusalem. Strategically speaking, the state is also blind to small Christian communities which, compared to the Druze, make no significant contribution to the national priorities of the state and, compared with the Muslims, pose little threat to the state's demographic concerns.

These instances of intra-communal violence demonstrate not only an important level of state indifference to Palestinian Christians in Israel but also the growing sense of vulnerability and existential threat experienced by Palestinian Christians. It is, ironically, the failure of the state to provide Palestinian Christians with adequate protection as equal citizens of the state which has contributed, in part, to voluntary Palestinian Christian conscription within the army. While other factors and motivations also exist, the necessity of acquiring a gun for the purposes of self-defence remains one of the most convincing explanations behind the conscription of Palestinian Christian villagers to the IDF. Nonetheless, the relatively small number of conscripts each year suggests that this phenomenon, while it exists, is not representative of the Palestinian Christian community as a whole. However, given the temporal significance of Druze attacks on Christians, with the majority occurring within the last decade, it should be anticipated that, if these attacks continue unabated, the number of Palestinian Christian voluntary conscripts to the army will increase, as will the number of violent confrontations between Druze and Christians in Israel.

8   Conclusion

This study has explored Israeli state attitudes towards Palestinian Christians in Israel. Through a critical examination of the literature together with an analysis of the varied perspectives offered by a cross-section of community representatives, opinion-makers and leaders in Israel, this study argues that the notion of state preferentialism which is often encountered within the literature and the media to describe the relationship between the Jewish state and its Palestinian Christian minority is, at best, flawed and, at worst, misleading.

Using state attitudes towards intra-communal conflict involving Palestinian Christians in Israel as a yardstick, this study finds that the state's attitudes towards Palestinian Christians are rather more complicated than has typically been suggested, often alternating, or fluctuating, between affirmation, indecision, indifference, antipathy and neglect, depending upon the shifting and limiting interplay of pragmatic and political demands, necessities and circumstances which define state–minority relations in a Jewish ethnocratic state. The political interests and strategic allegiances of the authorities during the conflict in Nazareth, for instance, or the biased and hesitant response of the authorities to conflicts involving Druze in several mixed villages, demonstrate that the state has, whether intentionally or unintentionally, overlooked and disregarded the needs and interests of the local Palestinian Christian population. The significance of this particular dynamic cannot be overstated as it has important consequences not only for intra-communal relations within the Palestinian Arab minority and for state–minority relations more generally, but, equally importantly, for the future status and prospects of Palestinian Christians in Israel.

This study does not, in any way, suggest that the authorities' direct and indirect support of Muslims or Druze in instances of intra-communal conflict involving Christians is indicative of an ideological or political rapprochement between the state and these two communities at the expense of Palestinian Christians. Indeed, as has been shown, this support, where it has been found to exist, has been either temporary (as with the state's instrumental support of the Islamic movement in Nazareth) or contingent upon the national priorities of the state (as can be seen with the swift and impartial response of the authorities in Shfar'amr). Moreover, this study has shown that while Palestinian Christians are firmly located within the state's pervasive system of control, they are by themselves not the primary object of it. Given that the prism through which the Palestinian Arab minority continues to be viewed by the state in Israel is not merely one that centralises the notion of a demographic and territorial 'Arab problem' that incorporates Muslim, Christian and Druze communities on an equal basis, but one that specifically associates the greatest level of threat to Jewish national interests and priorities with the majority of that minority, which happens to be Muslim, Israel's system of controlling its Palestinian Arab minority is primarily directed towards the control of its Muslim population.

What these instances of intra-communal conflict do nonetheless highlight is the irrelevance and political negligibility of the small, electorally weak Palestinian Christian population with regard to the central national priorities of the state: land, demography and, by extension, ethnicity and religion. The conflict which took place between the nominally Christian-led municipality and the Islamist move-ment in Nazareth and the role which successive Israeli governments have played in extending and exacerbating that conflict illustrates the continued political salience of demography and religion within Israeli politics as well as the erosive and corroding influence of politicised demography and religion upon the status of Palestinian Christians in Israel. Attempts to court the Arab (read Muslim) vote have, for obvious demographic reasons, sidelined Palestinian Christians. This has been compounded by the growing religiosity of Israeli society in general and of the parallel growth of anti-Christian religious antipathy within the increasingly powerful (Jewish) religious political establishment in Israel. Similarly, the recur-rence of intra-communal conflicts in a number of mixed Arab villages emphasises the political significance which remains attached to the performance, or rather the non-performance, of military service in Israel. Military service is hailed as the ultimate test of Arab loyalty in Israeli society, and its non-performance by the vast majority of Palestinian Christians in Israel has left this community not only outside of the normative consensus upon which Israeli society is based, but open to attack from some of their serving Druze neighbours who have used it as both a pretext and a means to vent their frustration at their relatively greater levels of socio-economic advantage and opportunity in society. , The vulnerability of sec-tions of the Palestinian Christian community in Israel, which is often unprotected by locally aligned police forces and denied legal due process by an impartial judi-cial system, has increased on a par with the increasing frequency and confidence of Druze attacks, contributing to the paradoxical phenomenon of Palestinian Christian voluntary conscription in the IDF. Without ignoring the role of other factors, the lure and necessity of acquiring a gun not only provides an important explanation for the relative growth of Palestinian Christian recruits, but unequivo-cally demonstrates the deeper significance of state indifference to the material and existential dilemmas of Palestinian Christians living in Israel.

While this study subscribes to a critical control perspective of Israeli state and society, this study's findings nonetheless challenge a number of the traditional assumptions surrounding theories of systemic control. The research identifies indifference and neglect as best describing the current nature of state attitudes towards Palestinian Christians in Israel. However, attitudes, particularly of indifference and neglect, are not easily reconciled within a theoretical framework of control which has generally been formulated on the basis of active, conscientious and direct strategies of control and intervention. While the various intra-communal conflicts analysed in this study demonstrate the continued salience and relevance of one of Lustick's 'techniques of control' – namely, the segmentation of the Palestinian Arab minority based on, in this case, the isolation and fragmentation of various religiously defined segments of the minority from each other – the application of the two other main strategies of state control which he outlined – co-optation and dependence – is more problematic with regard to contemporary analyses of the state's relationship with its Palestinian Christian population. The internal differentiation of the Palestinian Christian communal structure, together with the continued relevance of external links, has, in fact, reduced the practical capacity of the state to co-opt and control Palestinian Christians in Israel, and while it can be argued that the significance of national service for vulnerable and isolated Christian communities has increased the overall dependence of Palestinian Christians upon the state, the statistical insignificance of the overall number of Palestinian Arab recruits, whether Muslim or Christian, further undermines the notion of Christian dependency upon the state.

This study has, more precisely, uncovered two main areas of weakness concerning the literature on systemic control which must be addressed and challenged in order to better understand the nature of minority policy in Israel today and going forward. The first area of concern is the overly restrictive and narrow understanding of both the forms and mechanisms of control in an ethnocratic state. Methods of control which are passive as well as active, indirect as well as direct, conscious as well as unconscious, non-interventionist as well as interventionist, all require further and more balanced examination and analysis. As this study's findings on state attitudes of indifference and neglect towards Palestinian Christians in Israel show, it is essential that our assumptions concerning the nature and mechanisms of control in an ethnocratic state be constantly re-addressed if our analyses are to stay abreast of parallel paradigmatic shifts within the areas of Israeli national ideology, consensus and, by extension also, policy. Given the systemic and fluid nature of control, it is vital that control theories demonstrate a similar degree of flexibility.

This point is connected with a further area of weakness concerning control theories, which is an over-reliance on the concept of control itself. Is control always the only option open to ethnocratic states in their dealings with minorities? Given Yiftachel's description of an ethnocracy as an essentially non-democratic state, the range of possible policy options which were outlined by Smooha (which range between the two opposite extremes of ethnic cleansing and assimilation) need to be periodically re-considered and re-evaluated with respect to Israel as well. In fact, an investigation of the different possible forms of control open to an ethnocratic state in its dealings with its minority is as important today as the question of whether control need always be the primary objective or intention of state policy in the first place. Given the once marginal but now increasingly popular rhetoric of 'transfer' and 'population exchange' of Palestinian Arabs from Israel to the occupied territories of the West Bank, the assumption that control remains the only policy framework open to the Israeli state in its dealings with its Palestinian Arab citizens is no longer entirely credible or convincing. While control theories have made some of the most valuable contributions to our understanding of the nature of the state, state–minority relations and the state's minority policy, it is increasingly in danger of becoming stuck within its own terminological trappings. Given the continued salience and legitimacy of the definition of the state as a Jewish ethnocracy, it would perhaps be more useful to refer to the state's minority policy not within the exclusive boundaries of control but simply as 'ethnocratic policy' which would incorporate but not limit understandings of state policy to control.

This study's assessment of the impact of state indifference towards Palestinian Christians in Israel has the potential not only to significantly advance the theoretical literature on control itself but, more importantly, to challenge conceptions of state–minority relations in Israel in general. However, the findings of this study suggest that the decision to distinguish between what were deemed to be essentially secular and religious areas may not have been entirely necessary. The continued political deadlock between the Vatican and the State of Israel with regards to the implementation of the Fundamental Agreement of 1993 suggests not only a degradation of the political power of this important Christian institution but an increasingly independent and confident state which is less and less concerned with international opinion. What impact can this changing relationship be said to have on local Palestinian Christians who have traditionally been described as benefitting from the protection of such external powers? Could indifference also come to represent the state's attitudes towards the once politically powerful Christian churches? As such, future research on Palestinian Christians in Israel would do well to integrate, in a more balanced fashion, church scholarship with up-to-date analyses of issues relating to and affecting the Christian 'street' in Israel. For similar reasons, this study's findings could be strengthened by further research into the subject of state attitudes towards the Christian church school system in Israel. Given the political salience of education in Israel, the central role of relatively autonomous Christian religious institutions in providing Palestinian Arab youth with a competitive and alternative education to that which is provided by state-run public schools would have been an interesting avenue of research which could have either challenged or supported this study's findings that indifference and neglect constitute the primary state attitudes towards Palestinian Christians in Israel.

Similarly, further research into the area of current electoral politics within the Palestinian Arab minority in Israel could yield potentially rewarding results for our understanding of state–minority relations in Israel. With the abandonment of the policy of separate direct elections for the position of Prime Minister in 2001, the question of how relevant the 'Arab vote' and, particularly, the numerically superior Muslim contingent of it, is in Israel today has important consequences not only for the manner in which the state and mainstream Jewish parties engage with the Palestinian Arab minority but for the relative electoral power or strength of the various religious segments of that minority. Similarly, future research would be rewarded by a more in-depth empirical analysis of regional voting patterns within the Palestinian Arab minority and, particularly, within areas and localities which have significant Palestinian Christian populations, the findings of which have the potential to either support or contradict assumptions regarding the political outlook and orientations of Palestinian Christians in Israel.

By foregoing the exceptional approach which has traditionally characterised scholarship on Christians in the Middle East, a number of other potentially fertile avenues of future research into the subject of state–minority relations in Israel present themselves. As such, this study's examination of state attitudes towards Palestinian Christians in Israel not only provides a basis upon which the complicated relationship between the state and its Palestinian Christian population can be better understood, but provides an important test-case through which broader assumptions concerning the nature of the state, state–minority relations and state policy as a whole can be tested and analysed. While for some, Israeli state policies towards its minority have been unfairly spotlighted and disproportionately criticised, others have recognised the vital and symbiotic relationship which exists between the future maintenance and political stability of the state of Israel and the status of the Palestinian Arab minority within it. 'I am certain that the world will judge the Jewish state by what it will do with its Arab population, just as the Jewish people will be judged by what it does or fails to do in this state.' These prophetic words of warning which were penned by Israel's first President, Chaim Weizmann, more than half a century ago remain a poignant and accurate reminder today of the interlocked futures of the state of Israel and its Palestinian Arab minority and, by extension, of its Palestinian Christian population.

Notes

2 Society, state and minority policy in Israel

1 For an elaboration of this confusion between the concepts of ethnic group, nation and state, and the indiscriminate and misleading usage of the term 'nation-state' within the social and political sciences, see Connor (1994: 89–118). According to Connor, there are only 12 states in the world which can justifiably be described as nation-states, whereby a nation-state is defined as 'a state that has become largely identical with one people'.

2 Eisenstadt (1985: 158, 169, 186) considers Israel to be 'a basic parliamentary democratic State' while Landau (1993: 131) refers to Israel throughout his studies as a 'democratic regime'. Edelman (1987: 54) refers to it as 'a functioning democracy' that is 'comparable to that of other Western democracies', while Horowitz and Lissak (1989: 144) refer to it as a liberal and a parliamentary democracy. More recently, Peretz and Doron (1997: 2) have described Israel as 'one of the most democratic countries in the Middle Eastern region'.

3 The 'tyranny of the majority' is understood to be an abuse of the democratic concept of majority rule (Yiftachel 2006: 98).

4 *Herrenvolk* – which means 'ruling people' in German – was originally used to describe the system of apartheid rule in South Africa. It is generally understood to refer to the restriction of democratic rule, rights and citizenship to a dominant group.

5 The Koenig Report set out a bold strategy aimed at reducing the demographic presence and influence of Palestinian Arab citizens in the Galilee region through a range of political measures, including: undermining the political influence of the Arab Communist party (Rakah) by creating an alternative Labour affiliate party which could vie for Arab votes and be centrally controlled by Israeli authorities; finding a way to avoid the payment to Arab families of government subsidies for large families; discouraging Arab students from pursuing university education and encouraging them instead to acquire technical qualifications; and encouraging Arab students to study abroad while simultaneously making their re-entry into the state more difficult. See: MERIP (1976).

3 Profile of the Palestinian Christians in Israel

1 For more on nationalism and its variants, see: Gellner (1983: particularly, pp. 1–5), Anderson (1991: 3–8) or Hobsbawm (1990).

2 Notably: The Future Vision of the Palestinian Arabs in Israel (2006); The Haifa Declaration (2007); and The Democratic Constitution (2007).

3 According to the Explanatory Notes on Definitions and Sources provided by the CBS (2010) the category 'not classified by religion' is composed of (1) family members of Jewish immigrants who are usually non-Arab Christians, (2) about 400 members of other faiths (Buddhists, Hindus and Samaritans) who until 1995 were included in figures for

the Druze population and (3) approximately 2,500 Lebanese who entered Israel in 2000 with the flight of segments of the Southern Lebanese Army.

4 This figure excludes the 79 'unrecognised' Arab villages in Israel, 27 of which are located in the north of Israel. Email correspondence with the Association of Forty, 23/10/2008.

5 An Arab locality is understood to be any locality with a majority Arab population. Non-Arab localities are limited to two Circassian villages in the north (Rihanniya and Kfar Kama). The Circassians are a very small non-Jewish non-Arab Muslim minority which is, together with the Druze population, eligible for mandatory military service.

4 Writing the Palestinian Christians in Israel

1 See, for example, Haidar and Zureik (1987); Kimmerling (1992); Ram (1995); Lissak (1996); Ben-Yehuda (1997); Waxman (1997); Rosenhek (1998); Zureik (2003); Epstein (2004); Yair and Apeloig (2006) and Kalekin-Fishman (2006).

2 Schwarz (1959: 65); Smooha (1978: 47, 75, 83); Kaufman (1997: 3); Ghanem (2001: 166); Cook (2006: 31, 48) and Kanaaneh (2009: 2, 62).

3 The two main areas of dispute concern new visa restrictions faced by clergy, in particular Arab nuns and priests, as well as the issue of property tax. Traditionally, the churches were exempted from paying property tax (*arnona*), but the State has recently introduced the requirement that the churches should pay it, which, considering their vast property holdings, would financially cripple the churches. The Vatican has refused to pay this tax, arguing that it constitutes a violation not only of the *status quo* but of traditional Israeli policy.

Bibliography

Adalah: The Legal Centre for Arab Minority Rights in Israel. (2006) *Haifa District Court Issues Precedent-Setting Judgment that Considering Military Service Criterion in Allocation of Housing at Haifa University Discriminates Against Arab Students*, Available at http://www.adalah.org/newsletter/eng/jul-aug06/1.php (Accessed on 14 August 2008).

—— (2007a) *The Democratic Constitution*, Available at http://www.adalah.org/eng/ constitution.php (Accessed on 1 May 2007).

—— (2007b) *Adalah's Report to the UN CERD in Response to the List of Issues Presented to Israel*, Available at http://www.adalah.org/eng/cerd.php (Accessed on 13 January 2008).

—— (2008) *Haifa University to Adalah: The Law Imposes MilitaryService Requirement for Training Course for Commercial Fleet Officers; We Are Not Responsible for It*, Available at http://www.adalah.org/newsletter/eng/feb08/1.php (Accessed on 13 April 2008).

Amara, M. (2003) 'The Collective Identity of the Arabs in Israel in an Era of Peace', in Bligh, A. (ed.) *The Israeli Palestinians: An Arab Minority in the Jewish State*, London: Frank Cass.

Anderson, B. (1991) *Imagined Communities: Reflections on the Origin and Spread of Nationalism*, London: Verso.

Arab Association for Human Rights (Arab HRA). (1999a) *The Vicious Cycle: Discrimination in Funding for Arab Municipalities*, Available at http://www.arabhra.org/HRA/ SecondaryArticles/SecondaryArticlePage.aspx?SecondaryArticle=1414 (Accessed on 23 June 2008).

—— (1999b) *Poverty and the Palestinian Arab Minority*, Available at http://www.arabhra. org/HRA/SecondaryArticles/SecondaryArticlePage.aspx?SecondaryArticle=1418 (Accessed on 5 May 2008).

—— (1999c) *Bir'em and Iqrit: The Internally Displaced*, Available at http://www.arabhra. org/HRA/SecondaryArticles/SecondaryArticlePage.aspx?SecondaryArticle=1417> (Accessed on 12 September 2008).

—— (2000) *Nazareth: A Glimpse at the Arab Economic Crisis*, Available at http://www. arabhra.org/HRA/SecondaryArticles/SecondaryArticlePage.aspx?SecondaryArticle=14 29> (Accessed on 20 September 2006).

—— (2005a) *One Gunman, Many to Blame: Israel's Culture of Racism Prior to the Shefa'amr Massacre and the Role of the Attorney General*, Available at http://www. arabhra.org/HRA/SecondaryArticles/SecondaryArticlePage.aspx?SecondaryArticle=13 50 (Accessed on 15 June 2008).

—— (2005b) *Nazareth and Nazerat Illit: A Comparative Tour*, Available at http://www.

arabhra.org/HRA/SecondaryArticles/SecondaryArticlePage.aspx?SecondaryArticle=14 38 (Accessed on 14 September 2006).

—— (2006) *Attack on the Basilica of the Annunciation: Public Condemnation and Official Condonation*, Available at http://www.arabhra.org/HRA/SecondaryArticles/ SecondaryArticlePage.aspx?SecondaryArticle=1341 (Accessed on 31 August 2008).

Arab Centre for Alternative Planning (ACAP). (2007) *Database of Local Arab Municipalities and Towns in Israel* (Interactive Map), Available on http://www. ac-ap.org/files/ACAPmahozot20en.swf (Accessed on 5 September 2008).

Aronoff, M.J. (1999) 'Wars as Catalysts of Political and Cultural Change', in Lomsky-Feder, E. and Ben-Ari, E. (eds.) *The Military and Militarism in Israeli Society*, Albany: State University of New York Press.

Ashkenazi, A. (1988) *Israeli Policies and Palestinian Fragmentation: Political and Social Impacts in Israel and Jerusalem*, Jerusalem: Leonard Davis Institute for International Relations.

Asya, I. (2003) 'The Israeli Newspapers' Coverage of the Israeli Arabs during the Intifada', in Bligh, A. (ed.) *The Israeli Palestinians: An Arab Minority in the Jewish State*, London: Frank Cass.

Ateek, N. (2006) 'The Churches of the Holy Land: A Rich Mosaic', *Cornerstone*, 42: 3–5, Jerusalem: Sabeel, Available at http://www.sabeel.org/etemplate.php?id=5 (Accessed on 15 July 2008).

Avineri, S. (1981) *The Making of Modern Zionism: Intellectual Origins of the Jewish State*, New York: Basic Books.

Avishai, B. (1985) *The Tragedy of Zionism: Revolution and Democracy in the Land of Israel*, New York: Farrar Strauss Giroux.

BADIL Resource Centre. (2006) *Returning to Kafr Bir 'im*, Bethlehem: BADIL, Available at http://www.badil.org/index.php?page=shop.product_details&flypage=garden_flypage. tpl&product_id=2&category_id=2&vmcchk=1&option=com_virtuemart&Itemid=4 (Accessed on 12 August 2008).

Bailey, B.J. and Bailey, J.M. (2003) *Who are the Christians in the Middle East?* Cambridge: Wm B. Eerdmans Publishing Company.

Baladna Association for Arab Youth. (2008) *The Campaign Against Civil Service – Progress Report*, Available at www.momken.org/reports/ Campaign%20Against%20Civil%20Se rvice%20Final,%20Report.pdf (Accessed on 20 August 2008).

Bannoura, S. (2008) 'Arab Resident of Nazareth to be Imprisoned for Defending the Basilica of Annunciation Church', *The International Middle East Media Corner*, May 28, Available at http://www.imemc.org/article/55118 (Accessed on 12 November 2008).

Beinin, J. (2005) 'Forgetfulness for Memory: The Limits of the New Israeli History', *Journal of Palestine Studies*, 34: 6–23.

Ben-Ari, E. and Lomsky-Feder, E. (1999) 'Cultural Constructions of War and the Military in Israel', in Lomsky-Feder, E. and Ben-Ari, E. (eds.) *The Military and Militarism in Israeli Society*, Albany: State University of New York Press.

Ben-Dor, G. (1979) *The Druze in Israel: A Political Study – Political Innovation and Integration of a Middle Eastern Minority*, Jerusalem: Magnes Press.

Ben-Rafael, E. (1982) *The Emergence of Ethnicity: Cultural Groups and Social Conflict in Israel*, Westport, CT: Greenwood Press.

—— (1997) 'Critical versus Non-Critical Sociology: An Evaluation', *Israel Studies*, 2: 174–93.

Ben-Yehuda, N. (1997) 'The Dominance of the External: Israeli Sociology', *Contemporary Sociology*, 26: 271–5.

Benvenisti, M. (1987) 'The Second Republic', *Journal of Palestine Studies*, 16: 197–201.

Betts, R.B. (1978) *Christians in the Arab East*, Atlanta, GA: John Knox Press.

Bialer, U. (2005) *Cross on the Star of David: The Christian World in Israel's Foreign Policy, 1948–1967*, Bloomington: Indiana University Press.

Birnbaum, P. (1996) 'From Multiculturalism to Nationalism', *Political Theory*, 24: 33–45.

Bishara, A. (2000) '"A Double Responsibility": Palestinian Citizens of Israel and the Intifada', *Middle East Report, No. 217, Beyond Oslo: The New Uprising:* 26–9.

Bligh, A. (ed.) (2003) *The Israeli Palestinians: An Arab Minority in the Jewish State*, London: Frank Cass.

—— (2003) 'Israeli Arab Members of the 15th Knesset: Between Israeli Citizenship and their Palestinian National Identity', in Bligh, A. (ed.) *The Israeli Palestinians: An Arab Minority in the Jewish State*, London: Frank Cass.

Butenschon, N.A., Davis, U. and Hassassian, M. (eds.) (2000) *Citizenship and the State in the Middle East: Approaches and Applications*, Syracuse, NY: Syracuse University Press.

Central Bureau of Statistics (CBS). (2010a) *Statistical Abstract of Israel: No. 61*, Available at http://www.cbs.gov.il/reader/shnatonenew_site.htm (Accessed on 5 December 2010).

—— (2010b) *Introduction – Explanatory Notes, Definitions and Sources*, Available at http://www.cbs.gov.il/reader/ Accessed 5 December 2010).

Chacour, E. (2003) *Blood Brothers*, Grand Rapids, MI: Chosen Books.

Cohen, A. (1965) *Arab Border Villages in Israel: A Study of Continuity and Change in Social Organisation*, Manchester: Manchester University Press.

Cohen, S. (1995) 'The Israel Defense Forces (IDF): From a "People's Army" to a "Professional Military" – Causes and Implications', *Armed Forces and Society*, 21: 237–54.

Cohen-Almagor, R. (1995) 'Cultural Pluralism and the Israeli Nation-Building Ideology', *International Journal of Middle East Studies*, 27: 461–84.

—— (2001) 'Liberalism and the Limits of Multiculturalism', *Journal of Canadian Studies*, 36: 80–93.

Cohen-Hattab, K. and Shoval, N. (2007) 'Tourism Development and Cultural Conflict: The Case of "Nazareth 2000"', *Social and Cultural Geography*, 8: 701–17.

Colbi, S.P. (1969) *Christianity in the Holy Land: Past and Present*, Tel Aviv: Am Hassefer.

—— (1982) *The Christian Churches in the State of Israel: A Survey*, Jerusalem: Israel Economist.

Connor, W. (1994) *Ethnonationalism: The Quest for Understanding*, Princeton, NJ: Princeton University Press.

Cook, J. (2006a) *Blood and Religion: The Unmaking of the Jewish and Democratic State*, London: Pluto Press.

—— (2006b) 'Basilica Burning', *Al-Ahram*, March 9–15 March, Available at http://www.jkcook.net/Articles2/0234.htm (Accessed on 13 March 2008).

—— (2007) 'On the Wrong Side of the Clash of Civilizations: Israel's Purging of Palestinian Christians', *Counter Punch*, January 9, Available at http://www.counterpunch.org/cook01092007.html (Accessed on 20 March 2008).

—— (2009a) 'Arabs Left on the Wrong Side of the Tracks in Israel', *The National*, April 6, Available at http://www.jkcook.net/Articles2/0385.htm#Top (Accessed on 16 July 2010).

—— (2009b) 'Israel's Arab Students Are Crossing into Jordan', *The National*, June 10, Available at http://www.jkcook.net/Articles2/0386.htm#Top (Accessed on 16 July 2010).

Courbage, Y. and Fargues, P. (1997) *Christians and Jews under Islam*, London: I.B. Tauris.

Cragg, K. (1991) *The Arab Christian: A History in the Middle East*, Westminster: John Knox Press.

Davis, U. (2003) *Apartheid Israel: Possibilities for the Struggle Within*, London: Zed.

Dumper, M. (2002a) *The Politics of Sacred Space: The Old City of Jerusalem in the Middle East Conflict*, Boulder, CO: Lynne Rienner.

—— (2002b) 'Christian Churches of Jerusalem in the Post-Oslo Period', *Journal of Palestine Studies*, 31: 51–65.

—— (2006) 'Nazareth', in Dumper, M., Stanley, B.E. and Abu-Lughod, J.L. (eds.) *Cities of the Middle East and North Africa: A Historical Encyclopedia*, Santa Barbaara, CA: ABC-Clio.

Edelman, M. (1987) 'The Druze Courts in the Political System of Israel', *Middle East Review*, 19: 54–61.

Eisenstadt, S.N. (1967a) 'Israeli Identity: Problems in the Development of the Collective Identity of an Ideological Society', *Annals of the American Academy of Political and Social Science*, 370: 116–23.

—— (1967b) *Israeli Society*, London: Weidenfeld & Nicolson.

—— (1985) *The Transformation of Israeli Society*, London: Weidenfeld & Nicolson.

—— (1986) *The Development of the Ethnic Problem in Israeli Society: Observations and Suggestions for Research*, Jerusalem: Jerusalem Institute for Israel Studies.

Eldar, Y. (2003) *Focus on Israel – The Christian Communities of Israel*, Israeli Ministry of Foreign Affairs. Available at http://www.mfa.gov.il/MFA/Facts+About+Israel/People/Focus+on+Israel+-+The+Christian+Communities+of+Isr.htm (Accessed on 12 June 2006).

Eller, J.D. (1997) 'Anti-Anti-Multiculturalism', *American Anthropologist*, 99: 249–56.

Emmett, C. (1995) *Beyond the Basilica: Christians and Muslims in Nazareth*, London: University of Chicago Press.

—— (1997) 'Conflicting Loyalties and Local Politics in Nazareth', *Middle East Journal*, 51: 535–53.

Epstein, A.D. (2004) 'The Decline of Israeli Sociology', *Azure: Ideas for the Jewish Nation*, 16: 78–108.

Esman, M.J. and Rabinovich, I. (eds.) (1988) *Ethnicity, Pluralism and the State in the Middle East*, Ithaca, NY: Cornell University Press.

Estrada, K. and McLaren, P. (1993) 'Research News and Comment: A Dialogue on Multiculturalism and Democratic Culture', *Educational Researcher*, 22: 27–33.

Ettinger, Y. (2003) 'Urban plan seen as racist move in Arab sector' *Haaretz*, May 13, Available at http://www.haaretz.com/print-edition/features/urban-plan-seen-as-racist-move-in-arab-sector-1.10277 (Accessed on 20 August 2008).

Falah, G. (1991) 'Israeli "Judaisation" Policy in Galilee', *Journal of Palestine Studies*, 20: 69–85.

—— (1992) 'Land Fragmentation and Spatial Control in the Nazareth Metropolitan Area', *Professional Geographer*, 44: 30–44.

Fargues, P. (1998) *The Arab Christians of the Middle East: A Demographic Perspective*, Oxford: Oxford University Press.

Finer, S.E. (1970) *Comparative Government: An Introduction to the Study of Politics*, London: Allen Lane.

Firro, K. (2001) 'Reshaping Druze Particularism in Israel', *Journal of Palestine Studies*, 30: 40–53.

Forman, G. (2006) 'Military Rule, Political Manipulation and Jewish Settlement: Israeli Mechanisms for Controlling Nazareth in the 1950s', *The Journal of Israeli History*, 25: 335–59.

Friedlander, D. and Goldscheider, C. (1974) 'Peace and the Demographic Future of Israel', *The Journal of Conflict Resolution*, 18: 486–501.

Friedlander, D., Eisenbach, Z. and Goldscheider, C. (1979) 'Modernisation Patterns and Fertility Change: The Arab Populations of Israel and the Israel-Administered Territories', *Population Studies*, 33: 239–54.

Friedman, M. (1989) 'Israel as a Theological Dilemma', in Kimmerling, B. (ed.) *The Israeli State and Society: Boundaries and Frontiers*, Albany: State University of New York Press.

Friendly, A. (1972) *Israel's Oriental Immigrants and Druzes*, London: Minority Rights Group.

Frisch, H. (1993) 'The Druze Minority in the Israeli Military: Traditionalising an Ethnic Policing Role', *Armed Forces & Society*, 20: 51–67.

—— (1997) 'State Ethnicisation and the Crisis of Leadership Succession among Israel's Druze', *Ethnic and Racial Studies*, 20: 580–93.

—— (2001) 'The Arab Vote in the Israeli Elections: The Bid for Leadership', *Israel Affairs*, 7: 153–70.

Furnivall, J.S. (1948) *Colonial Policy and Practice: A Comparative Study of Burma and Netherlands India*, Cambridge: Cambridge University Press.

Gal, R. (1986) *A Portrait of the Israeli Soldier*, Westport, CT: Greenwood Press.

Gellner, E. (1983) *Nations and Nationalism*, 2nd edn, Oxford: Blackwell.

Ghanem, A. (1998) 'State and Minority in Israel: The Case of Ethnic State and the Predicament of its Minority', *Ethnic and Racial Studies*, 21: 428–48.

—— (2000) 'The Palestinian Minority in Israel: The "Challenge" of the Jewish State and its Implications', *Third World Quarterly*, 21: 87–104.

—— (2001) *The Palestinian-Arab Minority in Israel, 1948–2000: A Political Study*, Albany: State University of New York Press.

—— (2002) 'The Palestinians in Israel: Political Orientation and Aspirations', *International Journal of Intercultural Relations*, 26: 135–52.

Ghanem, A. and Mustafa, M. (2007) 'The Palestinians in Israel and the 2006 Knesset Elections: Political and Ideological Implications of Election Boycott', *Holy Land Studies: A Multidisciplinary Journal*, 6: 51–73.

Ghanem, A. and Ozacky-Lazar, S. (2003) 'The Status of the Palestinians in Israel in an Era of Peace: Part of the Problem but not Part of the Solution', in Bligh, A. (ed.) *The Israeli Palestinians: An Arab Minority in the Jewish State*, London: Frank Cass.

Ghanem, A., Rouhana, N. and Yiftachel, O. (1998) 'Questioning "Ethnic Democracy": A Response to Sammy Smooha', *Israel Studies*, 3: 253–67.

Gouldner, A.W. (1971) *The Coming Crisis of Western Sociology*, London: Heinemann.

Gutmann, A. (ed.) (1992) *Multiculturalism: Examining the Politics of Recognition*, Princeton, NJ: Princeton University Press.

Habermas, J. (1995) 'Address: Multiculturalism and the Liberal State', *Stanford Law Review*, 47: 849–53.

Hadawi, S. (1959) *Israel and the Arab Minority*, New York: Arab Information Centre.

Haidar, A. (1995) *On the Margins: The Arab Population in the Israeli Economy*, London: Hurst.

—— (ed.) (2009) *The 2008 Sikkuy Report: The Equality Index of Jewish and Arab Citizens in Israel*, Sikkuy: The Association for the Advancement of Civic Equality in

Israel, Available at http://www.sikkuy.org.il/english/reports.html (Accessed on 5 April 2010).

Haidar, A. and Zureik, E. (1987) 'The Palestinians Seen through the Israeli Cultural Paradigm', *Journal of Palestine Studies*, 16: 68–86.

Al-Haj, M. (1985) 'Ethnic Relations in an Arab Town in Israel', in Weingrod, A. (ed.) *Studies in Israeli Ethnicity: After the Ingathering*, New York: Gordon and Breach Science Publishers.

—— (1995a) *Education, Empowerment and Control: The Case of the Arabs in Israel*, Albany: State University of New York Press.

—— (1995b) 'The Political Behaviour of the Arabs in Israel in the 1992 Elections: Integration versus Segregation', in Arian, A. and Shamir, M. (eds.) *The Elections in Israel, 1992*, Albany: State University of New York Press.

—— (2002) 'Multiculturalism in Deeply Divided Societies: The Israeli Case', *International Journal of Intercultural Relations*, 26: 169–83.

—— (2004) 'The Political Culture of the 1990s Immigrants from the Former Soviet Union in Israel and Their Views toward the Indigenous Arab Minority: A Case of Ethnocratic Multiculturalism', *Journal of Ethnic and Migration Studies*, 30: 681–696.

—— (2005) 'National Ethos, Multicultural Education, and the New History Textbooks in Israel', *Curriculum Inquiry*, 35: 47–71.

Hajjar, L. (1996) 'Making Identity Policy: Israel's Interventions among the Druze', *Middle East Report: Minorities in the Middle East: Power and Politics of Difference*, 200: 2–6.

—— (2000) 'Speaking the Conflict, or How the Druze became Bilingual: A Study of Druze Translators in the Israeli Military Courts in the West Bank and Gaza', *Ethnic and Racial Studies*, 23: 299–328.

Harel, A. (2004) 'Number of Muslim, Christian Arab Volunteers in IDF Growing', *Haaretz*, 30 December, Available at http://www.haaretz.com/print-edition/news/number-of-muslim-christian-arab-volunteers-in-idf-growing-1.145565 (Accessed on 12 November 2008).

Herzog, H. (1985) 'Ethnicity as a Negotiated Issue in the Israeli Political Order: The "Ethnic Lists" to the Delegates' Assembly and the Knesset (1920–1977)', in Weingrod, A. *Studies in Israeli Ethnicity: After the Ingathering*, New York: Gordon and Breach Science Publishers.

Hobsbawm, E.J. (1992) *Nations and Nationalism Since 1780: Programme, Myth, Reality*, Cambridge: Cambridge University Press.

Horowitz, D.L. (1985) *Ethnic Groups in Conflict*, Berkeley: University of California Press.

Horowitz, D. and Lissak, M. (1989) *Trouble in Utopia: The Overburdened Polity of Israel*, Albany: State University of New York Press.

Huntington, S. (1993) 'The Clash of Civilisations?' *Foreign Affairs*, 72: 22–49.

Inglis, C. (1996) 'Multiculturalism: New Policy Responses to Diversity', MOST: UNESCO, Policy Paper No. 4, Available at http://www.unesco.org/most/pp4.htm (Accessed on 12 December 2006).

Institute for International Strategic Studies (IISS). (2009) *The Military Balance 2009*, Available to order at http://www.iiss.org/publications/military-balance/the-military-balance-2009/ (Accessed May 2009).

Institute for Palestine Studies. (1976) 'Rakah Victory in Nazareth', *Journal of Palestine Studies*, 5: 178–80.

—— (1978) 'The Squeeze on Nazareth', *Journal of Palestine Studies*, 8: 134–5.

Israeli, R. (2002) *Green Crescent over Nazareth: The Displacement of Christians by Muslims in the Holy Land*, London: Frank Cass.

—— (2003) *Islamikaze: Manifestations of Islamic Martyrology*, London: Frank Cass.

—— (2008) *Palestinians between Nationalism and Islam*, London: Vallentine Mitchell.

Izenberg, D. (2009) '12 charged in Shfaram shooter lynching', *Jerusalem Post, 7* June, Available at http://www.jpost.com/Israel/Article.aspx?id=144682 (Accessed on 15 June 2009).

Jabareen, Y. (2006) 'The Right to the City: The Case of the Shihab el-Din Crisis in Nazareth', *Makan: Adalah's Journal for Land, Planning and Justice*, Vol. 1, Available at www.adalah.org/publication/makan/MAK_ENG.pdf (Accessed on 15 August 2008).

Jamal, A. (2006) 'The Arab Leadership in Israel: Ascendance and Fragmentation', *Journal of Palestine Studies*, 34: 6–22.

Jerusalem Center for Jewish-Christian Relations (JCJCR). (2008) *Survey of Israeli-Jewish Attitudes towards Christianity*, Available at http://www.jcjcr.org/kyn_article_view.php?aid=221 (Accessed on 5 June 2010).

Jiryis, S. (1968) *The Arabs in Israel, 1948–1966*, Beirut: Institute for Palestine Studies.

—— (1979) 'The Arabs in Israel, 1973–79', *Journal of Palestine Studies*, 8: 31–56.

Jones, C. and Murphy, E.C. (2002) *Israel: Challenges to Identity, Democracy and the State*, London: Routledge.

Joppke, C. (2004) 'The Retreat of Multiculturalism in the Liberal State: Theory and Policy', *British Journal of Sociology*, 55: 237–57.

Kahane, M. (1987) *Uncomfortable Questions for Comfortable Jews*, Secaucus, NJ: Lyle Stuart.

Kalekin-Fishman, D. (2006) 'Making Sense of Constant Change: Israeli Sociology between Apologetics and Radical Critique', *Current Sociology*, 54: 63–76.

Kanaana, S. (1975) 'Survival Strategies of Arabs in Israel', *MERIP Reports, No. 41, Arabs in Israel:* 3–18.

Kanaaneh, H. (2008) *A Doctor in Galilee: The Life and Struggle of a Palestinian in Israel*, London: Pluto Press.

Kanaaneh, R.A. (2003) 'Embattled Identities: Palestinian Soldiers in the Israeli Military', *Journal of Palestine Studies*, 32: 5–20.

—— (2009) *Surrounded: Palestinian Soldiers in the Israeli Army*, Stanford, CA: Stanford University Press.

Karayanni, M. (2006) 'The Separate Nature for the Religious Accommodations for the Palestinian-Arab Minority in Israel', *Northwestern University Journal of International Human Rights*, 5: 42–71.

—— (2007) 'Multiculture Me No More! On Multicultural Qualifications and the Palestinian-Arab Minority of Israel', *Diogenes*, 54: 39–58.

Kashua, S. (2004) *Dancing Arabs*, New York: Grove Press.

Kaufman, I. (1997) *Arab National Communism in the Jewish State*, Gainesville: University of Florida.

—— (2003) 'Jews and Arabs in the State of Israel: Is there a Basis for a Unified Civic Identity?' in Bligh, A. (ed.) *The Israeli Palestinians: An Arab Minority in the Jewish State*, London: Frank Cass.

—— (2004) 'Ethnic Affirmation or Ethnic Manipulation: The Case of the Druze in Israel', *Nationalism and Ethnic Politics*, 9: 53–82.

Khalidi, R. (1988) *The Arab Economy in Israel: The Dynamics of a Region's Development*, London: Croom Helm.

Khoury, J. (2005a) 'Druze-Christian Clashes Cool Off in Maghar', *Haaretz*, February 11,

Available at http://www.haaretz.com/news/druze-christian-clashes-cool-off-in-maghar-1.150057 (Accessed on 6 March 2008).

—— (2005b) 'Four Druze policemen arrested for rioting in Maghar', *Haaretz*, February 16, Available at http://www.haaretz.com/news/four-druze-policemen-arrested-for-rioting-in-maghar-1.150427 (Accessed on 6 March 2008).

—— (2005c) 'Off-Duty Officers probed in Maghar rioting', *Haaretz*, February 16, Available at http://www.haaretz.com/print-edition/news/off-duty-officers-probed-in-maghar-rioting-1.150418 (Accessed on 6 March 2008).

—— (2005d) 'Government promises Maghar NIS 10m to repair riot damages', *Haaretz*, June 7, Available at http://www.haaretz.com/print-edition/news/government-promises-maghar-nis-10m-to-repair-riot-damages-1.160618 (Accessed on 6 March 2008).

—— (2009a) 'Shfaram calls strike after 12 charged with lynching Jewish terrorist', *Haaretz*, June 8, Available at http://www.haaretz.com/news/shfaram-calls-strike-after-12-charged-with-lynching-jewish-terrorist-1.277475 (Accessed on 13 June 2009).

—— (2009b) 'Israeli Arab town erupts in Christian-Druze riots', *Haaretz*, June 18, Available at http://www.haaretz.com/print-edition/news/israeli-arab-town-erupts-in-christian-druze-riots-1.278301 (Accessed on 20 June 2009).

—— (2009c) 'Youth arrested over YouTube clips that denigrate Druze community', *Haaretz*, June 26, Available at http://www.haaretz.com/news/youth-arrested-over-youtube-clips-that-denigrate-druze-community-1.278903 (Accessed on 28 June 2009).

Kimmerling, B. (1989) 'Boundaries and Frontiers of the Israeli Control System: Analytical Conclusions', in Kimmerling, B. (ed.) *The Israeli State and Society: Boundaries and Frontiers*, Albany: State University of New York Press.

—— (1992) 'Sociology, Ideology and Nation-Building: The Palestinians and their Meaning in Israeli Sociology', *American Sociological Review*, 57: 446–60.

—— (1999) 'Religion, Nationalism and Democracy in Israel', *Constellations*, 6: 339–363.

—— (2001) *The Invention and Decline of Israeliness: State, Society and the Military*, Berkeley, CA: University of California Press.

—— (2006) *Politicide: The Real Legacy of Ariel Sharon*, London: Verso.

Knesset, The. (2010) *Knesset Members Database: List of MKs by Knesset*, Available at www.knesset.gov.il/mk/eng/mkmain_eng.asp (Accessed on 5 February 2010).

Kook, R. (1995) 'Dilemmas of Ethnic Minorities in Democracies: The Effect of Peace on the Palestinians in Israel', *Politics & Society*, 23: 309–36.

—— (2000) 'Citizenship and its Discontents: Palestinians in Israel', in Butenschon, N.A., Davis, U. and Hassassian, M. (eds.) *Citizenship and the State in the Middle East: Approaches and Applications*, Syracuse, NY: Syracuse University Press.

Kretzmer, D. (1990) *The Legal Status of the Arabs in Israel.* Boulder, CO: Westview Press.

Kundnani, A. (2002) 'The Death of Multiculturalism', *Race and Class*, 43: 67–72.

Kuper, L. (1969) 'Plural Societies: Perspectives and Problems', in Kuper, L. and Smith, M.G. (eds.) *Pluralism in Africa*, Berkeley: University of California Press.

Kymlicka, W. (2000) *Politics in the Vernacular: Nationalism, Multiculturalism and Citizenship*, Oxford: Oxford University Press.

Landau, J. (1969) *The Arabs in Israel: A Political Study*, London: Oxford University Press.

—— (1976) *The Arabs and the Histadrut*, Tel Aviv: Histadrut ha-Kelalit shel ha-'ovdim be-Erets Yisra'el.

—— (1993) *The Arab Minority in Israel, 1967–1991: Political Aspects*, Oxford: Clarendon Press.

Lappin, Y. (2009) 'Police put Shfaram under lockdown after rioters open fire on officers', *Jerusalem Post*, June 17, Available at http://www.jpost.com/Israel/Article.aspx?id=145748 (Accessed on 20 June 2009).

Laqueur, W. (1972) *A History of Zionism*, London: Weidenfeld and Nicolson.

Lewin-Epstein, N. and Semyonov, M. (1993) *The Arab Minority in Israel's Economy: Patterns of Ethnic Inequality*, Boulder, CO: Westview Press.

Lijphart, A. (1993) 'Israeli Democracy and Democratic Reform in Comparative Perspective', in Sprinzak, E. and Diamond, L. (eds.) *Israeli Democracy Under Stress*, Boulder, CO and London: Lynne Rienner.

Lissak, M. (1969) *Social Mobility in Israel Society*, Jerusalem: Israel Universities Press.

—— (1996) '"Critical" Sociology and "Establishment" Sociology in the Israeli Academic Community: Ideological Struggles or Academic Discourse?' *Israel Studies*, 1: 247–94.

Litvak, M. (1996) *The Islamisation of Palestinian Identity: The Case of Hamas*, Tel Aviv: Moshe Dayan Centre for Middle Eastern and African Studies.

Lomsky-Feder, E. and Ben-Ari, E. (eds.) (1999) *The Military and Militarism in Israeli Society*, Albany: State University of New York Press.

Lustick, I. (1979) 'Stability in Deeply-Divided Societies: Consociationalism versus Control', *World Politics*, 31: 325–344.

—— (1980) *Arabs in the Jewish State: Israel's Control of a National Minority*, Austin: University of Texas Press.

—— (1989) 'The Political Road to Binationalism: Arabs in Jewish Politics', in Peleg, I. and Seliktar, O. (eds.) *The Emergence of a Binational Israel: The Second Republic in the Making*, Boulder, CO: Westview Press.

Mada al-Carmel. (2007) *The Haifa Declaration*, Available at www.adalah.org/newsletter/eng/may07/haifa.pdf (Accessed on 3 July 2007).

Mannheim, K. (1936) *Ideology and Utopia*, Orlando, FL: Harcourt Brace Jovanovich.

Mansour, A. (2004) *Narrow Gate Churches: The Christian Presence in the Holy Land under Muslim and Jewish Rule*, Pasadena, CA: Hope Publishing House.

—— (2006) 'Marginalised at Home', *Cornerstone: Issue 42: Have No Fear Little Flock*, Jerusalem: Sabeel, Available at http://www.sabeel.org/etemplate.php?id=5 (Accessed on 15 July 2008).

Masalha, N. (1999) 'A Galilee without Christians? Yosef Weitz and "Operation Yohanan" 1949–1954', in O'Mahony, A. (ed.) *Palestinian Christians: Religion, Politics and Society in the Holy Land*, London: Melisende.

—— (2005) *Catastrophe Remembered: Palestine, Israel and the Internal Refugees*, London: Zed Books.

MERIP. (1976) 'The Koenig Report: Demographic Racism in Israel', *MERIP Reports, No. 51:* 11–14.

Milton-Edwards, B. (1993) 'Façade Democracy and Jordan', *British Journal of Middle Eastern Studies*, 20: 191–203.

Ministry of Foreign Affairs (MFA). (1966) *The Arabs in Israel*, Jerusalem: Israel Ministry for Foreign Affairs, Information Department.

—— (1993) *The Fundamental Agreement between the Holy See and the State of Israel*, Available at http://www.mfa.gov.il/MFA/MFAArchive/1990_1999/1993/12/Fundamental%20Agreement%20-%20Israel-Holy%20See (Accessed on 20 May 2008).

—— (2010a) *History: The State of Israel*, Available at http://www.mfa.gov.il/MFA/Facts+About+Israel/History/HISTORY-+The+State+of+Israel.htm (Accessed on 1 December 2010).

—— (2010b) *The State: Political Structure*, Available at http://www.mfa.gov. il/MFA/Government/Facts+about+Israel-+The+State/THE%20STATE-%20 Political%20Structure (Accessed 1 December 2010).

Mitzna, A. (2005) 'There was a pogrom in Maghar', *Haaretz*, February 16, Available at http://www.haaretz.com/print-edition/opinion/there-was-a-pogrom-in-maghar-1.150451 (Accessed on 3 August 2008).

Morris, B. (2004) *The Birth of the Palestinian Refugee Problem Revisited*, Cambridge: Cambridge University Press.

Nakhleh, K. (1977) 'Anthropological and Sociological Studies on the Arabs in Israel: A Critique', *Journal of Palestine Studies*, 6: 41–70.

Nash, K. (2000) *Contemporary Political Sociology: Globalisation, Politics and Power*, Malden, MA: Blackwell Publishing.

Nasr, J. (2009) 'Video clip raises Christian-Druze tension in Israel', *Reuters*, June 18, Available at http://af.reuters.com/article/worldNews/idAFTRE55H1K820090618 (Accessed on 20 June 2009).

Nathan, S. (2005) *The Other Side of Israel: My Journey Across the Jewish-Arab Divide*, London: Harper Perennial.

National Committee for the Heads of the Arab Local Authorities in Israel, The. (2006) *The Future Vision of the Palestinian Arabs in Israel*, Available at http://www.adalah.org/ newsletter/eng/dec06/tasawor-mostaqbali.pdf (Accessed on February 12, 2007).

National Insurance Institute of Israel (NII). (2009) *Poverty and Social Gaps in 2008, Annual Report*, Available on http://www.btl.gov.il/English%20Homepage/Publications/ Poverty_Report/Pages/Poverty2008.aspx (Accessed on 15 November 2010).

O'Mahony, A. (ed.) (1999) *Palestinian Christians: Religion, Politics and Society in the Holy Land*, London: Melisende.

Oppenheimer, J. (1985) 'The Druze in Israel as Arabs and Non-Arabs: Manipulation of Categories of Identity in a Non-Civil State', in Weingrod, A. (ed.) *Studies in Israeli Ethnicity: After the Ingathering*, New York: Gordon and Breach Science Publishers.

Pacini, A. (ed.) (1998) *Christian Communities in the Arab Middle East: The Challenge of the Future*, Oxford: Clarendon Press.

Pappe, I. (2006) *A History of Modern Palestine: One Land, Two Peoples*, Cambridge: Cambridge University Press.

Peled, A. (1998) *A Question of Loyalty: Military Manpower Policy in Multiethnic States*, Ithaca, NY: Cornell University Press.

Peled, A.R. (2001a) *Debating Islam in the Jewish State: The Development of Policy toward Islamic Institutions in Israel*, New York: State University of New York.

—— (2001b) 'Towards Autonomy? The Islamist Movement's Quest for Control of Islamic Institutions in Israel', *Middle East Journal*, 3: 378–98.

Peled, M. (1975) 'The Arab Minority in Israel', *MERIP Reports, No. 41, Arabs in Israel*: 18–24.

Peled, Y. (1992) 'Ethnic Democracy and the Legal Construction of Citizenship: Arab Citizens of the Jewish State', *The American Political Science Review*, 86: 432–43.

—— (1998) 'Towards a Redefinition of Jewish Nationalism in Israel? The Enigma of Shas', *Ethnic and Racial Studies*, 21: 703–27.

Peleg, I. (2007) *Democratizing the Hegemonic State: Political Transformation in the Age of Identity*, Cambridge and New York: Cambridge University Press.

Peres, Y. (1971) 'Ethnic Relations in Israel', *American Journal of Sociology*, 76: 1021–47.

Peres, Y. and Levy, Z. (1969) 'Jews and Arabs: Ethnic Group Stereotypes in Israel', *Race*, 10: 479–92.

Peres, Y. and Yuval-Davis, N. (1969) 'Some Observations on the National Identity of the Israeli Arabs', *Human Relations*, 22: 219–33.

Peretz, D. (1958) *Israel and the Palestine Arabs*, Washington, DC: Middle East Institute.

—— (1979) *The Government and Politics of Israel*, Boulder, CO: Westview Press.

Peretz, D. and Doron, G. (1997) *The Government and Politics of Israel*, 3rd edn, Boulder, CO: Westview Press.

Rabinovich, I. (eds.) *Ethnicity, Pluralism and the State in the Middle East*, Ithaca, NY: Cornell University Press.

—— (2007) 'The Evolvement of an Arab-Palestinian National Minority in Israel', *Israel Studies*, 12: 1–28.

Rabinowitz, D. (1997) *Overlooking Nazareth: The Ethnography of Exclusion*, Cambridge: Cambridge University Press.

—— (2001a) 'Strife in Nazareth: Struggles over the Religious Meaning of Place', *Ethnography*, 2: 93–113.

—— (2001b) 'The Palestinian Citizens of Israel. The Concept of Trapped Minority and the Discourse of Transnationalism', *Ethnic and Racial Studies*, 24: 64–85.

Ram, U. (1995) *The Changing Agenda of Israeli Sociology: Theory, Ideology and Identity*, Albany: State University of New York Press.

Raved, A. (2009) 'Clashes break out in Shfaram between Christians, Druze', *YNet*, June 17, Available at http://www.ynetnews.com/articles/0,7340,L-3732585,00.html (Accessed on 20 June 2009).

Rekhess, E. (1988) 'Jews and Arabs in the Israeli Communist Party', in Esman, M.J. and Raz, J. (1994) 'Multiculturalism: A Liberal Perspective', *Dissent*, 41: 67–79.

Rex, J. (1986) *Race and Ethnicity* (Concepts in the Social Sciences series), Milton Keynes: Open University Press.

Ritzer, G. and Goodman, D.J. (2003) *Sociological Theory*, 6th edn, Boston: McCraw.

Rodinson, M. (1973) *Israel: A Colonial-Settler State?* New York: Monad Press.

Roffe-Ofir, S. (2006) 'Nazareth mayhem dies down', *YNet*, April 3, Available at http://www.ynetnews.com/articles/0,7340,L-3223475,00.html (Accessed on 30 August 2008).

Rolin, J. (2006) *Christians in Palestine*, Brooklyn, NY: IG Publishing.

Ronen, G. (2009) 'Druze Beat Out Jews in Recruitment to IDF', *Arutz Sheva*, April 4, Available on http://www.israelnationalnews.com/News/News.aspx/130757 (Accessed on 12 September 2009).

Rosenfeld, H. (1958) 'Processes of Structural Change within the Arab Village Extended Family', *American Anthropologist*, 60: 1127–39.

—— (1960) 'On Determinants of the Status of Arab Village Women', *Man*, 60: 66–70.

—— (1968) 'Change, Barriers to Change and Contradictions in the Arab Village Family', *American Anthropologist*, 70: 732–52.

—— (1978) 'The Class Situation of the Arab National Minority in Israel', *Comparative Studies in Society and History*, 20: 374–407.

—— (1987) 'Nazareth and Upper Nazareth in the Political Economy of Israel', in Hofman, J.E. (ed.) *Arab-Jewish Relations in Israel: A Quest in Human Understanding*, Bristol, IN: Wyndham Hall Press.

Rosenhek, Z. (1998) 'New developments in the sociology of Palestinian citizens of Israel: An analytical review', *Ethnic and Racial Studies*, 21: 558–78.

Rosenhek, Z. and Shalev, M. (2000) 'The Contradictions of Palestinian Citizenship in the Israeli Welfare State', in Butenschon, N.A., Davis, U. and Hassassian, M. (eds.) *Citizenship and the State in the Middle East: Approaches and Applications*, Syracuse, NY: Syracuse University Press.

Rossing, D. (1983) *The Ethnic Mosaic of Jerusalem: The Christian Communities*, Jerusalem: Jerusalem Institute for Israel Studies.

Rouhana, N. (1997) *Palestinian Citizens in an Ethnic Jewish State: Identities in Conflict*, New Haven, CT: Yale University Press.

—— (2006) '"Jewish and Democratic"? The Price of a National Self-Deception', *Journal of Palestine Studies*, 35: 64–74.

Rouhana, N. and Ghanem, A. (2007) 'The Crisis of Ethnic Minorities in Ethnic States: The Case of the Palestinian Citizens of Israel', *International Journal of Middle East Studies*, 30: 321–46.

Rouhana, N. and Sultany, N. (2003) 'Redrawing the Boundaries of Citizenship: Israel's New Hegemony', *Journal of Palestine Studies*, 33: 5–22.

Roy, S. (2007) 'Humanism, Scholarship and Politics: Writing on the Palestinian-Israeli Conflict', *Journal of Palestine Studies*, 36: 54–65.

Rudge, D. (1995) 'Probe of Bombing Incidents in two Galilee Arab villages', *Jerusalem Post, 7* February, Jerusalem Post Newspaper Archives.

—— (2005a) 'Galilee Druse, Christians brawl over "naked web photos" rumor', *Jerusalem Post*, 13 February, Jerusalem Post Newspaper Archives.

—— (2005b) 'Mughar Leaders struggle to reach "sulha" after riots', *Jerusalem Post*, 14 February, Jerusalem Post Newspaper Archives.

—— (2005c) 'Government pressed to compensate Christian families in Mughar', *Jerusalem Post*, 25 February, Jerusalem Post Newspaper Archives.

Sa'ar, A. (1998) 'Carefully on the Margins: Christian Palestinians in Haifa between Nation and State', *American Ethnologist*, 25: 215–39.

Sa'di, A.H. (2001) 'The Peculiarities of Israel's Democracy: Some Theoretical and Practical Implications for Jewish-Arab Relations', *International Journal of Intercultural Relations*, 26: 119–33.

—— (2003) 'The Koenig Report and the Israeli Policy towards the Palestinian Minority, 1965–1976: Old Wine in New Bottles', *Arab Studies Quarterly*, 25: 51–61.

—— (2004) 'Trends in Israeli Social Science Research on the National Identity of the Palestinian Citizens of Israel', *Asian Journal of Social Science*, 32: 140–60.

Sabeel Ecumenical Liberation Theology Centre. (2006) *The Sabeel Survey on Palestinian Christians in the West Bank and Israel: Historical Demographic Developments, Current Politics, and Attitudes towards Church, Society and Human Rights*, Available at http://www.sabeel.org/etemplate.php?id=25 (Accessed on 9 January 2007).

Schwarz, W. (1959) *The Arabs in Israel*, London: Faber and Faber.

Scott, J.W. (1992) 'Multiculturalism and the Politics of Identity', *October*, 61: The Identity Question: 12–19.

Sedan, G. (2005) 'Druse riot against Christian neighbours', *The Jewish Journal*, 24 February, Available at http://www.jewishjournal.com/world/article/druse_riot_against_christian_neighbors_20050225/ (Accessed on 20 April 2008).

Shafir, G. (1996) 'Israeli Decolonisation and Critical Sociology', *Journal of Palestine Studies*, 25: 23–35.

Shafir, G. and Peled, Y. (1998) 'Citizenship and Stratification in an Ethnic Democracy', *Ethnic and Racial Studies*, 21: 408–27.

—— (2002) *Being Israeli: The Dynamics of Multiple Citizenship*, Cambridge: Cambridge University Press.

Shihade, M. (2005) 'Internal Violence: State's Role and Society's Response', *Arab Studies Quarterly*, 27: 31–43.

Smith, A.D. (1988) *The Ethnic Origins of Nations*, Oxford: Blackwell Publishers.

Smith, M.G. (1969) 'Institutional and Political Conditions of Pluralism', in Kuper, L. and Smith, M.G. (eds.) *Pluralism in Africa*, Berkeley: University of California Press.

Smooha, S. (1975) 'Pluralism and Conflict: A Theoretical Explanation', *Plural Societies*, 6: 69–89.

—— (1978) *Israel: Pluralism and Conflict*, Berkeley: University of California Press.

—— (1982) 'Existing and Alternative Policy towards the Arabs in Israel', *Ethnic and Racial Studies*, 5: 71–98.

—— (1984) *The Orientation and Politicisation of the Arab Minority in Israel*, Haifa: University of Haifa, Institute of Middle Eastern Studies.

—— (1989) *Arabs and Jews in Israel: Conflicting and Shared Attitudes in a Divided Society*, Boulder, CO: Westview Press.

—— (1997) 'Ethnic Democracy: Israel as an Archetype', *Israel Studies*, 2: 198–241.

—— (2008) *Civic Service for Arabs in Israel: Findings of Attitude Survey of the Arab Public and Leadership in Fall 2007*, Jewish-Arab Centre and Unit for Social Responsibility: University of Haifa, Available at http://soc.haifa.ac.il/~s.smooha/page.php?pageId=166 (Accessed on 14 September 2008).

Soudah, R. (2006) 'Christians in the Holy Land', *Cornerstone*, 42: 1–3, Jerusalem: Sabeel, Available at http://www.sabeel.org/etemplate.php?id=5 (Accessed on 15 July 2008).

Srour, E.S. (2006) 'Ailaboun', *Cornerstone*, 42: 7–8, Jerusalem: Sabeel, Available at http://www.sabeel.org/etemplate.php?id=5 (Accessed on 15 July 2008).

Stein, R.L. and Swedenburg, T. (2004) 'Popular Culture, Relational History and the Question of Power in Palestine and Israel', *Journal of Palestine Studies*, 33: 5–20.

Stendel, O. (1968) *Arab Villages in Israel and Judea-Samaria (the West Bank): A Comparison in Social Development*, Jerusalem: Israel Economist.

—— (1973) *The Minorities in Israel: Trends in the Development of the Arab and Druze Communities, 1948–1973*, Jerusalem: Israel Economist.

—— (1996) *The Arabs in Israel*, Brighton: Sussex Academic.

Stern, Y. (2005) 'Christian Arabs / Second in Series: Israel's Christian Arabs don't want to fight to fit in', *Haaretz*, March 23, Available at http://www.haaretz.com/print-edition/news/christian-arabs-second-in-a-series-israel-s-christian-arabs-don-t-want-to-fight-to-fit-in-1.153786 (Accessed 6 July 2008).

Taylor, C. (1994) 'The Politics of Recognition', in Gutmann, A. (ed.) *Multiculturalism: Examining the Politics of Recognition*, Princeton, NJ: Princeton University Press.

Tsimhoni, D. (1978) 'The Arab Christians and the Palestinian Arab National Movement during the Formative Stage', in Ben-Dor, G. (ed.) *The Palestinians and the Middle East Conflict*, Jerusalem: Magnes Press.

—— (1983) *Demographic Trends of the Christian Population in Jerusalem and the West Bank, 1948–1978*, Jerusalem: Hebrew University of Jerusalem.

—— (1993) *Christian Communities in Jerusalem and the West Bank Since 1948: An Historical, Social and Political History*, Westport, CT: Praeger Publishers.

—— (1998) 'Palestinian Christians and the Peace Process: The Dilemma of a Minority', in Peleg, I. (ed.) *The Middle East Peace Process: Interdisciplinary Perspectives*, Albany: State University of New York Press.

—— (2002) 'The Christians in Israel: Aspects of Integration and the Search for Identity of a Minority within a Minority', in Ma'oz, M. and Sheffer, G. (eds.) *Middle Eastern Minorities and Diasporas*, Brighton: Sussex Academic Press.

Urquhart, C. (2005) 'Christians flee homes after Druze youths riot', *The Guardian*, 14 April, Available on http://www.guardian.co.uk/world/2005/mar/14/israel (Accessed July 2008).

U.S. Department of State. (2006) 'International Religious Freedom Report 2006: Israel and the Occupied Territories', Available at http://www.state.gov/g/drl/rls/irf/2006/71423. htm (Accessed on 12 November 2008).

Usher, G. (2000) 'Seeking Sanctuary: The "Church" vs. "Mosque" Dispute in Nazareth', *Middle East Report, No. 214, Critiquing NGOs: Assessing the Last Decade:* 2–4.

Van den Berghe, P.L. (1969) 'Pluralism and Polity: A Theoretical Explanation', in Kuper, L. and Smith, M.G. (eds.) *Pluralism in Africa*, Berkeley: University of California Press.

Wardi, C. (1950) *Christians in Israel: A Survey*, Jerusalem: Ministry of Religious Affairs, Government of Israel.

Waxman, C.I. (1997) 'Critical Sociology and the End of Ideology in Israel', *Israel Studies*, 2: 194–210.

Weitz, R. (2006) 'Israel and the Lebanon War: The Future of the IDF Reserve Component', *Defense Concepts: Journal of the Centre for Advanced Defense Studies*, 1: 26–39.

Wessels, A. (1995) *Arab and Christian: Christians in the Middle East*, Kampen, Netherlands: Kok Pharos.

Wieviorka, M. (1998) 'Is Multiculturalism the Solution?', *Ethnic and Racial Studies*, 21: 881–910.

Winckler, O. (2003) 'Fertility Transition in the Middle East: The Case of the Israeli Arabs', in Bligh, A. (ed.) *The Israeli Palestinians: An Arab Minority in the Jewish State*, London: Frank Cass.

Yair, G. and Apeloig, N. (2006) 'Israel and the Exile of Intellectual Caliber: Local Position and the Absence of Sociological Theory', *Sociology*, 40: 51–69.

Yiftachel, O. (1992) *Planning a Mixed Region in Israel*, Aldershot: Avebury.

—— (1995) 'Planning as Control: Policy and Resistance in a Deeply Divided Society', *Progress in Planning*, 44: 115–84.

—— (1999a) 'Between Nation and State: "Fractured" Regionalism among Palestinian-Arabs in Israel', *Political Geography*, 18: 285–307.

—— (1999b) '"Ethnocracy": The Politics of Judaising Israel/Palestine', *Constellations*, 6: 364–90.

—— (2006) *Ethnocracy: Land and Identity Politics in Israel/Palestine*, Philadelphia: University of Pennsylvania Press.

Yiftachel, O. and Segal, M. (1998) 'Jews and Druze in Israel: State Control and Ethnic Resistance', *Ethnic and Racial Studies*, 21: 476–506.

Yiftachel, O. and Ghanem, A. (2004) 'Understanding "Ethnocratic" Regimes: The Politics of Seizing Contested Territories', *Political Geography*, 23: 647–76.

Zarhi, S. and Achziera, A. (1966) *The Economic Conditions of the Arab Minority in Israel*, Givat Haviva: Centre for Arab and Afro-Asian Studies.

Zayyad, T. (1976) 'The Fate of the Arabs in Israel', *Journal of Palestine Studies*, 6: 92–103.

Zogby, J. (1994) 'The Unforgettable Tawfiq Zayyad', *Arab-American Institute*, 11 July, Available at http://www.aaiusa.org/dr-zogby/entry/w071194/ (Accessed on 6 August 2008).

Zureik, E. (1974) 'Arab Youth in Israel: Their Situation and Status Perceptions', *Journal of Palestine Studies*, 3: 97–108.

—— (1976) 'Transformation of Class Structure among the Arabs in Israel: From Peasantry to Proletariat', *Journal of Palestine Studies*, 6: 39–66.

—— (1977) 'Toward a Sociology of the Palestinians', *Journal of Palestine Studies*, 6: 3–16.

—— (1979) *The Palestinians in Israel: A Study in Internal Colonialism*, London: Routledge and Keegan Paul.

—— (2003) 'Theoretical and Methodological Considerations for the Study of Palestinian Society', *Comparative Studies of South Asia, Africa and the Middle East*, 23: 152–62.

Index